The Breton Lay
A Guide to Varieties

THE BRETON LAY:

A Guide to Varieties

Mortimer J. Donovan

Quod nos sumus sicut nanus positus super humeros gigantis

UNIVERSITY OF NOTRE DAME PRESS

Notre Dame   London

To My Wife Affectionately

PREFACE

THIS GENRE STUDY, which began almost twenty years ago, will be helpful in an age of aesthetic criticism. Although the reader may remain as general as ever, he will also be the student and the specialist intent on reading the 41 lays which have come down to us. In my assignment of space, strong bias favors the English lays, three chapters to the two for French lays; if the genre is at all misty, it may well be so in these, the English examples, which reflect the influence of competing forms.

Besides defining a genre and sketching examples thereof, this study may well be bibliographical. My bibliography includes publications which have proved substantial enough, yet not long necessarily. The recent contributors have been many: I list some whose publications have appeared regularly in the annual bibliographies during the past three or so decades, without whose help the present study would be difficult or untimely. I would single out no one kind of researcher—editor, literary historian or critic and no one kind of approach.

I express my thanks for a variety of kindnesses to Philip S. Moore, C.S.C., Paul E. Beichner, C.S.C., Joseph N. Garvin, C.S.C., Dr. A. L. Gabriel, O. Praem.; to my other colleagues, past and present, especially Professors F. D. Lazenby, Paul McLane, Robert Nuner and Edward Vasta; to Anne Kozak; to Professor F. P. Magoun, Jr., who long ago presented me with a copy of Warnke's *Lais*; to Professor B. J. Whiting, whose patience and help I can no more acknowledge adequately than I can my wife's.

To Mrs. William M. Burke, Miss C. Rulli, and Mrs. V. Schneck my thanks for typing the manuscript at various stages.

My thanks, finally, to the Governing Body, The Shrewsbury School, for permission to reproduce MS. VII, f. 200^r; to the authorities of the Bibliothèque Nationale for permission to reproduce MS. B. N. fr. 2168, f. 65^r; to Houghton-Mifflin Co. for permission to quote from F. N. Robinson, ed. *The Works of Geoffrey Chaucer*. Chapter 1, III, reprints with permission my article in *Speculum*, XXXVI (1961), 75–80 and Chapter 2, V, reprints with permission another, in *The Romanic Review*, XLIII (1952), 81–86.

ABBREVIATIONS

AJPh	*American Journal of Philology*
ALMA	*Arthurian Literature in the Middle Ages*, ed. R. S. Loomis (Oxford, 1959)
Archiv	Archiv für das Studium der Neueren Sprachen und Literaturen
DVLG	Deutsche Vierteljahrsschrift für Literaturwissenschaft und Geistesgeschichte
FFC	Folklore Fellows Communications
FR	*French Review*
MÆ	*Medium Ævum*
MED	*Middle English Dictionary*
MLN	*Modern Language Notes*
MLR	*Modern Language Review*
MP	*Modern Philology*
MS	*Mediaeval Studies* (Toronto)
PL	*Patrologia Latina*
RES	*Review of English Studies*
RF	Romanische Forschungen
RomN	Romance Notes
RPh	Romance Philology
RR	Romanic Review
RS	Research Studies, Washington State University
SATF	Société des anciens Textes français
SP	Studies in Philology
STS	Scottish Text Society
ZfSL	Zeitschrift für Französische Sprache und Literatur
ZfRPh	Zeitschrift für Romanische Philologie

CONTENTS

Contents

ILLUSTRATIONS

1

Marie de France
and the Breton Lay

I. GENERAL

WHEN JOSEPH RITSON referred to the "pretended *lais* of a certain Marie de France,"[1] he spoke more wisely than his contemporary, George Ellis, who answered: "A late critic (Mr. Ritson) has denied the Armorican origin of these lays; but it is quite needless to discuss his opinions concerning a work which he had manifestly neglected to read or was unable to understand."[2] If since 1802 Ritson has not been formally proved right, at least his implied warning has been respected: the connection between extant Breton lays and Celtic originals is not simple to establish, either in theory or practice.

---

[1] Joseph Ritson, *Ancient Engleish Metrical Romancees* (London, 1802), p. xxv.

[2] George Ellis, *Specimens of Early English Metrical Romances*, 3 vols. (London, 1805), I, 137.

1

Accordingly, certain Middle English poems of the fourteenth century—*Lai le Freine, Sir Orfeo, Sir Degare, Sir Launfal, The Erl of Tolous, Emare* and *Sir Gowther*[3]—have been grouped under the safe but somewhat ambiguous heading of "Breton lays." This classification not only springs from their "evident dependence on *Breton lais*—short poems of romantic content intended to be sung, represented best in the *lais* of Marie de France"[4]—but is based on a literal reading of the familiar prologue to Chaucer's *Franklin's Tale*:

> Thise olde gentil Britouns in hir dayes
> Of diverse aventures maden layes,
> Rymeyed in hir firste Briton tonge;
> Whiche layes with hir instrumentz they songe,
> Or elles redden hem for hir plesaunce,
> And oon of hem have I in remembraunce,
> Which I shal seyn with good wyl as I kan.[5]

In most of these Middle English poems, the writer explicitly acknowledges a debt to the ancient Britons. From them, so he claims, his story is derived. In the prologue in two manuscripts of *Sir Orfeo*, which in places resembles Chaucer's prologue to the *Franklin's Tale*, the writer refers to "Brytouns made her layes":

> We redyn ofte and fynde ywryte,
> As clerkes don us to wyte,
> Þe layes þat ben of harpyng
> Ben yfounde of frely þing.
> Sum ben of wel and sum of wo,

---

[3] John E. Wells, *A Manual of the Writings in Middle English 1050–1400* (New Haven, 1916), p. 125. Chaucer's *Franklin's Tale* is included, but possibly should not be, except as an imitation.

[4] Wells, pp. 124–125.

[5] *Canterbury Tales*, v (F) 709–715.

And sum of joy and merþe also,
Sum of trechery and sum of gyle,
And sum of happes, þat fallen by whyle,
Sum of bourdys and sum of rybaudy,
And sum þer ben of þe feyre.
Off alle þing þat men may se
Moost o lowe forsoþ þey be.
In Brytain þis layes arne ywryte,
Furst yfounde and forþe ygete,
Of aventures þat fillen by dayes
Wherof Brytouns made her layes,
When þey myght owher heryn
Of aventures þat þer weryn,
Þey take her harpys wiþ game,
Maden layes and þaf it name.
Of aventures, þat han befalle
Y can sum telle, but nought all.
Herken, lordynges, þat ben trewe,
And y wol ȝou telle of sir Orphewe.
                                    (ll. 1–24)

Simpler references to Breton sources are given in the other
Middle English lays:

Thys ys on of Brytayne layes,
That was used by olde dayes
              (Emare, 1031–32)

Yn Rome thys gest cronyculyd ys
A lay of Bretayn callyd ywys
       And evyr more schall bee.
              (Erl of Tolous, ll. 1219–21)

A lai of Breyten long y souȝt
And owt þerof a tale have brought,
       Þat lufly is to tell.
              (Sir Gowther, ll. 28–30)

3

Only the setting of *Sir Degare* is connected with Brittany:

> In Litel-Bretaygne was a kyng
> Of gret poer in alle þing,
> Stif in armes under sscheld
> And mochel idouted in the feld.
> (ll. 9–12)

Sir Launfal or *Launfalus Miles*, which develops the *Lanval* of Marie de France, gives a "lay" as its source:

> Be douȝty Artoures dawes
> Þot held Englelond in goode lawes,
> Þer fell a wondir cas
> Of a ley þat was ysette
> Þat hiȝt Launval and hatte ȝette
> Now herkeneþ how hit was.
> (ll. 1–6)

Sir Landeval, however, which is related to *Sir Launfal*, includes no reference to a Breton source.

These poems in Middle English belong to what has been described variously as a genre or "school."[6] To this over thirty Breton lays belong, the best known of which are the twelve composed by Marie de France in the twelfth century but before 1189. Like the English examples, many of these include the characteristic prologue and epilogue in which she cites her Breton source,[7] as she does at length in *Guigemar*:

---

[6] Karl Warnke, ed. *Die Lais der Marie de France*, Bibliotheca Normannica III, 3rd ed. (Halle, 1925), p. xxxviii, says that the lays of Marie de France "machten Schule." In *Les Lais de Marie de France* (Paris, 1935), p. 47, Ernest Hoepffner calls them a new genre, which Marie herself started. All quotations in this study are taken from Warnke's third edition.

[7] Hoepffner, *Les Lais*, p. 167: "Marie n' attribue en fait que huit lais sur douze à la tradition bretonne, et parmi ceux-ci la nature du sujet ne nous ramène qu'en partie à ce qu'on est convenu d'appeler des contes bretons.

> Les contes que jo sai verais,
> dunt li Bretun unt fait les lais,
> vos conterai assez briefment.
> El chief de cest comencement
> sulunc la letre e l'escriture
> vos mosterrai une aventure,
> ki en Bretaigne la Menur
> avint al tens ancienur.
>
> (*Guigemar*, ll. 19–26)

A half-century after Marie de France, an Old Norse translation of certain of her lays together with others not hers was prepared and given this introduction: "This book, which the worshipful King Hakon caused to be done into Norse out of the Romance language, may be called the 'Book of the Lays (*ljoða bok*)'." The king referred to was probably Hakon Hákonarson.[8] The translation consists of twenty-one short poems, eleven of which correspond to lays ascribed to Marie de France; only *Eliduc*, of her twelve, is missing. In addition to these eleven, six anonymous Old France lays are included in the Old Norse translation: *Desiré, Tydorel, Doon, Lecheor, Graalent* and *Nabaret*. But *Guingamar, Cor, Melion, Ignaure* and *Trot* are omitted.[9]

D'autres, par contre, ne se rattachent en rien, ni par leur sujet, ni par leur localisation, à des traditions specifiquement celtiques." See by the same author "The Breton Lais," *ALMA*, pp. 112–123.

[8] For an extended discussion of these literary relations, see Henry G. Leach, *Angevin Britain and Scandinavia*, Harvard Studies in Comparative Literature, vi (Cambridge, Mass., 1921), pp. 199 ff., and Phillip M. Mitchell, "Scandinavian Literature," *ALMA*, 467 ff.

[9] The canon of anonymous Old French lays varies considerably; Gröber, *Grundriss der romanischen Philologie* (Strasbourg, 1902), vol. ii, part 1, pp. 597–598, would add *Tyolet, Épine, Ombre* and *Conseil*. According to Lucien Foulet, the anonymous lays come after Marie de France and almost all imitate her: see *ZfRPh*, xxix (1905), 19–56, and Bédier's summary and

5

Their "common source" in Breton literature, then, has been the reason for grouping Breton lays of whatever language and for associating those in Middle English, however vaguely, with the earlier poems in French. At this time further points of resemblance between extant lays in English are so general as to add little to Wells' literary definition quoted earlier; modern research has until recently lingered understandably over individual poems to the neglect of the Breton lay as a form.

The difficulty in defining the Breton lay was expressed by the late Dorothy Everett, who saw in the common subject matter, love and fighting, sufficient reason for associating the Breton lay and the romance, but she remained less than satisfied after failing to distinguish structurally one form from the other:[10]

> Is there any essential difference in form between one of the tales in Gower's *Confessio Amantis* and a short romance? I think there is, but the difference is obscured by the existence of the Breton *lais*, some of which (notably those of Marie de France, the earliest known) are really

comments in *Romania*, xxxv (1906), 137. An attempt has been made to assign to Marie de France both *Guingamor* and *Tydorel* on the basis of style and content; see Friedrich Hiller's Rostock dissertation, *Tydorel, ein Lai der Marie de France* (1927). It is probable that many lays have not survived; for a discussion of losses, see R. M. Wilson, "More Lost Literature in Old and Middle English," *Leeds Studies*, v (1936), 25–26. See Harry F. Williams, "The Anonymous Breton Lays," *RS*, xxxii (1964), 76–84, for a recent study in which he lists and classifies thirteen such lays. I received too late to represent adequately Horst Baader, *Die Lais, zur Geschichte einer Gattung der altfranzösischen Kurzerzählung*, Analecta Romanica 16 (Frankfurt am Main, 1966).

[10] Dorothy Everett, "A Characterization of the English Medieval Romances," *Essays and Studies by Members of the English Association*, xv (1929), 120–121.

tales but are usually and naturally classified as romances because of the close connection in their subject matter with that of the romances. It must be admitted, however, that it is impossible to lay down detailed rules for differentiating the two.

When noting "difference in form," one recalls uneasily the warning sounded by W. P. Ker and echoed everywhere: "form is used in ways not only divergent, but contradictory. And all the ways are in turn justifiable."[11] The need for careful definition is clear. In this study *form* will be limited to specific internal and external characteristics. The latter will include the relative length of the poem, meter, organic structure with emphasis on prologues and epilogues while the former will focus on the development of a courtly theme or *sen*, for these characteristics are embodied in the first lays and place them as a type. It will become evident as we proceed that the type admits of a number of varieties: some are realistic, others not; some read like fabliaux, others like biography or saints' lives; some have little plot, others, a great deal; but all are concerned with an adventure, a human experience having, so the modern critic tells us, profound implications. The comparison of the Middle English Breton lay with those of Marie de France is inevitable. For practical purposes hers can be considered the first and set the standard.[12] Since sources in Celtic literature are oral, one is left to agree that

the growth, the development, the further composition of the 'matière de Bretaigne' is *predominantly French* [italics mine]. In France it grows; from France it passes on across the Rhine, across the Alps, then back to what may have

[11] W. P. Ker, *Form and Style in Poetry* (London, 1928), p. 95.
[12] To be designated *tale* or *short romance* unless a better word turns up.

been its old home across the British Channel. With equal ease on the wings of universal human interest it surmounts the Pyrenees. It would have crossed the ocean, had the New World been discovered.[13]

II. MARIE DE FRANCE

If not the first composer, at least the first distinguished composer of Breton lays is known. Though writing in an age of literary anonymity, Marie de France reveals in her three poems her personality and audience. In *Guigemar* (l. 3), the first of the lays, she asks that audience to hear "what Marie has to say." She appends her name to the epilogue of the *Fables:* "Marie ai num, si sui de France" (l. 4), and to the end of the *Purgatory of St. Patrick* (ll. 2297–3000), "Jo, Marie, ai mis en memoire / le livre de l'Espurgatoire en Romanz, qu'il seit entendables / a laie gent e covenables."[14] She knows the royal family intimately enough to dedicate poems to its members. In the Prologue to the lays (ll. 43–46), she writes "En l'onur de vus, nobles reis, / ki tant estes pruz e curteis, / a qui tute joie s'encline, / e en qui quer tuz biens racine." The *Fables* she translates from English into French, "Pur amur le cunte Willalme, / le plus vaillant de cest reialme" (Epilogue, ll. 9–10). It is remarkable that the woman who wrote these dedications is mentioned but once in contemporary literature, in *La Vie Seint Edmund le Rei*, by Denis Piramus, who tells how the lays of Dame Marie please

---

[13] Henry O. Taylor, *The Mediaeval Mind*, 4th ed. (London, 1925), I, 581.

[14] The editions used are: Karl Warnke, ed. *Die Fabeln der Marie de France*, Bibliotheca Normannica VI (Halle, 1898); *Das Buch vom Espurgatoire S. Patrice der Marie de France und seine Quelle*, Bibliotheca Normannica IX (Halle, 1938).

everyone, "Cunte, barun, e chivaler," and ladies as well.[15] If, as has been conjectured, Marie de France was not herself of noble birth, at least from this evidence she was writing specifically for the nobility.[16]

"Dame Marie" has been identified as Marie, the natural daughter of Geoffrey IV of Anjou, father of Henry II.[17] Ac-

---

[15] Ed. Florence L. Ravenel, Bryn Mawr College Monographs, v (1906), pp. 35–48.

[16] Hoepffner, p. 51, dismisses the suggestion that she was of noble birth: the submissive tone of the Prologue to the Lays does not support it.

[17] This identification is advanced in two studies by (Sir) John C. Fox entitled "Marie de France," The English Historical Review, xxv (1910), 303 ff., and xxvi (1911), 317 ff.; Constance Bullock-Davies, "Marie, Abbess of Shaftesbury, and her Brothers," EHR, lxxx (1965), 314–322. Although other identifications have been made since, these studies are still widely accepted. See Erich Nagel, Marie de France als dichterische Persönlichkeit (Halle, 1929), pp. 4–10. Nagel (pp. 10–12) rejects the other identifications made up to 1929, including Emil Winkler's developed in Französische Dichter des Mittelalters II. Marie de France (Vienna, 1918). Winkler maintains that her language is free of Anglo-Norman characteristics, that the English words in her poems (garualf, "werewolf," Bisclavret, l. 7; nihtegale, "nightingale," Laostic, l. 6; gotelef, "woodbine," Chievrefueil, l. 116; and in the Fables, wiblet, "gnat," 65:28; widecoc, "woodcock," 57:20; welke, "whelk," 12:3, 14, 18; sepande, "creator," 23:34) do not prove much, that rather she is to be identified with Marie de Champagne. Winkler, however, ignores the objection that the simple, sincere human love revealed in the lays differs radically from that of Andreas Capellanus' Tractatus Amoris, written to satisfy the wishes of Marie de Champagne.

In Studi sulle Opere di Maria di Francia (Florence, 1922) Ezio Levi considers Henry II (and his son, William Longsword, born to Rosamund Clifford) unworthy of the complimentary dedication discussed above. The king referred to must be "the Young King," Henry, born in 1155, crowned in 1170, and dead by 1183, who ruled Normandy, Maine and Anjou; and the "Cunte Willalme," his tutor, William the Marshall. Levi ignores the probability that the dedication may contain more prudent than accurate characterizations of these royal figures. An account of "the Young King" is given in Olin Moore, The Young King, Henry Plantagenet (1153–1183) in History, Literature and Tradition. [The Ohio State University] Studies, Vol. ii, no. 12, 1925. J. Wathelet-Willem, "Le Mystère chez Marie de France," Revue belge de philologie et

cording to an extant record of her foundation, she was abbess of Shaftesbury, probably from 1181 to 1216, and so could be appropriately addressed as *dame*. Thus she is the half-sister of Henry II, in spite of his reputation the monarch most eligible to be called "noble reis." In 1205, King John, son of Henry II, could call her "carissima amita," "dearest aunt on my father's side." Another nephew, William Longsword, Earl of Salisbury, at least once visited nearby Shaftesbury, according to a contemporary record in which "Dame Marie's" name appears, and of which he is a witness. He may be the Count William to whom she dedicates the *Fables*, not "en l'onur," but affectionately, "per amur." If the historical figure really is Marie de France, if she was born in Maine but lived in Norman England, her written language would conceivably resemble that of the literary Marie de France—Continental French with Anglo-Norman characteristics.

Assuming that the king to whom she dedicates the *Lais* is Henry II (1154–1189), then Marie de France may be counted among the occasional writers who enjoyed the patronage of the most capable administrator of Western Europe.[18] How his patronage was dispensed in a period of scattered intellectual centers, monasteries, cathedrals, universities and the court itself, is not clear. "Of the many books written by men

---

d'histoire, xxxix (1966), 661–686; F. N. Flum, "Additional Thoughts on Marie de France," *RomN*, iii (1962), 53–56.

[18] As a period of literary patronage the reign of Henry II has been effectively discussed in (Bishop) William Stubbs' two lectures, "Learning and Literature at the Court of Henry II," Chapters VI and VII of *Seventeen Lectures on Medieval and Modern History*, 3rd ed. (Oxford, 1900); and in Charles H. Haskins' "Henry II as a Patron of Literature," *Essays in Medieval History Presented to Thomas Frederick Tout* (Manchester, 1925). See also M. Dominica Legge, *Anglo-Norman Literature and Its Background* (Oxford, 1963), pp. 42–73.

of his court, a score or more were dedicated to him, including a little theology, some science and vernacular poetry, perhaps some medicine, much history both in Latin and French, and two works descriptive of his system of justice and finance, unique monuments to the high development of his administrative organization."[19] As meager as they are, dedications are the most valuable evidence for determining the relationship between author and patron. It is regrettable, however, that Marie's dedication, probably to Henry II, is matched in uncertainty only by the *curia regis*, itself "a vague term in literary as well as in an institutional sense."[20]

It is uncertain to what extent Marie de France participated in the development of Arthurian legend as a political device to glorify the new "imperialism" of Henry II. For the benefit of the Plantagenet court, Arthur would thus be characterized as a heroic figure comparable in stature to Charlemagne, in whom the Capetian kings across the Channel took pride. Among the lays, *Lanval* is only innocently Arthurian: Arthur is the "pruz e li curteis" (*Lanval*, l. 6) without any apparent political tag. If there was a movement of glorification,

[19] Charles H. Haskins, *The Renaissance of the Twelfth Century* (Cambridge, Mass., 1927), pp. 58–59.

[20] Haskins, "Henry II as a Patron of Literature," p. 72. The influence of Queen Elinor on the literature of the English court has been exaggerated. Stubbs, p. 139, says: "I confess that, as against the claims of her husband, Elinor's title to our gratitude depends very much on conjecture, and partly of a confusion between Aquitanian and Provençal civilisation. That Elinor was a clever and cultivated 'companion' for her husband we may accept as a matter of course, and she probably could have some share in the early education of her sons; but they were very soon removed from her influence, and after the year 1173 she probably saw very little of either them or her husband: whilst in England, court or country, her direct influence could never have been comparable with that of the king."

11

Lanval might have been part of it, but no one today can say so.[21]

Her poems are safer ground for discussion. She gives another king, Alfred, as the source of her *Fables*, probably erroneously:[22]

> Esope apele um cest livre,
> kil translata e fist escrivre,
> de Griu en Latin le turna.
> Le reis Alvrez, ki mult l'ama,
> li translata puis en Engleis,
> e jeo l'ai rime en Franceis,
> si cum jol truvai, proprement
> (Epilogue, ll. 13–19)

The *Fables*, the oldest Aesopic collection extant in a modern language, number one hundred and two, with a prologue and epilogue. From No. 1 through 40 they are derived from the so-called Romulus Nilantii, and the remaining from no one identifiable source. To what extent they are derivatives of

[21] In "Henry II as a Patron of Literature," p. 72, Haskins disagrees with those "who claim that . . . the romantic movement had its genesis in Henry's reign, and built upon the doubtful mention of later manuscripts a whole theory of royal encouragement of Celtic legend as the literary basis for a new British imperialism." But the discussion is continued by Gordon H. Gerould in "King Arthur and Politics," *Speculum*, ii (1927), 33–51, reviewed by William A. Nitze, *Speculum*, ii (1927), 317–321, who subscribes generally.

[22] There is no evidence to associate King Alfred with any translation of Aesop which she could have used. It may have been an understandable confusion of Alfreds. Karl Warnke, in "Die Quelle des Esope der Marie de France," *Festgabe für Hermann Suchier* (Halle, 1900), studies the complex of classical and medieval Aesopian fables and concludes, p. 254, that of Marie's 62 fables not from the *Romulus Nilantii* the greater number go back to antiquity, and the smaller number are of popular origin. *Romulus* here means a medieval collection in prose based on Phaedrus, a Roman fabulist of c. 15 B.C. to c. 50 A.D.; in 1709 F. Nilant published a collection of 67 such fables (Leiden, 1709). See also J. Wight Duff, *A Literary History of Rome in the Silver Age* (New York, 1935), pp. 136–137.

Aesop, the Samian slave, is uncertain. They range from 8 to 116 lines, all in octosyllabic couplets. In general form, they vary little, if at all: they open with a typical statement such as "Cit dit del lou e de l'aignel," then tell the fable proper, and being written "par moralité," conclude with a simple moral of from four to eight lines.

Her third poem, assuming that the lays came first, c. 1170 or earlier, and were followed by the fables, is a translation of *St. Patrick's Purgatory* of "H. of Saltrey." The date of this is c. 1190.[23] In thought and phrasing it remains close to the original, departing only as her purpose requires. As she is translating from Latin for the benefit of an Anglo-Norman laity, "qu'il seit entendables a laie gent e covenables," she simplifies and lightens the phrasing of the original, and the result is a translation which moves easily.[24] Her interest in a simplified style (below pp. 52–54) recaptures the "poetical simplicity," in Matthew Arnold's words, of Breton tales. This quality flows, not from her sources, but from her own workmanship, as it does in her *Espurgatoire*.

III. THE ANCIENTS AND THE TWELFTH CENTURY

Although Marie de France in lines 9–16 of the Prologue to the twelve lays refers somewhat ambiguously[25] to the Latin

[23] This order of composition is given in Warnke, *Espurgatoire S. Patrice,* pp. li and lii, and widely accepted. Urban T. Holmes summarizes the historic division of opinion in *A History of Old French Literature from the Origins to 1300* (New York, 1948), p. 188; "G. Paris and Julian Harris believe that the relative order of the *Lais, Fables,* and *Espurgatoire,* in date of composition, was F, L, E; Mall, Gustave Cohen, and T. A. Jenkins have placed them E, F, L: Warnke, Suchier, and Voretzsch arrange them L, F, E, and I agree with this. Ezio Levi is alone in the arrangement L, E, F."

[24] See Warnke, pp. xlvii–xlix, for a discussion of her style.

[25] A. Ewert, ed., *Marie de France, Lais* (Oxford, 1947), p. 163.

13

grammarian Priscian, who was widely read in the schools of
the twelfth century,[26] I feel that an explication of her lines
will illuminate the relationship of the twelfth century to
Priscian and the ancients generally.

> Custume fu as anciens,
> Ceo tes(ti)moine Preciens,
> Es livres ke jadis feseient
> Assez oscurement diseient
> Pur ceus ki a venir esteient
> E ki aprendre les deveient,
> K'i peussent gloser la lettre
> E de lur sen le surplus mettre.

(It was the custom among the Ancients—so testifies Priscianus—in the books which they wrote in olden days to put

---

[26] G. Paré, A. Brunet, P. Tremblay, *La Renaissance du XIIe siècle: Les Écoles
et l'enseignement,* Publications de l'Institut d'Études médiévales d'Ottawa
(Paris and Ottawa, 1933), p. 152; Hilda Buttenweiser "Popular Authors of the
Middle Ages; The Testimony of the Manuscripts," *Speculum,* xvii (1942),
53. In this study I quote from Professor Ewert's translation of Marie's Prologue, p. 163. This section reprints an article which appeared in *Speculum,*
xxxvi (1961), 75–80. Lately, and after receiving from the printer proofs of this
book, I found in my mail, thanks to its author, Hubert Silvestre, an offprint of
his study " 'Quanto iuniores, tanto perspicaciores,' Antécédents à la Querelle
des Anciens et des Modernes," in *Recueil Commémoratif du Xe Anniversaire
de la Faculté de Philosophie et Lettres,* Publications de l'Université Lovanium
de Kinshasa (Louvain and Paris, date unknown), pp. 231–255. In his study
(pp. 239–243) we find interpreted passages from medieval writers quoting or
paraphrasing Priscian and, among these, lines 9–16 of Marie's Prologue, where
the double interpretation of Priscian—the ambiguity—occurs. Whereas in the
original context *quanto iuniores, tanto perspicaciores* ("the more recent they
are, the more far-sighted") was construed in an active sense to describe the
advantage of moderns as they saw farther, Marie complicates Priscian with her
attribution of obscurity to the ancients and in so doing shifts emphasis to the
passive as she regards the material itself and not the person seeing: that
material, strictly, and not the person seeing, should be called *clear* or *obscure.*

14

their thoughts somewhat obscurely, so that those who were to come after them and who were to learn them, might construe their writing and add to it from their own ingenuity.)

According to modern editors, Marie in these lines is referring to the opening sentence of Priscian's *Institutiones*.[27] Here, as Priscian writes about generations of grammarians before him, he states that recent grammarians are more knowing and less obscure than ancient grammarians because they may draw on, correct and expand ancient works.

> Cum omnis eloquentiae doctrinam et omne studiorum genus sapientiae luce praefulgens a Graecorum fontibus derivatum Latinos proprio sermone invenio celebrasse et in omnibus illorum vestigia liberalibus consecutos artibus video, nec solum ea, quae emendate ab illis sunt prolata, sed etiam quosdam errores eorum amore doctorum deceptos imitari, in quibus maxime vetustissima grammatica ars arguitur peccasse, *cuius auctores, quanto sunt iuniores, tanto perspicaciores,* et ingeniis floruisse et diligentia valuisse omnium iudicio confirmantur eruditissimorum— quid enim Herodiani artibus certius, quid Apollonii scrupulosis quaestionibus enucleatius possit inveniri?—cum igitur eos omnis fere vitia, quaecumque antiquorum Graecorum commentariis sunt relicta artis grammaticae, expurgasse comperio certisque rationis legibus emendasse, nostrorum autem neminem post illos imitatorem eorum extitisse, quippe in neglegentiam cadentibus studiis literarum propter inopiam scriptorum, quamvis audacter, sed non impudenter, ut puto, conatus sum pro viribus rem arduam quidem, sed officio professionis non indebitam,

[27] Warkne, ed. *Die Lais*, pp. 259–260. Priscian's *Institutiones* has been edited by Martin Hertz in *Grammatici Latini*, ed. H. Keil (Leipsig, 1855), II, 1.

supra nominatorum praecepta virorum, quae congrua sunt
visa, in Latinum transferre sermonem.

(When I find that the Latins proclaimed in their own
language the teachings of all eloquence and every kind of
study derived from the sources of the Greeks and re-
splendent with the light of wisdom; and when I see that
they followed the steps of the Greeks in all the liberal arts
and imitated not only those studies which were handed
down by the Greeks without error, but also certain mis-
conceptions, having been biased by a love of Greek schol-
ars, among whom especially the most ancient art of
grammar is proved to have gone astray, an art whose
authors, the more recent they are, are so much the clearer,
and in the judgment of all the most learned, are acknowl-
edged to have flourished by their natural ability and to
have succeeded because of their diligence—for what could
be more definitive than the arts of Herodian or clearer
than the precise questions of Apollonius?—when, therefore, I find that these men purged almost all errors, whatever ones were left in the commentaries of the ancient
Greeks on the art of grammar, and made emendations
according to the fixed laws of reason, yet [when I find
that] none of us has since emerged as their imitator, to
counter a neglect of literary studies, which are declining
for want of writers, I have attempted, however boldly, yet
modestly, I think, and according to my strength, a difficult task surely, yet one befitting the office of my calling,
to translate into Latin idiom precepts of the above named
men which seemed fitting.)

That Marie in lines 9–16 is not paraphrasing Priscian is
clear enough. While Priscian is writing about ancient grammarians, Marie is writing about ancient writers, whatever
their subject matter. Secondly, while Priscian says that ancient grammarians wrote obscurely because they came early

in the history of grammar,[28] Marie does not account for the obscurity of ancient writers. Thirdly, while Priscian states that in the *Institutiones* he will correct the obscurity of ancient grammarians, Marie leaves her intention ambiguous: either she will rework clearly and meaningfully certain obscure Breton lays, or, as Meissner stated,[29] she considers the twelve lays in their present form as so obscure that future readers will want to add to them and clarify any meaning implicit in them. Thus the question arises: was Priscian's opening sentence given a new meaning before Marie's time, a meaning which would explain lines 9–16 of the General Prologue as we have them?

Not only Marie but other twelfth-century writers, particularly in prologues to long works, quote this opening sentence

[28] In its proper context, as Professor Klibansky observed, Priscian's long opening sentence "merely serves to justify the eclectical method of the author who reproaches his Roman predecessors for having neglected the comparatively younger Greek grammarians Herodian and Apollodor. . . . Priscian remarks in a schoolmasterly way that by correcting and adding to the works of his predecessors an author may bring his art nearer to perfection": "Standing on the Shoulders of Giants," *Isis*, xxvi (1936–37), 149.

[29] R. Meissner, *Die Strengleikar: Ein Beitrag zur Geschichte der altnordischen Prosaliteratur* (Halle, 1902), pp. 280 ff.; Leo Spitzer, "The Prologue to the *Lais* of Marie de France," *MP* xli (1943–44). Professor Spitzer observes: "Marie de France, thinking 'medievally' as did the Archpriest, sees her own book as only another 'text,' which will be 'glossed,' after the model of the Old Testament commented on by Tertullian, Augustine, Jerome, etc.— after the model of Virgil and Ovid 'moralized.' The *lur sen* (*sen* > Germ, *sinn*, 'sens') is obviously the 'Christian' attitude in which the interpreters consult the pagan authors—authors whose purpose it was (what a teleological bent she attributes to the imagination of the ancients!) to veil, with the obscurity of poetic form, the eternal verities; doubtless Marie feels constrained to excuse, in harmony with the apologists, the fictional matter of which she treats as well as the poetic form of her *lais*." For comment on Professor Spitzer's approach to the lays see H. Hatzfeld, "Esthetic Criticism Applied to Medieval Romance Literature," *Romance Philology*, i (1947–48), 319.

from Priscian and change its meaning much as Marie does. Such writers see themselves as "those coming later" as they both draw on and develop ancient writings. Although William of Conches, preceptor of Henry Plantagenet, does not mention this sentence in any prologue, he recognizes that after centuries Priscian's *Institutiones* is now obscure and that the glosses on Priscian of a generation earlier should be corrected; and he proposes to correct both Priscian and earlier *glossatores* than himself.[30]

> Quoniam in omni doctrina grammatica praecedit, de ea dicere proposuimus, quoniam, etsi Priscianus satis dicat, tamen obscuras dat definitiones, nec exponit causas, nec inventiones diversarum partium et diversorum accentuum in unaquaque praetermittit, antiqui glossatores satis bene litteram continuaverunt . . . sed in expositione accentuum erraverunt.

Of roughly the same period as William, the anonymous *Glosule* on Priscian's *Institutiones* demonstrates how present knowledge of grammar depends on knowledge derived earlier; according to the research of R. W. Hunt, the author of the *Glosule*, commenting on Priscian's opening sentence, states that the "*primus inuentor* perhaps spent his whole life in inventing four letters, whereas a younger man could learn them in a single day and then invent others. By successive additions grammar thus grew to perfection."[31] Dating from roughly the same time, Petrus Helias, master at Paris and

[30] *Patrologia Latina*, clxxii, 100. The *De Philosophia Mundi* is sometimes and incorrectly ascribed to Honorius of Autun. See *Dictionnaire de théologie catholique* (Paris, 1903), vii, 152.

[31] R. W. Hunt, "Studies on Priscian in the Eleventh and Twelfth Centuries," *Mediaeval and Renaissance Studies*, i (1941–43), 211–212. I have not examined any manuscript of the *Glosule*.

18

best known among commentators on Priscian, unfortunately does not mention Priscian's opening sentence, but drawing on earlier commentators—among them the author of the *Glosule*—shows the familiar awareness of the dependence of later writers on earlier ones who are incorrect or obscure.[32]

Priscian's opening sentence, however, was cited in the twelfth century in writings other than grammatical. Since it must have been familiar to all who studied grammar in the schools, it came to be applied by a chronicler who accepted the idea of progressively refined knowledge of whatever kind. Bishop Otto of Freising, who studied at Paris in 1128–33, opens Book V of his *Chronicon* with a free interpretation of the text, which he regards as a catchword familiar enough to schoolboys. The more advanced the age of the world, he says, the more knowing a generation is, and by implication the more accurate the writing of history in the present age.[33]

Inter prima elementorum rudimenta ac grammaticae artis praecepta audire solent pueri, quod 'quanto iuniores, tanto sint perspicaciores.' Quod non inconvenienter dictum puto, dum et priorum, qui ante nos sapientiae studuerunt, scriptis et institutis informamur, ac processu temporum et experientiis rerum tanto maturius, quanto in provectiori orbis aevo positi edocemur, per nos quoque hiis quae ante nos sunt inventa, comprehensis, eodem quo et illi spiritu nova inveniri possumus. Hanc in senio mundi ex his quas dixi causis sapientiam fore multi-

---

[32] Charles Thurot, *Notices et extraits de divers manuscrits latins pour servir à l'historie des doctrines grammaticales au moyen âge: Notices et extraits des manuscrits de la bibliothèque impériale*, No. 22 (Paris, 1868), pp. 214–215. The opening sentence of Priscian's work does not appear to be discussed in the commentary of Petrus Helias, which at the present time is unedited.

[33] Otto of Freising, *Chronicon*, ed. G. H. Pertz, *Monumenta Germaniae Historica*, xx (Hanover, 1868), 213–214. See Klibansky, p. 149.

plicandam propheta praevidet, qui ait: *Pertransibunt plurimi, et multiplex erit scientia* (Daniel xii.4).

Expanding on what he calls a catchword, Bishop Otto then says that many things hidden to past generations have with the passage of time become clear. The modern chronicler may now record that the Roman empire, which the pagans had thought eternal, came to utter ruin; the pagans had written with an obscurity which may now end.

> Hinc est quod multae antecessores nostros, praeclarae sapientiae ac excellentium ingeniorum viros, latuerunt causae, quae nobis processu temporum ac eventu rerum patere coeperunt. Proinde Romanum imperium, quod pro sui excellentia a paganis aeternum, a nostris pene divum putabatur iam ad quid devenerit, ab omnibus videtur.

Andrew of St. Victor, who wrote in the middle of Bishop Otto's century, does not accept the catchword from Priscian's opening sentence. As Beryl Smalley has stated, "Andrew quotes the famous phrase from Priscian; but he puts it as a question expecting the answer 'no': are we, because younger, more farsighted than our elders? Andrew prefers to justify himself by the very nature of truth. She is unfathomable. There is always something fresh to discover."[34] The importance of this dissent in the present survey is that Andrew in fact abandons an apparently accepted interpretation of Priscian's sentence, as a writer of independence might well be expected to do. His subject matter, a commentary on the Bible, is different from Bishop Otto's or from writings on Priscian.

---

[34] This passage is taken from Andrew's Prologue to Isaias, preserved in MS. Mazarine 175, Paris, f. 40ª, and printed in Beryl Smalley, *The Study of the Bible in the Middle Ages* (New York, 1952), p. 378; for discussion see p. 123.

A final example remains to be cited. The unedited *philosophia* of the little known Henricus Brito, dating from the thirteenth century, juxtaposes Priscian's catchword and another, made famous by John of Salisbury, which tends to explain the greatness and at the same time the obscurity of ancient writers in the eyes of their medieval admirers. Henricus Brito admits that the younger a writer is, so much the clearer he is; yet he adds that a modern writer going to ancient sources is like a dwarf placed on the shoulders of a giant, because, just as a dwarf can see whatever the giant can see and more in addition, so a modern can see whatever was invented by the ancients and add anything new as well.[35]

> huic etiam consonat verbum Prisciani in principio Maioris, ubi dicit quod quanto moderniores tanto perspicaciores et ingenio magis floruisse videntur. Supra quod dicit Petrus Heliae, quod nos sumus sicut nanus positus super humeros gigantis, quia sicut potest videre quicquid gigas et adhuc plus, sic moderni possunt videre quicquid inventum est ab antiquis et si quid novi poterunt addere.

This ancient simile is well known, as is its adaptation in the fable of the wren which flies higher than the eagle.

Unfortunately, there is wanting a more pointed use of Priscian's sentence in a prologue similar in purpose to Marie's and of the same historical period. Yet the interpretation of the writers surveyed is quite consistent. Each writer quoting the text places himself, or refuses to, in the position of a mod-

---

[35] Klibansky, p. 149, prints in part the unedited work of Henricus Brito from Corpus Christi College MS. 283, Cambr., f. 147ra. Other studies of "standing on the shoulders of giants" include: Foster E. Guyer, "The Dwarf on the Giant's Shoulders," *MLN*, xlv (1930), 398–402; George Sarton, "Standing on the Shoulders of Giants," *Isis*, xxiv (1935–36), 107–109; and J. de Ghellinck, "Nani et Gigantes," *Bulletin du Cange*, xviii (1945), 25–29.

ern whose present writing is the more fully informed and less obscure than his ancient source. Consequently, it must be determined from the lays whether Marie's understanding of Priscian is different from that of her contemporaries.

In her Prologue the reference to Priscian follows lines 1–4, which treat in general terms the obligation of the writer not to remain silent if he discovers in himself the talent to write: "Whom God has granted knowledge and fair eloquence of speech, he must not be mute or secretive; rather he shall readily reveal himself." Lines 5–8 go on to develop with floral imagery the conventional thought that "when a thing of great virtue is heard by the many, then for the first time does it blossom forth, and when it is praised by the multitude, then has it burst into full bloom." The obscurity of lines 9–16, which come next with their reference to Priscian, derives in large part from Marie's abrupt shift in thought. The foremost question in this study might well be: do lines 9 and following continue in the same general terms the subject of writing and from a writer's viewpoint, or do they introduce a new but related topic; namely how the lays are to be interpreted by generations of readers coming after Marie, as Meissner originally proposed?

The wording of lines 9–16 is admittedly ambiguous, even in Professor Ewert's careful translation: "It was the custom among the Ancients—so testifies Priscianus—in the books which they wrote in olden days to put their thoughts somewhat obscurely, so that those who were to come after them and who were to learn them, might construe their writings and add to them from their own ingenuity." Ewert (p. 163) thus reads *custume* (as *anciēns*) as "custom," a word implying obfuscation or deliberate veiling of the truth in ancient writings. We know, of course, from Macrobius' commentary that fabulous narratives are one way of avoiding an open exposition of Nature, whose secrets even in life are not revealed directly.[36] Yet, thanks to the mention of Priscian in Marie's Prologue, we know also that the ancients, as the twelfth-century writer came to regard them, wrote obscurely only because they lived too early to see their meaning developed more fully; it was their practice to write obscurely, something they continued to do, but not deliberately obscurely. Thus, for the modern writer, in Marie's words, "to gloss the letter and to place from his own sense a fuller meaning on a text," as I interpret lines 15 and 16, simply typifies the work of the twelfth-century modern as he cleared up obscurities or corrected or generally reworked his sources in whatever ways. As Nitze observed of *Perceval*, "the exegesis or interpretation of traditional material according to the *sensus* (OF *sens*) it might have in the mind of the poet thus became the common practice of those writing romances."[37] To the me-

---

[36] J. W. H. Atkins, *English Literary Criticism: The Medieval Phase* (New York and Cambridge, 1943), pp. 30 ff., surveys from Jerome onward the tradition that poetry is "a means of conveying hidden truths to the initiated . . . an art of telling lies skillfully." A recent expression of the view that the ancients "deliberately composed their works with a certain obscurity" is found in D. W. Robertson, Jr., "Marie de France, *Lais*, Prologue, 13–16," *MLN*, LXIV (1949), 336.

[37] The present reading of Priscian's text is, of course, not really new at all. See William A. Nitze, "Perceval and the Holy Grail: An Essay on the Romance of Chrétien de Troyes," *University of California Publications in Modern Philology*, 28 (Berkeley and Los Angeles, 1944), p. 288: "The method of composition Chrétien employed has already been indicated. It sprang from the Alexandrian interpretation of the Old Testament as practiced by Philo the Jew and supported by the Liber Sapientiae or Book of Wisdom, chapters VII and VIII of which were used by Chrétien in the *Erec* prologue. *The exegesis or interpretation of traditional material according to the sensus (OF sens) it might have in the mind of the poet thus became the common practice of*

23

diaeval reader of Marie's Prologue the reference to Priscian must have sounded familiar enough. It must have prepared him for her reworking of the ancient sources of the lays—a reworking actually accomplished in the lays as we have them.

If we examine the outline of Marie's Prologue, we shall see its three main divisions: generalized reasons for writing, which might be called public and personal reasons (ll. 1–27); Marie's materials (ll. 28–42); her dedication (ll. 43–56). The misunderstood text from Priscian, which is found in the first division, contrasts the modern of the twelfth century with the ancients, who did not live to witness the development of meaning implicit in their writings. Since this text was quoted in the twelfth century, it was, so far as I know, nowhere used in association with the idea that the ancients wrote obscurely on purpose; nor in any work in which the text is found is the reader directed to gloss that work and impose thereon his own meaning. I conclude that the long unrecognized catchword from Priscian fixed for Marie, as it did her contemporaries, the position of the modern surveying his relations with the ancients, on whom he depended for matter which he proceeded to develop as he saw fit.[38]

For Marie de France, the ancients were the Bretons of the distant past whose tales or *contes*, traditional in character,

those writing romances. And the elaboration the author give his story material was justified by it."

[38] Marie's reference to Priscian must be viewed as a commonplace, perhaps similar to her reference to the Song of Songs, iii, 9–10, in *Guigemar*, 170–182. Though her "l'uevre Salemon" seems to reflect biblical scholarship, G. D. West, in *MLR*, xlix (1954), 176–182, shows that the reference is common in contemporary and later romances and chansons de geste as a "purely literary expression." For further on the influence of other works on Marie de France, see Hoepffner, *Les Lais de Marie de France*, pp. 1–48, which discusses contemporary and slightly earlier romance.

24

were now recast as reading for a feudal society of her own day. To describe her contribution to the genre would not be easy; yet, as the tales themselves suggest at a glance, there are common elements in theme and setting.

GUIGEMAR (886 ll.)

Guigemar serves at the court of King Hoels of Brittany and is there dubbed a knight. Though attractive to women he takes no interest in love and is regarded as backward. He goes hunting, wounds a hind and is himself hurt when his arrow rebounds and enters his thigh. Thereupon the wounded hind warns him that he will not recover until he is helped by a woman who for love of him will suffer great pain. Rather than die he goes off in search of her. When he comes to the sea he finds a boat along the shore and, seeing a bed aboard it, lies down and falls asleep. Awakening later, he notices that the boat has been sailing for some time and is about to reach a strange land. There along the coast a jealous old lord lives with his beautiful wife, whom he has locked up in a garden approachable only by boat. When Guigemar, again asleep, approaches, the lady and her attendant rescue him and bring him to a rich chamber, where she cares for his wound. Immediately he realizes that he has fallen in love with her and that his new torment is caused by love. The lady returns his love. To insure that it will last, they make a pact. She will plait his tunic, and, if any other woman can undo the plait, she may have his love. Guigemar then gives her a girdle: whoever can open it without a knife may enjoy her. But through a chamberlain the old lord discovers his wife's secret love and immediately causes Guigemar to leave in the same boat. Guigemar returns to Brittany. The wife is again locked up.

But she soon escapes and travelling by boat reaches Brittany. There she is sheltered by Meriadus, a Breton noble, who falls in love with her, but she is faithful to her pledge. Presently she hears of Guigemar's whereabouts, and he of hers, through their tokens, which are known everywhere. When Meriadus refuses to give her up, Guigemar sides with enemies besieging the latter's castle and forces him to give up the lady, whom Guigemar happily takes away.

EQUITAN (320 ll.)

The pleasure-seeking of Equitan, king of Nantes, knows no moderation. While hunting he contrives to pass the night at the castle of his loyal seneschal, whose attractive wife he desires. During the night he feels the pain of love and pretending to be ill is nursed by her. When, however, she realizes their difference in social status, she pauses and hears him offer himself as her servant in love. They presently exchange rings. Because the seneschal stands in their way, they plot to kill him during the king's next visit to the castle. On that occasion, when the king and his seneschal bathe, the latter will be given a tub of scalding water. The plan miscarries. Unexpectedly finding the king and his own wife in an embrace, the seneschal shames the king, who, unclothed and confused, seeks cover in one of the tubs, that with the scalding water. Then the seneschal throws his wife in after her lover, and both die.

LE FRAISNE (536 ll.)

In Brittany a knight becomes the father of twins. Happily he tells his neighbor. Instead of rejoicing the neighbor's wife laughs, because twins are born only of unfaithfulness. But within a year she herself has twin daughters and in her shame plans secretly to dispose of one of them. The child is abandoned in an ash tree just outside an abbey with only a ring and a silk cloth to indicate its noble birth. When the abbess receives the child from the porter, who has discovered it, she agrees to adopt it as her niece. When, later, Le Fraisne becomes the fairest maiden of Brittany, a knight who seeks her love takes her off to his castle. There she remains until the knight is encouraged to take a lawful wife. The bride of his choice is Le Fraisne's twin sister. Faithful and submissive even now, Le Fraisne places on the marriage bed the silk cloth that covered her years before as an abandoned child. This her mother, now repentant, recognizes, and seeing the ring also, knows Le Fraisne to be her own child. Though the knight has meanwhile been married, he is separated next morning by the archbishop and marries Le Fraisne, whose noble birth is now recognized.

BISCLAVRET (318 ll.)

In Brittany a happily married baron perplexes his wife by his absence three days each week. When she inquires, he explains that he becomes a werewolf and lives in the forest; after shedding his clothing he carefully hides it in a hollow stone near an old chapel, since to lose it would mean that he would forever remain a werewolf. To be married to a werewolf is unthinkable, and so his wife seeks another lover. In protecting herself she suggests securing the werewolf's human clothing. For a year the werewolf remains in the forest, unable to become man again. During a hunt he is chased by the king, and, brought to bay, begs for mercy. Thereafter he is affectionate. One day, to everyone's surprise, he savagely bites the guilty knight, who has married his wife. When his wife appears, he bites off her nose. About to be slain, the werewolf is saved by an old counsellor, who believes that the animal's hatred is reasonable. And so it happens that after questioning, the lady and her lover confess the betrayal of the missing baron. They are banished, and the werewolf, given his clothing, again becomes man.

LANVAL (664 ll.)

During Arthur's stay at Carlyle, generous Lanval is sad, because, having given everything away, he is destitute and receives no help from the King. For pleasure he rides out of the city until he comes to a clear stream in a meadow. His horse, suddenly frightened, will not cross over. Lanval dismounts and lets him graze, while he himself lies down to rest. Two maidens then come and escort him to their mistress. She is beautiful and rich and willing to make Lanval her lover, but on one condition: that he agree to keep their love a secret. He agrees and is suddenly made rich. That same year, Lanval, again at court, meets Queen Guinevere, who offers him her love. When Lanval refuses it and claims that he loves someone far more beautiful, the Queen is displeased, and spitefully tells Arthur that Lanval tried to force his love on her. Lanval is tried before his peers. He denies the Queen's charge, but in doing so reveals his love for the maiden and thus breaks his agreement. He has one chance to save himself: if the maiden will appear before the court, and if she is more beautiful than the Queen, the evidence will stand and Lanval will be adjudged innocent. The maiden comes, the most beautiful in the world, and confirms Lanval's boast. When Lanval is cleared of the charge, she and he mount a palfrey and ride off to Avalon.

Les Dous Amanz (254 ll.)

In Normandy, a king's only child, a daughter, is a great comfort to him. To discourage suitors, he imposes a trial: whoever would marry her must first carry her in his arms up a nearby mountain. Several try, but all fail. A youth who loves her goes to her aunt in Salerno for a potion which will increase his strength during the climb. Returning to Normandy, he offers himself to the King as a suitor. At first he moves swiftly up the mountain, since the princess has fasted and dressed lightly. When she offers him the potion, he refuses it and continues to climb. Finally, reaching the summit, he falls. When she again offers the potion, he does not take it, because he has died of exhaustion. She follows him, dying of a broken heart, and both are buried on the mountain.

Yonec (562 ll.)

The elderly governor of Caerwent marries before it is too late to have an heir. His young wife he incloses in a tower, where she sees no one and for seven years watches her beauty fade. One day as she desires a fairy lover, a falcon flies in through the window and is transformed into a knight, who professes love. At once her color returns. When the old man grows suspicious, and his watchful sister confirms his suspicions, he sets some spikes around the window to impale the falcon. The trap works, and the knight is wounded. Though in pain, he sees the lady again and tells her that a child will come from their love, who will avenge his death. Returning to his castle, he dies. Years later, Yonec, the promised avenger, now grown to manhood, stops over at an abbey with his mother and the old lord. There they happen on the grave of the slain knight. When the mother learns whose grave it is, she tells Yonec about his father. Yonec then avenges his father's death by killing the old lord.

Laostic (160 ll.)

The lay is called *Laostic*, which means "nightingale." It is about two knights, one married and the other single, who live in adjacent dwellings in Saint-Malo. The wife of the first is loved by her neighbor, but can see him only at night from the window of her chamber, where she also is visible to him. Nights when her testy husband asks why she is getting up and where she is going, she replies that whoever fails to hear the nightingale enjoys none of the world's pleasure. Angrily the husband has the nightingale caught, so that everyone can rest in quiet at night. Then, before his wife's eyes, he twists the neck of the bird, flings its body at her and stalks out. Cursing all bird-limers and fearing that her lover will think her false, she picks up the bird and sends it with a note to her lover. He has a small casket made for it, which he carries about with him to remind him of his love.

Milun (534 ll.)

Milun's reputation as a knight spreads far beyond his birthplace in South Wales. He succeeds also in love, and when his mistress bears him a son, he agrees to send him secretly to her sister in Northumbria, where he will be safe. Then, Milun leaves the country to seek rewards. His mistress, whom he leaves with her father, fears that she will have to marry someone of her father's choice before Milun returns. When Milun returns and finds her married, he sends her as a gift a swan which will carry letters back and forth between them. For twenty years they communicate in secret, using the swan as their messenger. Meanwhile their son has developed into a promising knight. When he goes abroad and in Brittany is called "the Peerless," Milun, still strong and agile and not recognizing his son, decides to challenge him. They fight, and Milun is unhorsed. On inquiry he finds that his opponent is his son, whom he can be proud of. On return to their own country they learn that Milun's mistress is now a widow. The lovers and their son are happily united.

CHAITIVEL (240 ll.)

Chaitivel, or *The Four Sorrows*, relates an adventure which took place in Nantes in Brittany. A lady there of beauty, learning and carriage is loved by so many that, rather than hurt her suitors by rejecting any of them, she shows each good will. Four who are vying for her love engage in the tournament at Easter outside Nantes. Three are killed. The fourth, seriously wounded, she takes into her chamber and nurses. One day during the following summer she tells him that she will compose a lay about her four lovers and call it *The Four Sorrows*. But he pleads that it should be called *Chaitivel*, "the unfortunate one," because, though allowed to live, he finds unfulfilled love more bitter than his comrades do the grave.

CHIEVREFUEIL (118 ll.)

Tristram is banished from Cornwall when his love for the Queen becomes known. For a year he lives in South Wales in sorrow. Then he secretly returns, living with peasants until he finds that at Pentecost King Mark will hold court at Tintagel. In an attempt to intercept the Queen on her journey to Tintagel, he leaves a marker along the road which she will recognize. It is a hazel-tree branch, and on it his name is written. It is a hazel-tree because the two lovers are like the clinging honeysuckle and the hazel: when these are intertwined, they thrive; when torn from each other, they die. As soon as the Queen recognizes the marker, she moves off the road with her attendant and there spends a short but happy time with Tristram. They part presently, and Tristram returns to South Wales, where he remains until recalled to court.

ELIDUC (1184 ll.)

Eliduc, a valiant knight of Brittany, is happily married to a wife of noble birth and serves his king faithfully. Because of jealousy at court he is banished, leaves his wife and lands, and heads abroad for Logres. He meets near Exeter a king who lives with a daughter and is hard pressed by his enemies. So well does Eliduc defend him that after a year he becomes the king's seneschal. Soon he falls in love with the princess, Guilliadun, but is tormented by his duty to his wife. When word comes that his own king needs him, he breaks away regretfully and returns to Brittany. But again he leaves his homeland after claiming that he has given his word to protect the other king overseas. He sets sail, travels to the court in disguise and by a stratagem succeeds in carrying off Guilliadun. During the passage back to Brittany a storm arises, and the seamen want to throw her overboard. When in their remonstrations they suggest that Eliduc is already married, Guilliadun faints and is thought dead. On disembarcation she is taken to a chapel in the forest and laid on a bed before the altar. Eliduc meanwhile returns to his home nearby. When he seems sad, his wife investigates his visits to the chapel.

Going there herself, she discovers Guilliadun and is so moved by her beauty that she no longer wonders at her husband's sadness. Guilliadun is revived by a red flower placed in her mouth, a remedy which a weasel just then used to revive its mate on the floor of the chapel. Once again Eliduc is happy. He releases his wife from her marriage vow so that she may become a religious. Eliduc and Guilliadun are married, and later both retire to the religious life.

It is clear from the summaries above that certain lays of the twelve may be described as realistic. These would include *Equitan, Le Fraisne, Les Dous Amanz, Milun, Chaitivel* and *Eliduc* and probably *Laostic* and *Chievrefueil.*[39] Except for the potion in *Les Dous Amanz* and the red flower in *Eliduc* none of the poems contains elements of the marvelous, the fantastic and the supernatural in the same sense in which these occur in *Guigemar, Bisclavret, Lanval* and *Yonec.* In a recent study in which two worlds found in the lays are described as structural elements not to be confused, one is *féerique* and the other *courtois:* but the distinction is not entirely new, as further discussion will show (pp. 54–63 below). Any definition of the Breton lay, therefore, has to be broad enough to allow for both the realistic and the marvelous.[40]

[39] S. Foster Damon, "Marie de France: Psychologist of Courtly Love," *PMLA,* xliv (1929), 970 ff., omits *Laostic* and *Chievrefueil* from his list of "realistic" lays.

[40] Nagel, pp. 44–49, recognizes that life as presented in the lays is idealized to varying degrees. For a discussion of the occurrence of the marvellous in related literature, see Marguerite Hallauer, *Das Wunderbare Element in den Chansons de Geste,* (Diss. Basel, 1918). She collects and classifies elements of Christian origin, from the Celtic world of fairies and from the oriental art of magic.

The summaries might also lead one to the discovery of a principle which unifies each lay, not history or tradition, but, as in some of the long romances, a single idea.[41] The idea varies with the individual lay, but always relates to man's love for woman. (The statements printed in the Appendix illustrate unifying ideas according to Leo Spitzer.) Further, functional in the design of each lay is the concept of *aventure*. For each one represents a human experience, seen first dimly as if controlled by Fortune, but later explicated as part of the divine plan, as conflict is followed by calm and understanding.[42]

Love is thus represented as a fatal power which man controls with difficulty. "Es ist ein Welt passiven, zum Verzicht bereiten Menschentums and elegisch—träumerischer Stimmung, eine Welt ganz aus dem Blickwinkel einer Frau gesehen."[43] Marie de France wrote, however, without accepting the tradition of Courtly Love. For her, love is "le sentiment naturel, naif et spontané, . . . exaltant les courages, poussant aux exploits heroiques et aux sacrifices sublimes, mais aussi

[41] See Luise Lerner, *Studien zur Komposition des höfischen Romans im 13. Jahrhunderts* (Münster in Westf., 1936), pp. 1–7, for a discussion of composition and its application to courtly romance.

[42] They are quoted from Leo Spitzer, "Marie de France—Dichterin von Problemmärchen," *ZfRPh*, L (1930), 29–38. His provocative article and another by Friedrich Schürr, "Komposition und Symbolik in den Lais der Marie de France," *ZfRPh*, L (1930), 556–582, as well as S. Foster Damon's study referred to above, deserve mention here, since they have enriched the text considerably. See also Bartina H. Wind, "L'idéologie courtoise dans les lais de Marie de France," *Mélanges de linguistique romane et de philologie médiévale offerts à M. Maurice Delbouille* (Gembloux, 1964), II, 741–748. John A. Frey, "Linguistic and Psychological Couplings in the Lays of Marie de France," *SP*, LXI (1964), 3–18, builds on S. Foster Damon's study with interesting results.

[43] Schürr, p. 566.

aux crimes les plus abominables."[44] Although she is amused in *Chaitivel* by the casuistry of love, she seems to withdraw to the background of the story and elsewhere is satisfied to identify herself with her characters and to experience their lot as they react to a blind, sometimes fatal passion. She differs again from writers following the tradition of Courtly Love when she tolerates adulterous love "only in one instance—that of the badly married, when the woman is the innocent victim of a forced marriage and of a jealous and ill-natured husband."[45]

Just as in theme each lay possesses unity, similarly the twelve together make up a whole. They all treat of human love and are presented within a frame, the frame of memory:

> Ne dutai pas, bien le saveie,
> que pur remembrance les firent
> des aventures qu'il oirent
> cil ki primes les comencierent
> e ki avant les enveierent.
> (Prologue, ll. 34–38)

Although the adventures happened in the past, they are brought together in time and place by the recalling mind, which shows a calculated leisureliness:

> Quant des lais faire m'entremet,
> ne vueil ublier Bisclavret.
> (*Bisclavret*, ll. 1–2)

The process of recalling, further, is done under guidance.

[44] Ernest Hoepffner, *Aux Origines de la Nouvelle Française* (Oxford, 1939), p. 20.

[45] P. 36. Hoepffner's judgment ignores *Chievrefueil*. For a fuller discussion see Emil Schiött, *L'Amour et les Amoureux dans les Lais de Marie de France* (Lund, 1889).

Marie, according to a recent comment, chooses a "specific concrete object as the centre of her *lai* which shall develop, within the poem, new varieties of symbolic content."[46] Where no such content is intended, the danger obviously is that of reading what may be inadmissible to all; how certain can one be, for example, of the following interpretation of the werewolf's return to the society of his wife in *Bisclavret?*

> We might even go farther and say that his return, after his beastly adventures, to the chapel for his clothes suggests confession, after which he emerges clothed and in his right mind.[47]

Other lays are better examples: (1) *Chievrefueil* and *Laostic* and (2) *Guigemar* and *Milun.* In the first group the concrete object, because of its importance in the narrative, is centrally placed. In the second it is given less emphasis.

In *Chievrefueil* the presence of a consciously contrived object is undisputed. When Tristram and the Queen are compared to a hazel intwined by a honeysuckle vine, the narrative suddenly halts and the reader is preoccupied with a static image:

> D'els dous fu il tut altresi
> cume del chievrefueil esteit
> ki a la coldre se perneit:
> quant il s'i est laciez e pris
> e tut entur le fust s'est mis,
> ensemble poeent bien durer,
> mes ki puis les vuelt desevrer,
> la coldre muert hastivement

---

[46] Anna Granville Hatcher, "Lai du Chievrefueil, 61–78; 107–113," *Romania,* LXXI (1950), 339.

[47] Damon, p. 977.

> e li chievrefueilz ensement.
> 'Bele amie, si est de nus:
> ne vus senz mei ne jeo senz vus!'
> (ll. 68–78)

So that the point of her object will not be lost, Marie de France glosses *chievrefueil* with the English *gotelef* and so explains its meaning to an Anglo-Norman living in England and learning botanical terms from native Englishmen. The comparison, introduced by *altresi*, is of course unoriginal. In the *Heroides*, V, 46–48, Ovid reads: "miscuimus lacrimas maestus uterque suas; non sic adpositis vincitur vitibus ulmus, ut tua sunt collo bracchia nexa meo."[48] In *Chievrefueil* the comparison is given such prominence that only one idea stays with the reader: "Lovers belong together; if they are separated by fate, they must die." He realizes that the object in this poem has two functions: it is a figurative as well as a literal element of the story.[49]

In *Laostic*, the nightingale, which is the means of uniting the lovers, has symbolically two separate lives, one coming before and the other after its physical death. It stands at first for the love of the knight for his neighbor's wife. When the jealous husband kills it, it lives on as a reminder of their love. It receives the same care as a saint's relic:

> Un vaisselet a fet forgier.
> Unkes n'i ot fer ne acier:
> tuz fu d'or fin od bones pieres,
> mult precieuses et mult chieres.
> (ll. 149–152)

---

[48] *Heroides and Amores*, tr. Grant Showerman, *LCL* (London and New York, 1925). To this particular analogue no significance need be attached. It simply turned up, as others, even better, might.

[49] Spitzer, pp. 44–45.

Its life memorializes their love: "Even if *vilenie* kills love, yet the betrayal of lovers is base, and true love is eternal and indestructible," as the nightingale is the indispensable means of carrying through the idea of the poem.[50]

Only *Chievrefueil* and *Laostic*, of all the twelve lays, are built so prominently around a single object. In the other poems objects are used, but for other purposes. They are, for example, devices by which Marie de France prepares the reader for coming events. Thus the meaning of the poem or of individual incidents and situations is brought to the level of consciousness by mirrorings.[51] Examples are found in *Guigemar*. Stolid Guigemar, up to this time unmoved by love, is wounded by a ricocheting arrow while hunting. No gloss is needed to clarify the reference: Guigemar's arrow recalls Cupid's. Later on, when Guigemar is in the chamber of his beloved, he can see Venus in a mural as she throws Ovid's *Remedia Amoris* into the fire. Though a conventional decoration, this also shows the direction in which Guigemar is moving, as the fire of love is kindled.

In *Milun* and *Eliduc*, events to follow are forecast, but the concrete objects may be indistinguishable from traditional ones having no special purpose. Milun's swan, like the nightingale in *Laostic*, unites the lovers by carrying their messages back and forth during their separation. After the father and the son fight, and presently recognize each other, the son takes the swan's place and brings his father to his beloved, this time physically. In *Eliduc*, the remedy which the weasel applies to revive its mate works when later applied to Guilliadun.

Her mastery of the arts of poetry reveals how close she is

[50] Spitzer, pp. 58–59.
[51] Schürr, pp. 567–568.

to the literary practices of her age. With Marie de France and with Chrétien de Troyes, "a tradition of conscious literature begins. It makes its appeal to a society largely dominated by women, which has found leisure to cultivate the arts of peace, and has learnt to take a pleasure in the decoration of verse, as well as in its subject matter."[52] The "decoration of verse" implies a contrast with the plainness of the *chansons de geste*, which developed earlier, and which fitted an unadorned style to a representation of men in physical action, often fighting Saracens, in a world usually without women or courtly amenities.[53] In the greater of the two writers, Chrétien de Troyes, "the courtly style reaches its fulfillment": of his contemporaries none surpasses him in the arts of rhetoric. He employs these abundantly and richly with a calculated awareness of their effect.[54] Although it is difficult to set Marie de France alongside Chrétien, since the two write in different forms, yet a comparison is plausible and may bring out the richness of the twelve lays.[55]

[52] E. K. Chambers, *Arthur of Britain* (London, 1927), p. 142.

[53] William W. Comfort, "The Essential Difference between a *Chanson de Geste* and a *Roman d'Aventure,*" *PMLA*, xix (1904), 64–74. See also E. E. Kellett, *Fashions in Literature* (London, 1931), p. 110: "When a writer begins to know what he is doing—and he criticizes his own work—he can no longer write as he used to write." That Marie de France was ever aware as a conscious artist of the vast difference between a Breton tale and an artistic work is discussed by Stith Thompson, *The Folktale* (New York, 1946), pp. 181, 406.

[54] See Hennig Brinkmann, *Zu Wesen und Form Mittelalterlicher Poesie* (Halle, 1928), p. 114, for detailed discussion; also p. 97 for meaning of rhetoric: "Dass dichterischer und rhetorischer Stil den Poetiken dasselbe bedeuten, haben wir gesehen. Der Stil hat ornamentalen Charakter . . . ; die Dichter selbst sprechen von malen, blühmen. Die sprachliche Ausformung ist ein Dekorieren mit den Mitteln des Worts. . . ."

[55] The paragraphs that follow in this section on her style are based largely on Erich Nagel's study, already cited. Nagel refers occasionally to R. Grosse, *Der Stil Chrestiens von Troies* (Franz. Studien, i, 1881) and to A. Hilka,

The limitations imposed on the two by their contrasting forms, the short lay and the full-length romance of several thousand lines, appear in their descriptive passages. To keep her narrative moving, Marie de France is in general satisfied to write *assez briefment*, to use only single words to describe, though fairly long passages come in *Yonec* (ll. 504–515), where the monastery is revealed to the reader and in *Guigemar* (ll. 153–159; 170–177), where one sees a magic boat befitting even Solomon in his glory.[56] Her heroes are presented by means of epithets, as well as by their action: "Equitan fu mult de grant pris" (*Equitan*, l. 13). Her women in this respect fall into two groups. Those not *fées* are described briefly in much the same way as men: "Une dame de halt parage,/franche, curteise, bele e sage" (*Guigemar*, ll. 211–212). Not surprisingly, the supernatural women in her lays command her greatest powers of description. In *Lanval* (ll. 94–96, 105–106, and 300–304) she shows no restraint:

> Le cors ot gent, basse la hanche,
> le col plus blanc que neif sur branche;
> les uiz ot vairs e blanc le vis,
> bele buche, nes bien asis,
> les surcilz bruns e bel le frunt
> e le chief cresp e alkes blunt;

Die direkte Rede als stilistische Kuntsmittel in den Romanen des Chrestien von Troyes (Breslau, 1902). See M. Wilmotte, "Marie de France et Chrétien de Troyes," *Romania*, LII (1926), 353–355.

[56] Nagel, pp. 85–89. Brinkmann, pp. 82–84, discusses the universalizing tendency in medieval descriptions. Only the general is vital in medieval art because only it reflects what is important in life: "True reality for man in the middle ages is that resting in God," and since man is His reflection, man should be presented without distracting traits peculiar to the individual. See also Jean I. Hamilton, *Landschaftsverwertung im Bau höfischer Epen* (Diss. Bonn, 1932), which studies landscapes in courtly romances.

fils d'or ne gete tel luur
cum si chevel cuntre le jur.

(ll. 569–576)

But the effectiveness of her characterization arises, not from
formal descriptions like these, but from the action she relates:

> In all the lays, there is not one main character which does
> not stand out distinctly from all the others. At first glance,
> of course, they all look alike. All the knights are *pruz*
> and *curteis*, all the ladies *beles* and *sages*; but these are
> only the stock ideals with which lovers even of today
> endow their beloved. The real test comes in how they
> act, not in how they first appear through the glamour of
> an emotion notoriously deceptive.[57]

Her handling of discourse, also, fits the exigencies of the
short narrative poem, which has no space for long speeches.
In this respect she is guided by convention. The courtly literature of her period, which abhors the heavy stylized discourse
of the *chansons de geste*, favors fewer direct statements than
indirect.[58] When Marie de France uses direct discourse, she
makes it life-like. Her speeches are longer than those of Chrétien de Troyes; she fails to master realistic dialogue in the form

[57] Damon, p. 969. Descriptions in the romances of Chrétien de Troyes run
as a rule much longer: *Erec*, ll. 411–441; 1590–1630; 1655–67; 6743–6809;
Cligès, ll. 778–845; 2760–92; *Ivain*, ll. 1462–1506. They show little com-
pression, since they appear in reflective narratives which move at a leisurely
pace. Descriptions in the lays are objective in the sense that Marie de France
does not reveal that these are *her* impressions of persons and things. But the
lay is certainly written without the impersonality of a form like the ballad of
tradition. Occasionally, like Chrétien de Troyes, she addresses the reader
(*Lanval*, ll. 2, 35; *Le Fraisne*, ll. 162–163). When Lanval is saved from
distress, she remarks, "Ore est Lanval en dreit veie!" and so convinces the
reader that there is a living author behind the text (*Lanval*, l. 134).
[58] Werner W. Günther, "Probleme der Rededarstellung," *Die neueren
Sprachen*, Beiheft No. 13 (1928), p. 25.

of question and answer coming within the narrow frame of a single verse: "Comant a non?" "Mes sire Yvains" (*Ivain*, l. 1815) shows an economy unparalleled in the lays.[59]

Her figures of speech show a restraint which would appeal to a sophisticated audience.[60] The *fée's* tent and her equipage in *Lanval* are unsurpassed in richness:

> La reine Semiramis
> quant ele ot unkes plus aveir
> e plus puissance e plus saveir,
> ne l'emperere Octavian
> n'eslijassent le destre pan
> (*Lanval*, ll. 82–86)

The lovers of her stories are treated with warmth and an occasional metaphor: ("Or est sis quers en grant prisun" (*Eliduc*, l. 466). Both she and Chrétien de Troyes use plant life in developing their comparisons: "En la flur de son meillur pris" (*Guigemar*, l. 69). Both poets personify love, nature, the heart, fortune, death, but in Marie de France there is no personification of the abstract terms of knighthood such as are found in Chrétien: *Proesce, Hardemenz, Largesce* (*Lancelot*, l. 5770; *Ivain*, l. 1296; *Erec*, l. 4641); perhaps she is betraying a woman's lack of interest in these details.

Like Chrétien de Troyes, she exaggerates for rhetorical effect. In *Milun* (l. 141) one reads: "Mielz me vendreit murir que vivre." Certain examples of *anaphora* are memorable:

> Lanval donout les riches duns,
> Lanval aquitout les prisuns,
> Lanval vesteit les jugleurs,
> Lanval faseit les granz honeurs,

[59] Nagel, pp. 25 ff.
[60] Pp. 63–73.

42

Lanval despendeit largement,
Lanval donout or e argent.
(*Lanval*, ll. 209–214)

Both use the octosyllabic couplet but differ in specific technique. They live in a period when the monotony of the endstopped couplet with its "fusion of thought and line" is slowly being eliminated. The result is a change in poetic rhythm:[61]

A sentence begun with the first line of a couplet would be finished on the first line of the following couplet or couplets or one begun with the second line would finish with the first or second line of succeeding couplets. In this way phrases of three, five, or seven lines would be formed, and incidentally, overflow between the couplets would appear.

Statistically, in the lays as a whole there is "an average of about 10 per cent for broken couplets and 34 per cent for three line sentences which follow the break. . . ." In contrast Chrétien de Troyes usually breaks every third couplet.[62]

This characterization of Marie de France as an artist may help define the lay as it left her hands to become a model for various imitators. Foremost, it is a narrative form intended for a cultivated audience that would appreciate literary sophistication. Its theme is human love, contrasting with the Courtly Love of contemporary literature. The poetic arts which Chré-

---

[61] For a discussion of the couplet in the poetry of Chrétien de Troyes see Otto Borrman, *Das kurze Reimpaar bei Chrestien de Troyes mit besonderer Berücksichtigung des Wilhelm von England* (Erlangen, 1907), p. 41. The quotation is taken from F. M. Warren, "Some Features of Style in Early French Narrative Poetry (1150–70)," *MP* vi (1907), 662 ff. M. Dominica Legge, *Anglo-Norman in the Cloisters* (Edinburgh, 1950), pp. 137–151, summarizes scholarship on Anglo-Norman versification.

[62] See p. 668 but the first 3000 lines of *Erec* are not included in this generalization.

tien de Troyes used to excellent advantage are a preoccupation of Marie de France, who is always a conscious literary artist. So far the chief difference between the lay and the medium and the long romance is a consequence of length: the lay, which is shorter, forces its author to compress and to tell the narrative directly, without reflective digressions and asides.

IV. THE LAY

The term *lay* applied to a narrative poem of from one hundred to one thousand lines may fail to record the narrative emphasis proper to the form. Ordinarily one thinks of the first meaning of *lay*: "a short lyric or narrative poem intended to be sung," and its etymology might support this meaning.[63] Because of isolated lines of music in the *Graelent* manuscript (see illustration) for a time it was speculated that Breton lays, even in their present form, might have been sung. But this interpretation has since been questioned in the light of better understanding of romances, long and short, of which the lay is a species.[64] The twelve poems of Marie de France in their pres-

[63] *OED*, 6¹. The etymology of the word is debatable: "The most likely view is that formed by M. Gaston Paris, that the word is of Teut[onic] origin, an adoption of some form of the word represented by OHG., MHG. *leich*, play, melody, song. The ON. *lag* . . . used in the sense of 'tune' would also be phonetically a possible source. Connexion with Teut[onic] *leuþo* (OE. *leoþ*, Ger. *lied*) is out of the question, as are the Celtic words commonly cited: the Irish *laoidh* is believed to represent an OCeltic type *ludi—*; the Welsh *llais*, voice, sound, is too remote a meaning, and the assumed Breton equivalent is non-existent." Professor Ewert, p. x, remarks that *lai* "is probably of Celtic origin."

[64] See Wells, Chapter I, "Romances." Pp. 124–138 of this section are devoted to the Breton lays. For a discussion of how the lays were rendered see Ernest Brugger's review of Karl Warnke's (1925) edition of Marie's lays in ZFSL, xlix (1927), 127. For a study of the oral delivery of Middle Eng-

MS. B. N. fr. 2168, f. 65ʳ

"*Aucassin et Nicolette* follows immediately the lay [*Graelent*]
and I wonder if the scribe did not begin to note the music for
the chantefable and then change his mind and write the lay of
Graelent, leaving the five lines that he had put there for musical
notation of the chantefable. . . . It seems to me that the five lines
at the beginnings of *Graelent* are very doubtful proof that the
lays were sung."

Grimes, *The Lays of Desiré, Graelent and Melion*, p. 44.

ent form were probably not sung; like the longer romances they were read, either aloud by a practiced reader or to oneself.

The claim that they were sung has turned attention to the exact wording of the prologues and epilogues of the lays of Marie de France. A significant passage occurs in Guigmar[65] edited usually as the first of her collection:

> Les contes que jo sai verais,
> dont li Bretun unt fait les lais,
> vos conterai assez briefment.
> (ll. 19–21)

If in this quotation *contes* is translated by "tales," she must be pointing to two different kinds of composition, the traditional tale, or *conte*, told simply as a narrative, and the *lai*, a lyrical or narrative form presumably intended to be sung. The *conte* seems here to be the earlier of the two: from it Breton minstrels derived material for lays and presented with harp and rote (*Guigemar*, l. 885) the same story as Marie de France prefers to relate (*conter*), that is, not in song.

---

lish romances see Ruth Crosby, "Oral Delivery in the Middle Ages," *Speculum*, xi (1936), 88–110, and "Chaucer and the Custom of Oral Delivery," *Speculum*, xiii (1938), 413–432. For a discussion of oral delivery as it relates to the theory of composition by formulas and themes, see A. C. Baugh, "Improvisation in the Middle English Romance," *Proceedings of the American Philosophical Society*, ciii (1959), 418–454; for a general survey of other applications of this theory, see M. Curschmann, "Oral Poetry in Mediaeval English, French, and German Literature: Some Notes on Recent Research," *Speculum*, xlii (1967), 36–52, where studies of the *chanson de geste* and of the *fabliau* are reported.

[65] Other pertinent passages are: General Prologue, ll. 33–42; *Guigemar*, ll. 883–886; *Equitan*, ll. 1–12; 311–314; *Le Fraisne*, ll. 1–2; 533–536; *Bisclavret*, ll. 315–318; *Lanval*, ll. 1–4; *Les Dous Amanz*, ll. 5, 6; 253–254; *Yonec*, ll. 551–554; *Laostic*, ll. 1–2; 159–160; *Milun*, ll. 5–8; 531–532; *Chaitivel*, ll. 1–2; *Chievrefueil*, ll. 107–118; *Eliduc*, ll. 1–4; 1181–84.

A. THE LYRIC LAY

This important distinction preserves for *lai* the meaning of "song." But it also points to the lines in *Chievrefueil* (ll. 117–118), "Dit vus en ai la verité/*del lai que j'al ici cunte* [italics mine]." In this quotation the term *lai* is applied directly to the *conte*-form of the same story as the Bretons rendered musically. With Marie de France, then, if not earlier, the term must have taken on a second meaning, that of a *conte* based on the same story as a lyric Breton lay.[66] For purposes of convenience separate terms have been adopted to designate the two forms: the *narrative lay* and the *lyric lay*.[67]

Recently the accuracy of this distinction, lyric and narrative lay, has been questioned; and the narrative lay has been found to lack a firm basis in the writings of Marie de France.[68] Historically, there was first the *aventure*, the fated experience, which was to become the substance of the tale or *conte*. Almost invariably Marie says that she is retelling the *conte* associated

[66] Hoepffner, *Les Lais de Marie de France*, p. 47, in explaining this change, says: "Ainsi, par un de ces phénomènes d'extension du sens, bien connu des linguistes, le mot de lai élargit sa signification primitive, restreinte à la composition musicale, et s'adjoint un sens nouveau, très different du premier, désignant à présent aussi le conte d'où provenait le lai musical." For an account of similar changes in the meaning of the word *romance* see Reinald Hoops, *Der Begriff 'Romance' in der mittelenglischer und frühenglischer Literatur* (Heidelberg, 1929), pp. 1–46.

[67] Identified by Warnke in his edition as "erzählende Lais" and "Harfenlieder." This discussion does not concern the artistic lay developed from the twelfth to the fifteenth century. See Friedrich Gennrich, *Grundriss einer Formenlehre des mittelalterlichen Liedes* (Halle, 1932), pp. 96–231. Gennrich elaborates the theory of F. Wolf, *Ueber die Lais, Sequenzen und Leiche* (Heidelberg, 1841), who believes that the artistic lay and its variants are derived from the sequence of Church liturgy. They are musical compositions, with words, which follow the Alleluia of the Mass, and show a highly complex musical and poetic structure. Warnke, p. xxxvii, allows the possibility that they may be related to the lyric Breton lay.

with an *aventure;* where she says that she is composing a lay, her real intention can be determined, as in *Fraisne,* ll. 1 and 2. According to MS. Harley 978 the reading is,

> *Le lai* del Freisne vus dirai
> Sulunc le cunte que jeo sai.

The reading of another MS. (B. N. n. a. 1104) is the same except that line 1 begins "Du lai," "I shall tell of the lay," etc.[68] It might be pointed out in the discussion of the lays which came after Marie de France whether the use of *aventure, conte* and *lai* bears out this interpretation.

Unfortunately the characteristics of the lyric poems which Marie de France says the Bretons composed have not been ascertained. As to how they existed, the manuscripts needed for study are now unknown; further, the lyric lays "were not translated, either into French or English, because they were untranslatable on account of their dependence on music."[69] Possibly the mysterious "loss" may be in part explained by the strong oral tradition among the Bretons, as among other Celts.[70]

The conjectural nature of the lyric Breton lay has at least enlivened discussion. This has centered around the following question: did Marie de France in her lifetime ever hear a Breton lay rendered "with harp and rote"? Contemporary literature offers an interesting reference in *Roman de Renart,* written before 1200, in which Renard is disguised as a Breton

---

[68] Martín de Riquer, "La 'aventure,' el 'lai' y el 'conte' en Maria de Francia," *Filologia Romanza,* anno ii, fasc. l, no. 5, 1955, pp. 1–19.

[69] See Brugger's review of Warnke's edition of the lays, p. 123.

[70] This opinion is based on the well-known passage in Caesar's *De Bello Gallico,* Book VI, Chapter xiv, wherein Caesar explains that students of Celtic poetry commit long passages to memory for two reasons, "quod neque in

minstrel and renders lyric lays.[71] Her own testimony is conflicting:

> De cests cunte qu'oi avez
> fu Guigemar li lai trovez,
> que hum dit en harpe e en rote;
> bone en est a oir la note.
> (*Guigemar*, ll. 883–886)

But in the Prologue to the lays she literally says that she heard
the story related:

> Plusurs en ai oiz conter,
> nes vueil laissier ne oblier.
> (ll. 39–40)[72]

From this evidence two divergent opinions have developed.
The first is that she probably never heard the Breton harpers,
who had lived in the distant past, long before her time. Her
stories she developed from Breton *contes*, common in her time,
which "had already lived a long life and experienced more than
one transformation before reaching" her.[73] The *contes*, at first
oral, had circulated simultaneously with lyric lays, which were
first of all melodies, possibly with accompanying words; they
shared with the lyric lays only a title. In the twelfth century,
when Marie de France heard the title of a lyric lay, by this
time existing only as a title, she recalled the corresponding
conte, which she then retold, and retained as good advertising

vulgum disciplinam efferri velint neque eos qui discunt litteris confisos minus
memoriae studere; quod fere plerisque accidit ut praesidio litterarum dili-
gentiam in perdiscendo ac memoriam remittant."

[71] *Le Roman de Renart*, ed. Ernest Martin, 3 vols. (Strasbourg, 1882), I,
66, ll. 2371 ff.

[72] See also *Le Fraisne*, ll. 1–2; *Laostic*, ll. 157–158; *Chaitivel*, ll. 1–2. Her
meaning in these passages is that she heard the story related and not sung.

[73] Lucien Foulet, "Marie de France et les Lais bretons," pp. 319–320.

the title of the lyric, which struck a pleasant response in her listeners. Her sources were any *contes*, oral or written, available to her, and these she used to best advantage.[74]

If Marie de France, contrary to her statement, never heard a Breton lay rendered with harp and rote during her lifetime, she would hardly be consistent with the person of station identified as the Abbess of Shaftesbury and the half-sister of Henry II. But there is another interpretation of her statement, although a weak one, that, as she affirms, she actually heard lyric lays. Beginning with the simple assumption that as a moral person she must be telling the truth, it explains away any conflicting details by reconstructing a lyric lay which answers the description she gives of it.[75] Before the presentation of a lyric lay, which was musical-vocal, a narrator would relate in prose the details of the story, so that there would be no misunderstanding or lack of appreciation in the audience. According to this interpretation, the story itself would correspond to the term *conte*, which she gives as her source (*Le Fraisne*, ll. 1–2); the *lai*, or musical composition in verse, which theoretically followed, would correspond to her term *lai*.

Although the practice of juxtaposing verse and prose within a single work is known in later medieval literature, its occurrence in early Irish literature is more than significant. Here the origin and development of a prose-in-verse form in Celtic literature is plainly traceable and can be satisfactorily studied.[76] In order of development the verse came before the prose. It con-

---

[74] See, for example, *Chievrefueil*, ll. 5–6: "Plusurs le m'unt cunte e dit e jeo l'ai trove en escrit"; also in *Milun*, ll. 533–534, the tantalizing "e jeo ki l'ai mis en escrit el recunter mult me delit."

[75] Warnke, "Introduction," pp. xxxvi and xxxvii.

[76] Well-known works in European literature in which verse is mingled with prose are: Petronius, *Satyricon*; Boethius, *De Consolatione Philosophiae*; *Aucassin et Nicolette*. The material of this paragraph is made available in an

sists of lyrical and dramatic passages which, because of their emotional value, are lifted from traditional sagas in verse and presented as independent works. Since they would be meaningless if unrelated to a definite time, place and context, they are introduced by a passage in prose explaining any necessary details which the audience should possess. In the early examples the prose passages are short, yet always indispensable. In time, they lengthen, probably as the traditions on which the sagas are based become unfamiliar. Finally, as emphasis shifts from the lyric to the narrative elements, they become more important than the verse, which in the final stages merely ornaments the artistic work.

Whether a parallel development occurs in the lyric lay of Breton literature will probably remain unknown. It is interesting at this point to note a resemblance between the lay as reconstructed above and a familiar Provençal form. This consists of a short passage in prose, the *razo*, which precedes certain songs of the Troubadours.[77] When the *razo* is known, the passage in verse which follows presents no difficulty of understanding. Similarly, Marie de France might have heard or read a story arranged in the form of prosimetrum. In *Eliduc* she says:

> D'un mult ancien lai Bretun
> le cunte e tute la raisun
> vus dirai, si cum jeo entent
>   (ll. 1–3)

unpublished Radcliffe College dissertation (1935) by Marie L. Edel and summarized in "The Relations between Prose and Metrical Composition in Early Irish Literature," *Radcliffe College Summaries of Theses, 1935–1938* (Cambridge, 1938), pp. 33–35. See R. Bromwich, "A Note on the Breton Lays," *MÆ*, xxvi (1957), 36–38, for a parallel development in Welsh literature.

[77] Hoepffner, *Les Lais de Marie de France*, p. 46.

It is simple and safe to equate *raisun* with *razo*. And if this reconstruction of the Breton lay is correct, still another, but undiscussed, passage would become meaningful. It occurs in *Yonec* (ll. 1–2): "Les aventures que jeo sai *tut par rime* les conterai." She is saying either that the entire lay will be in couplets, and not partly in prose, as was her original, or perhaps that she is rejecting Latin hexameters.

B. THE NARRATIVE LAY

Whatever its origin in Breton or Old French literature, the narrative lay remains the earliest Breton lay to survive. Those disinclined to theorize may well say that the present study should start from this point, omitting references to the lyric lay. Yet the concept of a lyric lay enables the modern reader to understand the evolution of the narrative lay and to see in this form the dignity assured it by the extreme age of the lyric lay.

Of the features which suggest its affinity to a lyric lay, the most distinctive is the studied simplicity of the narrative lay. In all twelve instances, Marie de France tells a simple story, sometimes comparable to the short story of today, varying from about one hundred to one thousand lines. The shortest, *Chievrefueil* (118 lines), *Laostic* (160 lines), *Les Dous Amanz* (254 lines), become mere anecdotes in comparison with *Lai le Fraisne* (536 lines), which approximates a full-length biography. In presenting a situation, as in *Chievrefueil*, in relating an anecdote as in *Chaitivel* or in telling events from a lifetime, as in *Eliduc*, the narrative lay shows a remarkable economy of detail. There are no digressions or asides to delay the plot; all emphasis is placed on a single "adventure" told chronologically and unspoiled by sentimentality.

This simplicity can be misunderstood. It is surprising to read

that "in some of the lays of Marie de France, and in the fragments of the poems about Tristram, there is a kind of simplicity, *partly due to want of skill* [italics mine], but in its
effect impressive enough."[78] This criticism fails to consider
what Marie de France was trying to do. She was simplifying
the contents of a *conte*, so that her audience would understand perfectly. In fact, she remarks in *Milun:*

> Ki divers cuntes vuelt traitier,
> diversement deit comencier
> e parler se *raisnablement*
> que il seit plaisible a la gent.
>
> (ll. 1–4)

To speak understandably means the avoidance of complicating
detail from her plots, as well as the use of language understandable to her audience. If her sources were a variety of tales each
unique in subject matter and problems of composition, she
must vary the opening of each of the twelve in keeping with
the poetic practice of her day.

In yet another way the narrative lay reveals a detail of style
which might recall the lyric lays. As their designation implies,
these are supposed to have been basically lyric. They are associated with a single adventure and culminate in an emotional
passage in which the protagonist, succeeding or failing in love,
expresses his feelings. "Embedded" lyric passages can be found
in two narrative lays by Marie de France.

One passage comes in *Chievrefueil*, where Tristram secretly
returns from exile in South Wales and by a stratagem succeeds
in meeting the Queen. His pleasure is unbounded:

> Pur la joie qu'il ot eue
> de s'amie qu'il ot veue

---

[78] W. P. Ker, *Epic and Romance* (London, 1922), p. 336.

53

> e pur ceo qu'il aveit escrit,
> si cum la reine l'ot dit,
> pur les paroles remembrer,
> Tristram ki bien saveit harper,
> en aveit fet un nuvel lai.
> (ll. 107–113)

If the entire lyric lay consisted of a prose passage followed by the lyric proper, Marie's *Chievrefueil* would correspond to the *argumentum* or prose passage preparing the scene for whatever lyric Tristram would render.

A similar passage can be found in *Chaitivel* (ll. 201–230), where the lady's reticence yields to an outburst of feeling. Up to this point she has been visited by her four suitors, all of whom she loves equally. When three die in a tournament after a display of bravery, and the fourth is left seriously wounded, she speaks out:

> Pur ceo que tant vus ai amez,
> vueil que mis doels seit remembrez.
> De vus quatre ferai un lai,
> e Quatre Dols le numerai.
> (ll. 201–204)

Her wounded suitor is pleased and replies:

> Dame, fetes le lai novel,
> si l'apelez Le Chaitivel!
> E jeo vus vueil mustrer resun
> que il deit issi aveir nun.
> (ll. 207–210)

After this preparation the reader might feel that he will hear the lyric lay itself. The expectation is real. He should not be disappointed, however, if he does not hear one, for the purpose of *Chaitivel* is to relate the details of a story *briefment* and to go no further.[79]

Though it may bear features of the lyric lay, the narrative lay can best be understood if it is regarded for what it is, a narrative form with definite characteristics distinguishing it from other forms of the time: the long romance, the Ovidian *conte*, the fabliau and the saint's life. Merely to say that it implies "not so much a given range of material as a manner of presenting it"[80] adds slightly to one's understanding, and may even be inaccurate, because the "range of material," of uncertain origin, is really limited to stories of love; and "manner of presenting it" is unspecific. Rather the beginnings of a positive definition can be reached by an association of the narrative lay with the *style courtois* of the twelfth century, which reached its greatness in Chrétien de Troyes. It is a style "more individual, more lively, more varied, more picturesque, more artistic" than anything which preceded it in French literature.[81]

In point of time the narrative lay as a form appeared during the same creative period as the great romances.[82] Generally the subject matter, ideal love and adventure, as well as their spirit is much the same. Though the two forms were designed for

[79] *Chaitivel* is less suitable than *Chievrefueil* as an illustration of a narrative lay containing a lyric situation. The tournament outside Nantes suggests that Marie de France was describing a contemporary incident, though it is possible that she was adapting an older story to a modern setting.

[80] Walter H. French, *Essays on King Horn* (Ithaca, N. Y., 1940), p. 6.

[81] Gunnar Biller, *Étude sur le Style des Premier Romans Français en Vers (1150–1175)* (Göteborg, 1916), p. 15.

[82] It is doubtful whether Marie de France was familiar with the "new type of Arthurian romance developed by Chrétien de Troyes." Hoepffner, *Les Lais de Marie de France*, p. 53, thinks that she did not know the type, at least at the time she was composing the lays. But see note 38, above p. 24.

the entertainment of a courtly audience, they differ in specific purpose. The narrative lay is intended for entertainment during a shorter reading period than the full-length romance. It can be read in a "single sitting," since it usually contains fewer than one thousand lines. The long romance, on the other hand, is far more extensive, sometimes reaching many thousand lines, and far less compact, since it wanders in tracing the fortunes of its hero and, instead of one or two, has several scenes. While the romance is the ancestor of the modern novel, the narrative lay suggests the short story. Yet as fiction the two forms have a similar general purpose and, in matter and technique, are from the same quarry.[83]

C. Related Forms

The narrative lay, in external form, is hardly distinguishable from *contes courtois* modeled on Ovid, "the master poet of love, and the greatest poet who . . . ever told of marvels—miraculous transformations and weird adventures mostly motivated by sex."[84] These include *Piramus et Tisbé*, *Narcissus* and *Philomena*, attributed to Chrétien de Troyes, and probably others now lost.[85] All dating from the twelfth century, they are around one thousand lines long, in octosyllabic couplets, and relate a simple story of love. They are derived from a common source: Ovid's *Metamorphoses*. In this study they have one clear significance. They show that in the age of Marie de

[83] Hoepffner, *Les Lais de Marie de France*, pp. 47–48.
[84] Gilbert Highet, *The Classical Tradition* (New York and London, 1949), p. 59.
[85] *Piramus et Tisbe*, ed. C. de Boer (Paris, 1921); "Der altfranzösische Narcisuslai," ed. Alfons Hilka, ZfRPh, xlix (1929), 633–675; and *Philomena: conte raconté d'après Ovide par Chrétien de Troyes*, ed. C. de Boer (Paris, 1909).

France a literary model for the narrative lay was not lacking. Their general closeness to the *Metamorphoses* is accepted.[86] *Piramus et Tisbé,* a Norman poem, "elaborates" the classical legend (*Metamorphoses,* IV, 55–156) in 921 lines, adding chiefly complaints by Piramus and Thisbé. It sets a pattern for Old French tales based on Ovid by its use of psychological observations, allegory and stylistic devices taken from the source.[87] Resembling it as a psychological study is the *Narcissus* (after *Metamorphoses,* III, 339–510) in the Picard dialect. It moves further from Ovid, being independent of its model in its treatment of love. *Philomena* (after *Metamorphoses,* VI, 424–674) reaches 1468 lines and is a short psychological romance not at all unworthy of Chrétien de Troyes.[88]

That the *Narcissus* should be called by a modern editor a *lai* is hardly significant.[89] The three poems are merely episodes from Ovid, who was widely read in the schools of the twelfth century.[90] It is not easy, however, to pass by their general resemblance to the narrative lay which Marie de France wrote at about the same time and for a similarly sophisticated audience. Thus one wonders whether she had considered writing

[86] Karl Voretzsch, *Introduction to the Study of Old French Literature,* tr. Francis du Mont (New York, 1931), pp. 244–248.

[87] Edmond Faral, *Recherches sur les sources latines des contes et romans courtois du moyen âge* (Paris, 1913), p. 410. Faral's thesis, which is compelling, finds in the literary productivity of the twelfth century large traces of classical influence.

[88] de Boer, p. cii.

[89] George Lyman Kittredge, "Sir Orfeo," *AJPh,* VII (1886), 182–183: the three "poems [based on Ovid] have nothing to do with Brittany. . . . The word *lay* does not occur in any of them."

[90] J. J. A. Frantzen, "Uber den Einfluss der mittellateinischen Literatur auf die französische und die deutsche Poesie des Mittelalters," *Neophilologus,* IV (1918–19), 363. See also Brinkmann, p. 109, and Giovanni Pansa, *Ovidio nel Medioevo e nella Tradizione Popolare* (Sulmona, 1924), *passim.*

a series of stories based on the *Metamorphoses* and about love before she began to search Breton literature for material:

> Pur ceo comencai a penser
> d'alkune bone estoire faire
> e de Latin en Romanz traire;
> mais ne me fust guaire de pris:
> itant s'en sunt altre entremis.
>
> (Prologue, ll. 28–32)

Though she rejected the Latin source and chose to retell popular tales handed down by the "Bretons," her treatment is literary and places her alongside the poets of the three *contes* writing in the *Aetas Ovidiana* with a similar purpose and for a similar audience.[91]

The Ovidian *contes* should be kept on their proper literary level, however, because, as though to perplex, they have their counterpart in popular Celtic literature. Tales taken from Ovid are known to have circulated among the Celts of the Middle Ages. Yet these are hardly distinguished from traditional tales, which, "in the magic of their beauty," they resemble.[92] In Thomas' poem, when Tristram entertains with his harp, he renders *Graelent*, and then, importuned, satisfies the King with an encore, "le lai de la courtoise Thisbé de l'ancienne Babylone."[93] There must also have been a French version of the Middle English Breton lay *Sir Orfeo*, which in outline resembles Ovid's story of Orphaeus and Eurydice. If

---

[91] Joseph Engels, *Études sur l'Ovide Moralisé* (Diss. Gronigen, 1945), p. 65, discusses the widespread interest in Ovid coming before the *Ovide Moralisé*.

[92] Brinkmann, p. 106.

[93] Joseph Bédier, ed. *Le Roman de Tristan* (Paris, 1902), I, 52. This version of the Pyramus and Thisbe story may well be a lyric lay, following as it does *Graelent*, described as "cette melodie."

so, like the English *Sir Orfeo* it would reveal the effect of popular handling in its passage from Ovid through Breton to medieval French.[94]

The narrative lay of Marie de France has one prominent feature distinguishing it from the Ovidian *conte*. The claim, frequently stated, is that she is telling stories taken from the Breton past.[95] Whether or not it is as conventional as the remarks in the opening and closing lines of medieval romances is hard to decide; but the claim is made and, since it is the reason for associating Breton lays with Celtic sources, deserves comment.[96] In the General Prologue she says:

> De lais pensai qu'oiz aveie.
> Ne dutai pas, bien le saveie,
> que pur remembrance les firent
> des aventures qu'il oirent
> cil ki primes les comencierent
> et ke avant les enveierent.

[94] See Kittredge, "Sir Orfeo," p. 185: "Our Breton harper . . . got the story by word of mouth and in no very accurate shape; and in making it over into a lay, he must inevitably have changed the story still further to make it square with his own beliefs and traditions and those of his auditors. In this process, such parts of the classic myth as were within his circle of ideas were retained with least alteration; such things as he could not understand were cast aside or forgotten; many points were misunderstood or unwittingly misrepresented. In short, the Ovidian story became a Breton lay in every sense—short, romantic, Celtic. This the French translator must have rendered without much change, his aim being to tell the tale of a favorite lay, not to restore an antique. And from this French version came our English Orfeo; freely handled, no doubt, but with no essential variation."

[95] Gröber, *Grundriss*, vol. ii part I, p. 597, describes the special prologue and epilogue as a peculiarity of the narrative lay. Since the fact of a "special prologue and epilogue" is meaningless by itself, it seems necessary to dwell hereafter on the specific contents of these features.

[96] See Parley A. Cristensen, "The Beginnings and Endings of the Middle English Metrical Romances," *Stanford University Abstracts of Dissertations*, ii (1928), 105–110.

Plusurs en ai oiz conter,
nes vueil laissier ne oublier.
(ll. 33–40)

In her individual lays, the mention of a source is never specific. *Guigemar* (ll. 19–26) adds that the people of ancient Brittany "made lays from stories which I know to be true"; so also *Equitan* (ll. 1–12), where the Bretons composed "par pruesce, par curteisie, e par noblesce." Then, according to *Les Dous Amanz* (l. 1), the adventure happened in the past ("jadis").

The temptation is great, but unrewarding, to wrest a definite meaning from her lines. She is relating an adventure about which Bretons, or others, made a lay. She notes both that the adventure took place in the ancient past and that her stories are true, including *Bisclavret* with its werewolf. By "true" she may conceivably mean "accurately reported" or, probably, the moral, the sentiment and the situations of her stories are true to life.[97]

Her acknowledgement of a debt to the Bretons, rather than to a Latin author, perhaps Ovid, whom she might have translated, indicates that she had a choice of more than one source. Does the possibility of a choice, which she mentions, show an indifference to which it would be? For her purpose, either would serve, since either in her hands would soon become a

[97] For a comparison see Paul J. Jones, *Prologue and Epilogue in Old French Lives of Saints before 1400* (Philadelphia, 1933), pp. 12–13. "The claim to absolute veracity that we find in the lives of the saints is found in the prologues to the epic in Old French, and some critics would have us believe that the phrases are mere conventions in both cases. This may be true in the epic. Summoned to produce his pretended documents, or to name them, the author of the *chanson de geste* would have been much embarrassed. Not so with our authors." Ewert, ed. *Marie de France: Lais*, p. 165, defines *true* in the lays as meaning "authenticated by tradition."

vehicle for the expression of ideas and sentiments about love and adventure; it would soon cease to be the prime material which she took over. By her own admission, very simply, she chooses the stories told in the lays only because they are fresher than any others available; in the General Prologue (l. 32) she says that many before her translated from Latin and preempted the field; she must search elsewhere.

If the formal claim that her source is Breton appeared in each of the twelve poems, it could be considered a characteristic of the narrative lay. In *Le Fraisne*, *Bisclavret*, *Yonec*, *Milun* and *Chaitivel* it is not made at all; whether it was originally intended, but omitted just to "vary the opening lines" is uncertain. Since the setting of these five poems is Brittany for at least part of their story, however, it can be concluded that either a Breton setting or a claim to a Breton setting or a claim to a Breton source is sufficient to identify the form. Imitations, which will be considered in Chapter 2, may simply call themselves Breton lays without referring to a Breton source or setting.

Marie de France reshaped available stories at a time when borrowing reflected little on an author's originality. How she reshaped these is more important than where she found them. In the process she respects the separateness, such as it was, of medieval literary forms, the fabliau, the saint's life, the fable, each with its own purpose.

At least two of her narrative lays present fabliau situations: *Equitan* and *Bisclavret*. In these adulterous lovers are detected and punished, but without the unpitying humor of the fabliau. Her purpose is not to make one laugh, but to represent an aspect of ideal love, here tragic. In *Les Dous Amanz*, a father who desires to keep his daughter from mar-

riage sets before any suitors an impossible test; his motive is
to enjoy the companionship of his only daughter without
having to share her affections with a son-in-law.

> Li reis ot une fille, bele
> e mult curteise dameisele.
> Fiz ne fille fors li n'aveit;
> forment l'amout e cherisseit.
> (ll. 21–24)

A father's love for an only daughter, which occurs as a theme
in popular analogues, is often presented as incestuous. Marie
de France prefers to ennoble it, although she knows the
nature of the relationship as it is found elsewhere; she has
heard fabliaux, which were not always offensive.[98] She avoids
the painful realism of this form and presents the father, if
not as completely good, at least as no worse than old and
selfish. For her the motifs found in one type of narrative are
applicable to another; they demonstrate in this instance the
difficulty of defining the narrative lay in terms of motifs,
Breton or otherwise.

The saint's life, in glorifying the life, death and miracles
of a holy person, assumes any number of forms in medieval
literature and can be distinguished from the narrative lay by
its purpose, to edify.[99] It is designed as devotional literature,

[98] Joseph Bédier, *Les Fabliaux*, 4th ed. (Paris, 1925), p. 116. For a discussion of who heard fabliaux, see pp. 371–385. Fabliaux are short, from 18 to 1200 verses, usually of from three to four hundred. Their unpolished octosyllabic couplets go well with their contents. Unlike the narrative lay they are realistic poems written without any pretensions to literary standing. Their dialogue is easy and natural. See pp. 341–357 for comments on style. Frappier, "Remarques," pp. 24–27, finds a demarcation between lay and fabliaux hard to establish.

[99] Gordon H. Gerould, *Saints' Legends* (Boston and New York, 1916), pp. 1–5.

purely and simply, and achieves its purpose by holding up for imitation someone eminent for his holiness. In tracing the subject's lifetime it may resemble *Le Fraisne, Milun* and *Eliduc,* which are the only lays of the twelve to relate major parts of a lifetime. The significance of this comparison, involving two very dissimilar forms, is to anticipate the merging of a saint's life and a narrative lay in *Emare* and *Sir Gowther,* which will be considered in Chapter 5.

The Aesopian fable, of which Marie de France was a translator, is distinguished from the narrative lay in purpose as well as in method: it instructs its reader by telling a story which has a moral.[100] Specifically, it relates a brief, concrete action from which a moral or lesson in worldly wisdom can be derived. Ordinarily, the shorter the action, the more pointed the lesson; and the more concrete it is, the greater its probability and effectiveness. It has no emotional appeal, since it is designed to address the reason. Its relative brevity recalls the narrative lay; so also does its unification by means of its single idea, though the idea is far more explicit in the fable and surpasses in emphasis the story accompanying it. In other respects the two forms have little or nothing in common.

Thus the Breton lay of Marie de France is a short narrative poem of between one hundred and one thousand lines, about ideal love and designed as reading for the court of England of the twelfth century. Although its origin in Celtic literature is uncertain, it may even be a simplified *conte* accompanying

[100] Walter Wienert, *Die Typen der griechisch-römischen Fabel mit einer Einleitung über das Wesen der Fabel,* F F Communications No. 56 (Helsinki, 1925), presents in his introduction definitions of the fable.

a Breton lay, which is believed to have been a musical-vocal composition; its conscious simplification is extended to plot and language. Considered externally, the narrative lay contains, besides the story proper, a prologue and epilogue, in which either a Breton source is claimed or the setting is given as Brittany. It is written in octosyllabic couplets, in the vernacular rather than Latin. Artistically it shows both a knowledge of the arts of rhetoric and a conscious attempt at elegance, which does not necessarily conflict with the author's desire for simplification. Its unity is derived from the single idea about love which it develops; but love in the narrative lay is a simpler, more natural emotion than that associated with Courtly Love. In scope it may vary within a limited range by presenting (1) a simple dramatic situation without much action, (2) an anecdote or (3) a biography in brief.

2

The Later Breton Lay in French

ALTHOUGH THE BRETON lay, modeled on the twelve poems of
Marie de France, continued to be written through the year
1270, her imitators because of a lack of skill more often than
not failed.[1] To assure dignity and an audience, the more in-
ventive of them applied to short didactic love poems and elevated examples of the fabliau the designation of *lay*. Finally,
some called any short and serious narrative poems Breton lay
regardless of their source or setting. These developments in
Old French form a part of the background of the Middle

---

[1] Lucien Foulet, "Marie de France et la Légende de Tristan," *ZfRPh*,
XXXII (1908), 263–264, traces the narrative lay as far back as Marie de France,
with whom the form begins. Warnke, *Lais*, p. xxi, is less positive: the most
important composer of the narrative lay "ist die Dichterin Marie de France.
Dem Beispiel, das Marie gegeben hatte, folgten andere Dichter unbekannten
Namens." Axel Ahlström, "Marie de France et les Lais Narratifs," *Kungl.
Vetenskaps-och-Vitterhets-Samhälles, Handlingar*, 3rd Series, XXIX (Göteborg;
1925), No. 3, p. 27, thinks that she began a new literary form.

English lays. Two other theories, each recent and each dependent on its own principle, should also be mentioned. According to the first, which distinguishes between recurring story-patterns, there are three types of supernatural lay: Type I (*Lanval, Graelent, Guingamor*); Type II, differing from Type I in that the mortal and fairy have a child (*Tydorel, Desiré*); Type III, the Sohrab and Rustum story (*Milun, Doon, Sir Degare*).[2] According to the second classification, there are three kinds: anecdotes, realistic lays and supernatural lays (Williams, pp. 76–84).

I. ANONYMOUS BRETON LAYS

Usually the closest imitators reveal only a "pâle reflet" of their model and a fatal preoccupation with favorite motifs, phrases and such externals as the prologue and epilogue of the Breton lay.[3] Although in the thirteenth century these borrowed advantages must have done much to insure an audience, they poorly make up for the story of love unified by a predominant idea. Motivation was unsure or changed. If recognizable at all *courtoisie* in the anonymous Breton lays becomes little more than a mechanical ascription of *bonté, pitié, largesse, joie*; and love, not necessarily Courtly Love, fails to enjoy the prominence which Marie de France gave it in her twelve poems.

The anonymous Breton lays, however, should be considered

[2] G. V. Smithers, "Story-patterns in Some Breton Lays," *MÆ*, xxii (1953), 62 ff. Doubtless studies of the Breton lay written after Marie de France will be affected by current interest in composition by formulas such as have been identified in the OE. and ME. poetry, the OF. fabliau and epic (Curschmann, pp. 36–38).

[3] Foulet, "Marie de France et les Lais bretons," p. 321.

individually, or if grouped at all, should be shown in their relationship to analogous poems of Marie de France. Three, *Desiré*, *Graelent* and *Guingamor*, tell how a knight falls in love with a *fée* in much the same way as Lanval, and show among themselves various degrees of artistic skill.

DESIRÉ

Desiré has the outward appearance of a Breton lay.[4] Brief, containing 822 lines in octosyllabic couplets, it has also the typical prologue and epilogue, which should be quoted in full:

> M'entente i ai mise et ma cure
> A raconter une aventure
> Dont cil qui a ce tens vesquirent,
> Por remembrance ·j· lai en firent.
> (ll. 1–4)

> Cil qui sorent cest aventure,
> En avoient ·j· lai trouvé
> Qu'il en apelent Desirré.
> (ll. 820–822)

It develops the theme of love, to which prowess is subordinate: in Calatir near the Blanche Lande of Scotland, a couple remain childless until they make a pilgrimage to St. Gilles in Provence. When their son Desiré grows up, he seeks adventure in Normandy and Brittany, and then returns to serve his king. One day he goes to the Blanche Lande to be counselled by a hermit. On the way he meets and falls in love with a *fée* more beautiful than Venus, who gives him wealth as well as a ring which will disappear from his finger if he reveals their love. Desiré then goes off tourneying. Returning later to the

---

[4] *The Lays of Desiré, Graelent and Melion*, pp. 48–85.

hermit, he happens to mention in confession his secret love and at once loses the ring. For over a year he grieves until one day the *fée* comes and in pity forgives him: she then reveals herself as a Christian who will be with him always, even at divine service. Returning to court Desiré goes hunting and comes upon a child who, greeting him as father, returns the lost ring. When the child flees into the forest, Desiré follows until he meets a dwarf, who leads him to his *amie*, the mother of the child. After returning years later to the court, Desiré is surprised at Pentecost to see before the king his *fée* with their two children, the boy now old enough for knighthood and a maiden ready for marriage. When the *fée* asks for help, the king dubs the youth a knight and takes the maiden as his own queen. Then Desiré and the *fée* are married and go off to a home in the Blanche Lande.

This poem fails to represent human love in the tradition of the Breton lay. The ennobling force noted in the lays of Marie de France is missing from *Desiré*. Though love as an interest remains prominent and certainly unifies the poem, it betrays a poet who nervously awaits the day when the lovers will be united with the full blessings of the Church; only then will his obligation to Church as well as to art be discharged. His handling of supernatural elements is not always skillful; "son surnaturel est de qualité inférieure, il consiste surtout à introduire des incidents inexplicable suivant les lois ordinaires de la vraisemblance; mais d'y mettre une intention d'art ou à vrai dire une intention quelconque, c'est ce dont l'auteur est incapable" (Foulet, p. 37). The unexplained dwarf is a vestigial character from the story on which the poet drew: he serves no purpose other than to satisfy an interest in the supernatural or unnatural.

GRAELENT

Graelent (756 lines; octosyllabic couplets) is based on a tale from which the Bretons derived a lay.[5]

> L'aventure de Graelent
> Vos dirai si com je l'entent:
> Bons en est li lais a oir,
> Et les notes a retenir
> (ll. 1–4)

> ·I·lai en firent li Breton,
> Graelent Muer l'apele l'on.
> (ll. 755–756)

It varies slightly the story of Marie's *Lanval*, but lacks the Arthurian setting as well as "every trace of her literary style . . . and every effect of her skill as a storyteller."[6] When Graelent honorably refuses the Queen's offer of love, he so angers her that she persuades the King of Brittany to deprive him of rewards. Destitute, Graelent leaves the Court and goes off into the forest. There he meets a *fée* who becomes his mistress, but only on his promise that he will keep their love a secret; in return, she gives him wealth and accoutrements. They live together until Graelent returns to court. One day,

---

[5] *The Lays of Desiré, Graelent and Melion*, pp. 76–101.

[6] Though sources are somewhat beyond the scope of this study, one cannot ignore the disagreement over the relationship of *Graelent* to *Lanval*. Foulet, "Marie de France et les Lais bretons," p. 25, concludes: "Nous pouvons dès maintenant conclure que l'auteur de *Graelent* n'a pas eu, en ce qui concerne la légende de *Lanval*, d'autre source que Marie (*Eliduc, Lanval*)." William C. Stokoe, Jr., "The Sources of *Sir Launfal: Lanval* and *Graelent*," PMLA, LXIII (1948), 493, argues that *Graelent*, which has "all the characteristics of unaltered folklore," could have been derived from Marie de France only by a redactor who "took the greater trouble of changing it back, altering the names, removing every trace of her literary style and destroying every effect of her skill as a storyteller. The assumption is absurd."

as the others praise the Queen's beauty, Graelent alone disagrees and says that he loves someone far more beautiful.
Incensed, the King tells him to produce her. Graelent is disturbed because he remembers his promise, now broken by his
boasting. At the proper moment his *amie* saves him by walking in so that everyone can see her beauty. After his vindica-
tion, Graelent accompanies her back into the forest. When
she crosses a river, he goes along against her wishes and is
almost drowned before she rescues him and takes him to the
farther bank. There they live together; Graelent's horse, still
on the opposite bank of the river, grieves for his master.

It is interesting to note that some humor appears in *Graelent*, unlike both the other lays resembling *Launfal* or those
of Marie de France. Happening on the maiden as she bathes
in the spring, Graelent is anxious not to disturb her. She
notices him only when he seizes her clothes:

> "Graelent, lai mes dras ester,
> Ne t'em puez gueres amender;
> Se tu o toi les en partoies,
> Et ainsi nue lessoies,
> Trop seroit povre covoitise.
> Rendez moi seviaus ma chemise,
> Li mantiaus puet bien estre tuen,
> Deniers en pren, car il est buens."

> "Ne sui pas filz de marcheant,
> Ne borjois, por vendre mantiaus;
> S'il valoit ore iij chastiaus,
> Ne l'en porteroie je mie;
> Issiez hors de cele eue, amie,
> Prenez vos dras, si vos vestez,
> Pri vos qu'ensemble o moi parlez."

> "Je n'en veil pas," fet cele, "issir,
> Que de moi vos puissiez sesir;
> N'ai cure de vostre parole,
> Ne sui mie de vostre escole."
> (ll. 243–261)

This passage, with its sly reference to bourgeois dealers in secondhand clothing, is an early indication of a development to come: the application of lay to the *fabliau* (see below, pp. 94–100).

GUINGAMOR

The third poem in the group, *Guingamor*, might pass as the work of Marie de France.[7] It consists of 678 lines in octosyllabic couplets with prologue and epilogue:

> D'un lai vos dirai l'aventure:
> Nel tenez pas a troveure,
> Veritez est ce que dirai;
> Guingamor apele on le lai.
> (ll. 1–4)

> Por l'aventure recorder
> En fist li rois un lai trover:
> De Guingamor retint le non;
> Einsi l'apelent li Breton.
> (ll. 675–678)

After his royal uncle goes hunting, Guingamor is approached

---

[7] *Le Lai de Guingamor, Le Lai de Tydorel,* ed. Erhard Lommatzsch and Max L. Wagner (Berlin, 1922), pp. 1–20. Peter Kusel, *Guingamor: Ein Lai der Marie de France* (Rostock, 1922) attempts to show that this poem belongs to Marie de France, especially on the basis of language and prosody. When the third edition of the *Lais* was published in 1925, it included with Warnke's approval *Guingamor* as the thirteenth Breton lay of Marie de France.

71

at court by the Queen, who offers him her love. He rejects it. Fearing that her dishonesty will become known to the King, the Queen conspires to get rid of Guingamor and so encourages him to hunt for the white boar in an adventurous land beyond the perilous river. She promises him two packs of hounds belonging to the king. After a long hunt Guingamor comes upon a castle and then a spring at the foot of an olive tree. When he sees a maiden bathing in the spring he seizes her clothes. She calls out and invites him to live with her. At her palace he meets the others of his party, from whom he was separated. He is so comfortable that he stays for three hundred years, which seem like only three. When he decides to visit his uncle, he is warned not to eat anything while away. Back in his own country he meets a charcoal burner and from him learns that his uncle died centuries earlier. Being hungry he eats a wild apple growing along a road and so, in keeping with the warning, shrivels up and remains so until rescued by the *fée*, who whisks him back to the land of the fairies.

Doon

Certain other narrative lays show the influence of Marie de France. *Doon* (288 lines; octosyllabic couplets) recalls *Milun*.[8] Its prologue and epilogue are significant because they state clearly the distinction between a lyric and narrative lay:

> Doon, cest lai sevent plusor:
> N'a gueres bon harpeor
> Ne sache les notes harper;
> Mes je vos voil dire et conter

[8] G. Paris, "Lais inédits de Tyolet, de Guingamor, de Doon, du Lecheor et de Tydorel," *Romania*, viii (1879), 59–64.

L'aventure dunt li Breton
Apelerent cest lai Doon.

(ll. 1–6)

Firent les notes li Breton
Du lay c'om apele Doon.

(ll. 287–288)

Like countless other suitors Doon of Brittany attempts to win the maiden of Edinburgh by performing the two pre-scribed tests. He rides in a single day from Southampton to Edinburgh, but, unlike the other suitors, remains alive by not using the lethal bed which the maiden has prepared for her exhausted suitors. He succeeds in the second test by follow-ing the flight of a swan during the course of a single day. Then he and the maiden marry. Before returning to Brit-tany he gives her a ring by which he can identify the son she will bear him. In an encounter years later at Mont San Michel, Doon is unhorsed by a young knight, who with the ring identifies himself as Doon's son. Accompanied by his son, Doon then rejoins his beloved in Edinburgh.

Doon is unworthy of Marie de France. It consists of two parts unskillfully joined: (1) the test which the exhausted hero performs in not yielding to the temptation of sleep; (2) the long ride from Southampton to Edinburgh and its sequel, following the swan for a day.[9] Fascinated by these, the poet goes on to borrow the father-son combat, feeling certain that, since it worked in *Milun*, it will here also. He sometimes fails to assign motives: for no good reason at all Doon departs for Brittany three days after his marriage. Love,

---

[9] Paris, pp. 59–61.

which should be prominent, is less so than the tests which Doon performs to win his lady.

MELION

Melion, like *Doon*, is a slight poem, certainly recalling Marie de France, but not hers.[10] It develops in 594 lines of octosyllabic couplets the werewolf story of *Bisclavret*, which must have been popular. Yet, in spite of the added Arthurian setting, it is inferior to *Bisclavret*.

> Vrai est li lais de Melion;
> Ce dient bien tot il baron.
> (ll. 591–592)

After Melion antagonizes the ladies of Arthur's court by vowing to love none who has been loved before, he remains unhappy until Arthur gives him a castle of his own. One day while hunting he comes upon an Irish princess who has never before been loved and is now willing to have Melion as her lover. After their marriage they go hunting with a squire and locate a stag. When the princess craves a piece of its meat, Melion with a special ring transforms himself into a werewolf in order to hunt better. While he is off by himself, his wife and the squire leave him and hurry to Dublin, taking with them the ring. Unable now to change back, Melion pursues them as a werewolf, reaches Ireland by stowing away aboard ship and joins a pack of ten wolves. When all ten are killed, Melion takes refuge with King Arthur, who has just arrived to make peace with the King of Ireland. Lying meekly at Arthur's feet, Melion suddenly sees the squire who betrayed

[10] *The Lays of Desiré, Graelent and Melion*, pp. 102–122. For variants of the werewolf story see Charles W. Dunn, *William of Palerne, History, Legend and Romance* (Harvard University dissertation, 1947), especially p. 196.

him. Attacking him savagely, Melion is saved by Arthur's
intervention from the revenge of those present. When the
squire confesses the princess' and his own perfidy, Melion
is identified as Arthur's lost baron. By means of the ring,
which his wife still has, he regains human form and leaves
Ireland with Arthur, making sure, however, that the Irish
princess stays behind.

ÉPINE

Épine seems to have been written merely to satisfy interest
in poems of this style.[11] It contains 514 lines in octosyllabic
couplets and a prologue, which protests that the adventure
really happened (ll. 1–15) and goes on to cite as proof a
manuscript at St. Aaron's in Caerleon. In the epilogue the
author announces a departure; instead of naming his work
after the subject of the adventure, he gives only the alternate
title:

> De l'aventure que dite ai,
> Li Breton en firent un lai.
> Por ce que il avint au gue,
> En ont li Breton esgarde
> Que li lais ne recevroit non
> De rien se de l'espine non.
> Ne l'ont pas des enfanz nomme
> Ainz l'ont de l'espine apele,
> Si a non li lais de l'espine
> Qui bel comence et bel define.
> (ll. 505–514)

In verses 165–186, he recaptures the atmosphere of the Breton

---

[11] Rudolf Zenker, "Le Lai de l'Épine," *ZfRPh*, xviii (1893), 232–255.
For an evaluation of the poem see Foulet, "Marie de France et les lais bretons," p. 29.

lay as he describes the entertainment of the knights eight days before the feast of St. John. They hear the lay of Aelis and the lay of Orphai, which may be related to the Middle English *Sir Orfeo* (below, pp. 146–158). The natural son of a king and the queen's daughter by an earlier marriage are allowed to grow up together as children and are separated only when discovered in an innocent embrace. As the years pass, their separation does little to kill their love. The son, on the vigil of the feast of St. John, goes off on an adventure as a knight. During the night he lies awake at the Perilous Ford, near which a thorn-tree grows. His beloved at the same time enters her garden and rests under a grafted fruit tree. When she prays that she may be near her lover, she is suddenly united with him at the Perilous Ford. He proves his strength before her against a knight in red armor, who appears on the opposite side of the water riding a white horse with red ears. After defeating the knight, he takes the horse, which will disappear as soon as its bridle is removed. He meets in combat two other knights and then returns with his beloved to court, where he describes his adventure and is married. He keeps the magical horse until one day his lady out of curiosity removes its bridle and causes the animal to disappear.

The erotic symbols of the poem have not been satisfactorily explained: the youthful embrace, the removal of the maiden while she is seated under the grafted fruit-tree as in *Sir Orfeo*, the meeting near a thorn-tree alongside a ford, the knight in red armor, mounted on a white horse with red ears and the magical bridle. More so than the symbols in other Breton lays these might be called irrational and point to a poet more interested in magic than in the continuity of his love story. His treatment of love, which is prominent throughout, presents difficulties. As the poem opens, love between the children is discouraged, but develops without hindrance after the incident at the ford: there is no dramatic conflict in the hero, no real challenge except the physical one, which he successfully meets in defeating the knight. Like *Doon*, *Épine* is by an imitator who fails to grasp the unity of the Breton lay, but who should not, for his disappointing effort, be styled "plagiaire médiocre."[12]

TYDOREL

Of a high quality, *Tydorel* comes close to the art of Marie de France without being hers.[13] It opens its 490 lines by referring to the new lay about *Tydorel*:

> L'aventure d'un lai novel,
> Que l'en apele Tydorel,
> Vous conterai comme ele avint
> (ll. 1–3)

> Ceste conte tienent a verai
> Li Breton qui firent le lai
> (ll. 489–490)

Tydorel falls into two parts. For the first ten years of their marriage the King and Queen of Brittany live happily, but

---

[12] Foulet, "Marie de France et les Lais bretons," p. 36.

[13] E. Lommatzsch and M. W. Wagner, *Le Lai de Guingamor, Le Lai de Tydorel*, pp. 23–36. Friedrich Hiller, *Tydorel, ein Lai der Marie de France*, on the basis of prosody style, vocabulary and composition, attributes the poem to Marie de France. M. B. Ogle, "The Orchard Scene in Tydorel and *Sir Gowther*," *The Romanic Review*, XIII (1922), 40–41, finds *Tydorel* "certainly posterior to Marie's *Yonec* and influenced by it." Interestingly, Ogle would see in the poem the faint outline of the apocryphal story of Anna, wife of Joachim. Alexander H. Krappe, "The Celtic Provenance of 'The Lay of Tydorel,'" *MLR*, XXIV (1929), 204, thinks that the story reached France from a Celtic-speaking country.

without children. One summer day, while the King is hunting, the Queen retires to the orchard with her women and for relaxation lies down under a tree. Left alone for a moment she sees a handsome knight approach and offer his love. She immediately accepts and becomes his secret lover. Leaving the orchard with him by horse, she rides as far as a lake and there dismounts, but the knight continues to ride into the lake, right over his head, and disappears for as long as it would take to go four miles. Returning, he tells her that she will bear him a son, who will rule Brittany, and who at night, since he will never sleep, will have to be entertained with songs and stories. She will also bear a daughter, who in her marriage to a count will have two children, from whom Count Alains and his son Conains will spring. The knight then takes her back to the orchard and departs. When the Queen gives birth to Tydorel, the King is pleased to accept him as his own. In the second part of the lay, Tydorel, true to the prediction, lives without sleep, requiring at night only entertainment. He replaces his deceased father as king. One night, when a sick widow's only son is called on to entertain, he demurs because he can repeat nothing except the axiom that no human being goes without sleep. When the puzzled King reflects on his sleeplessness, his mother tells him who his father was and describes in detail the incident in the orchard leading to his birth. No sooner has Tydorel heard her than he hurries off to the lake, into which, like his father, he rides and never returns.

Tydorel has the appearance of an occasional poem. Alains and his son Conains (ll. 147–148), who are descendants of Tydorel's sister, have been identified as Alain III (1008–40) and Conan II (1040–66), or Alain Fergent (1084–1113) and

Conan le Gros (1113–48).[14] To what extent a supernatural ancestor would flatter these figures is uncertain. A more understandable identification, however, can be made. Conains might be Conan III, who ruled Brittany from 1113 to 1148 and married Matilda, daughter of Henry I of England, by whom he *believed* that he had two children—Noel and Bertha; but "suspecting his wife of infidelity, he protested on his death-bed that Noel was not his son."[15] There is a further question. Would the descendants of Conan III be pleased by a poetic explanation offered after their ancestor's death to remove a taint from the pages of history? The character of Tydorel's father would certainly be flattering enough: "though no longer a god, the mysterious lover is still a creature of beauty and charm, who bends mortals to his will and holds them in awe lest they pry too curiously into the hidden things he may not reveal."[16]

The anonymous author of *Tydorel* intended first to write a Breton lay, which had a ready audience. In comparison with Marie de France he is less successful in handling the form. The poem is made up of two parts, and "the lack of unity . . . is doubtless open to severe criticism . . ." (p. 171). In the first part the Queen, who recalls the lady in *Yonec*, gladly receives a supernatural lover, although she has had a devoted husband. All she wants is a child, regardless of who the father is, and regardless also of whether love outside marriage is less

[14] Paris, "Lais Inédits de Tyolet, de Guingamor, de Doon, de Lecheor et de Tydorel," pp. 66.

[15] The second of these identifications seems to be made here for the first time. See Baring-Gould Sabine, *A Book of Brittany*, revised by Ivan Daniel (London, 1932), p. 24, which says nothing about *Tydorel*, but discusses Conan III and his doubts.

[16] Florence L. Ravenel, "*Tydorel and Sir Gowther*," PMLA, xx (1905), 177.

virtuous than fruitful. Since in *Yonec* the lady is unloved—her husband is old and cruel, the motivation of the two poems is different. In *Tydorel* love is far less than the ennobling emotion which Marie de France represents; it is practical and begets a son. In the second part, love is ignored except incidentally; so is *courtoisie*. Though Tydorel presumably is an ideal courtly character, attention is centered, not on his nobility, but on his supernatural origin and the question of how soon it will be detected: the treatment of suspense is masterful, but more appropriate to the fabliau. The introduction of the widow's son is practical, but inappropriate also: he is a bourgeois goldsmith, and on him the poet spends lavishly in sympathy and narrative skill, and it is his proverb which neatly determines the outcome of the entire story—a story about a king.

TYOLET

Like *Tydorel*, *Tyolet* consists of two separate stories made into a Breton lay.[17] It opens its 704 lines with an account of how and why Breton lays are written, which ends:

> Bretons en firent lais plusors
> Si con dient nos ancessors,
> Un en firent que vos dirai,
> Selonc le conte que je sai,
> D'un vallet bel et engingnos,
> Hardi et fier et coragos.
> (ll. 35–40)

In the first part Tyolet, the son of a widow, lives in a remote forest where he has never seen an armed knight. He supports

[17] Paris, "Lais Inédits de Tylolet, de Guingamor, de Doon, du Lecheor, et de Tydorel," pp. 41–50.

his mother by killing game, which he attracts by whistling. One day while hunting he comes upon a kid, which is transformed before his eyes into an armed knight. He asks the knight to explain his equipment, and the knight agrees. When Tyolet returns and tells his mother of his experience, he receives from her both the arms which belonged to his deceased father and encouragement to serve under King Arthur as a knight. Riding into court, he declares his intention and is accepted. He then attempts to win the princess of Logres by fetching the leg of a white stag. He locates the stag with the help of her favorite hound and by whistling brings the animal close enough for a kill. Thus he wins the maiden and later on becomes King of Logres.

Tyolet, "an ancient tradition," resembles *Conte del Graal* of Chrétien de Troyes.[18] In both a youth is raised by his mother in complete ignorance of chivalry. Meeting a knight he is attracted by a life of *courtoisie* and goes to King Arthur's court. Neither poem is derived from the other, both having a common twelfth-century source. *Tyolet*, however, is not so clearly or simply told. The connection between its two parts is unnecessary: in the second part the only use which the poet makes of Tyolet's background comes when Tyolet the hunter whistles to attract the white stag, much as he did in his youth.

As a love poem *Tyolet* is close to the lays of Marie de France, but with a difference. It presents love as its chief interest, and courage only as a means of demonstrating a worthiness to love and be loved. Thus Tyolet climaxes his ascent at court by winning the hand of the princess. When he performs the prescribed test, which is the only adventure in

---

[18] Pp. 40–41.

the poem, he receives her as his bride and settles down to a life of contentment and majesty. The formula of love and adventure breaks down only where there is no emphasis of the effects of love: Tyolet goes through the physical development, but not the psychological, which the reader is left to fill in for himself.

If *Desiré, Graelent, Guingamor, Doon, Melion, Épine, Tydorel* and *Toylet* were not written under the direct inspiration of Marie de France, they were at least attempts to make the most of the form which she had developed. Between 1170 and 1250 there was a general interest in any poem called a Breton lay, lyric or narrative.[19] As late as the Anglo-Norman *Horn*, written in the last years of the twelfth century, Horn can distinguish himself by presenting a lyric lay:

> Sur toz homes ke sunt · fet cist a merueiller
> Quant ses notes ot fait · si la prent amunter.
> Et tut par autres cordes · les cordes fait soner.
> Mut se merueillent tuit · qu'il la sout si bailler.
> E quant il out issi fait · si cummence a noter
> Le lai dunt orains dis · de Baltof haut e cler,
> Si cum sunt cil Bretun · ditiel fait costumier.[20]
>
> (ll. 2385–91)

Unfortunately it is impossible to determine how much Marie de France and "cil Bretun" each contributed to the total interest in the lay either as a lyric form or narrative. The important fact is that this interest, which was real, was sustained by literary artists during the thirteenth century, and manu-

---

[19] Foulet, "Marie de France et la Légende de Tristan," pp. 263–264, gives a detailed, but debatable breakdown of these years and assigns poems to periods.

[20] *Das Anglonormanische Lied vom wackern Ritter Horns*, ed. R. Brede and E. Stengel (Marburg, 1883).

scripts of narrative lays in Old French continued to be copied even later.[21] The recently noted Shrewsbury School MS. VII, f. 200, dating after 1270, which includes in its list of sixty-seven titles *Bisclavret*, *Le Fraisne*, *Lanval*, *Eliduc*, *Chievrefueil*, *Milun* and *Yonec*, as well as the anonymous *Doon*, *Lai d'Haveloc*, *Tydorel* and *Nabaret*, is certain evidence of continued vogue.[22]

The geographical area in which the twenty extant Breton lays were written, twelve by Marie de France and eight anonymous, is surprisingly limited, to judge from dialect alone. All "bear the marks of Norman French,"[23] but show individual characteristics. Since Marie de France probably wrote in England, this area would comprise Norman England as well as Normandy: Bretons "as allies of the Normans and as kinsmen of the Welsh and Cornish"[24] were free to travel on both sides of the Channel and so to circulate their stories— if these were not already widespread before the period of Norman political supremacy. Although in the lays the elusive term *Bretaigne* usually means "Brittany,"[25] the area in

[21] Two of the most important manuscripts date from the second half of the thirteenth century, British Museum MS. *Harley 978* and Bibliothèque Nationale MS. *Nouvelles Acquisitions du Fonds Français No. 1104*. Another, in the latter library, MS. Fr. 24432, containing *Yonec*, was prepared in the fourteenth century. For a convenient account see Ewert, *Marie de France: Lais*, pp. xviii ff.

[22] Georgine H. Brereton, "A Thirteenth-Century List of French Lays and Other Narrative Poems," *MLR*, xlv (1950), 40–45, adds as probable identifications *Desiré*, *Ignaure*, *Guiron*, *Chaitivel* and *Guigemar* or *Guingamor*. She dates the MS. "after 1270, because a list of English kings on f. 203v. ends with the words: "Henricus tercius regnauit quinquaginta annis."

[23] Gaston Paris, "Le Lai de L'Espervier," *Romania*, vii (1878), 2.

[24] Roger Sherman Loomis, *Arthurian Tradition & Chrétien de Troyes* (New York, 1949), p. 32.

[25] E. Brugger, "Über die Bedeutung von Bretagne und Breton in mittelalterlichen Texten," *ZfSL*, xx (1898), 79–162.

which narrative lays were written would ironically exclude Brittany and would seem today so small as to emphasize the nature of the Breton lay in Old French literature: a literary form fashionable among Norman audiences between around 1170 and the middle of the thirteenth century.

During its period of imitation and decline, as the Breton lay met competition, especially from the fable and the fabliau, it began to show the characteristics of other forms and to lose its identity almost completely. Some significance attaches to the fact that Shrewsbury School *Manuscript VII* includes in its list of lays poems like "Lay sent brandan," presumably a saint's life, but designated a *lay*. In the remaining pages of this chapter, three offshoot forms, all related to the Breton lay, will be considered: the didactic lay, the elevated fabliau and the nondescript short poem framed as a Breton lay just to attract readers.

II. THE DIDACTIC LAY

Of these three forms, the didactic lay developed the most naturally. Written to teach *courtoisie*, it results from stressing the idea or *sen* of a Breton lay with a proportionate de-emphasis of other elements: its idea is so explicitly stated that the poem becomes primarily didactic. Extant examples are *Lai du Trot, Lai de l'Oiselet, Lai du Conseil* and *Lai de l'Ombre.*

Lai du Trot

Lai du Trot should be considered first because it comes close to the Breton lay in form and shows how the didactic tend-

ency was first worked out.[26] Its 304 lines of octosyllabic
couplets include a typical prologue and epilogue:

> Une aventure vos voil dire
> Molt bien rimee, tire a tire,
> Com il avint vos conterai
> Ne ja ne vos en mentirai
> L'aventure fu molt estraigne,
> Si avint jadis en Bretaigne
> A ·j· molt riche chevalier,
> Hardi et coragous et fier
> De la table reonde estoit.
> (ll. 1–9)

> Un lay en fisent li Breton
> Le lay del trot l'apele l'on.
> (ll. 303–304)

It opens in Brittany as Lorois, a knight of the Round Table,
arises early just to hear the nightingale. As he approaches a
forest he sees twenty-four happy damsels, lavishly clad, who
are riding swiftly and smoothly on white palfreys and are
accompanied by devoted lovers. They are followed by a dismal
train of *puceles*, dressed in black, whose lean cart-horses move
at a bumpy trot. Lorois is disturbed by their appearance. As
a lady of the latter group approaches, he questions her and
learns that the first group in life rendered service to Love
and are now being rewarded, but that the second, who can
only complain, sigh and trot along without lovers, disdained
Love. The speaker herself repented too late and now must

---

[26] Evie M. Grimes, "Le Lay du Trot," *Romanic Review*, xxvi (1935),
317–321. For a discussion of similar treatments of virginity and its perils see
B. J. Whiting, "Old Maids Lead Apes in Hell," *Englische Studien*, lxx
(1935–36), 337–351.

suffer. Lorois is so moved by this adventure that on returning to his castle he tells every detail.

The author of this poem, recognizing the "fundamental
equivalence between the immaterial and the material"[27] in
medieval art, tells a simple story to illustrate the system of
rewards and punishments under Courtly Love. Whatever his
source, he has removed its primitive quality and given it a
thirteenth-century chivalric meaning. He incidentally entertains his reader, but first urges him to act according to rule;
he stresses first the idea of the poem, the story of the wise
and foolish virgins.

LAI DE L'OISELET

The idea of *Lai de l'Oiselet* (390 lines; octosyllabic couplets)[28]
is equally apparent: *courtoisie* receives divine sanction. As a
didactic lay, however, this poem differs specifically from *Trot*:
it is called a *lay*, but lacks both a Breton setting and the characteristics of a Breton lay except these: it is a *short, serious
narrative* poem of a nonreligious nature. A greedy villain
visits the shady garden on his well-cultivated farm. On a limb
above his head a small bird is singing its message: love God
and realize that He thinks ill of *vilenie* but well of *courtoisie*.
Unmoved by its song, he catches it in a trap. Then the talk-
ing bird plans its escape. In return for its freedom it will tell
the villain three truths which no one of his class ever before
knew. When released it flies to a tree and there says that no
one should believe everything he hears, or cry over what he
does not have, or throw away what he has. Knowing these

---

[27] C. S. Lewis, *The Allegory of Love* (Oxford, 1936), p. 44.

[28] Raymond Weeks, "Le Lai de l'Oiselet," *Medieval Studies in Memory of
Gertrude Schoepperle Loomis* (Paris and New York, 1927), pp. 341–353.

already, the villain feels himself hoodwinked, and by a bird. The bird then asks why he ever believed his prisoner in the first place. To embarrass him further, it then tells him about the precious stone in his stomach. When the villain is more miserable than ever, the bird then warns him not to believe everything he hears, including this, not to cry over what he never had, or to throw away what he has. After giving this advice it flies away. The garden withers; the villain grows unhappy: he who covets all loses all.

Oiselet differs from its closest analogue,[29] yet retains certain characteristics of the *fable*. It has a setting in thirteenth-century France and enforces a courtly idea at the expense of a villain who is greedy and otherwise devoid of the ideals of court. The garden takes on a spiritual tone: everything in it is beautiful if only the observer has the qualities of soul to appreciate beauty, and these are vouchsafed only to the nobility. Instead of the malicious bird of the traditional tale, there is "un être surnaturel sorte de génie ailé," the instrument of God's will, which deals effectively with the villain. Even God has a courtly prejudice: He thinks well of *courtoisie*, but ill of *vilenie*. In spite of these changes, however, the poem is still distinguishable as a fable. It ends, as a fable should, with a clearly stated moral: "he who covets all loses all."

LAI DU CONSEIL

The two remaining didactic lays show the influence of other forms than the fable. *Lai du Conseil* (868 lines; octosyllabic couplets) is first of all a lay: "Cis lais nous conte sanz mentir"

---

[29] Gaston Paris, ed. *Le Lai de l'Oiselet* (Paris, 1884), pp. 49–52.

(4).[30] In its prologue it explicitly states its didactic purpose, which distinguishes it from the Breton lay of Marie de France:

> Uns chevaliers qui ne vout mie
> Que l'aventure fust perie,
> Nous a cest lai mis en romanz
> Por enseignier les vrais amanz
> Le plus bel que il pot, l'a fet
> L'un mot apres l'autres retret
> Mes mout se puet esmerueillier
> Que il ne se set conseillier
> D'un amor dont il est sorpris,
> Ainz dit qu'il est autressi pris
> Con cil qui en la bee maint.
>
> (ll. 855–865)

It opens on Chrismas eve at the court of a noble. Among the guests a lady who is sought after by three knights remains without a lover because she cannot decide on which of the three to have. When she notices a knight sitting apart from the others she puts her dilemma before him, describing the three in detail and their respective qualifications. No sooner has she heard him discourse on love than she forgets the first three suitors in her enthusiasm for a newly found fourth. Since he has all the qualities of a knight as well as eloquence, she correctly accepts him. According to a modern study, *Lai du Conseil* shows the influence of the *jeu parti* (p. 826). It presents a dilemma in that form: what can a woman do who is loved by three knights and responds with the same affec-

[30] Albert Barth, "Le Lai du Conseil," RF, xxxi (1911–2), 831–860. The curious coupling of *lais* and *contes* is a medieval example of the confusion which de Riquer says we should not associate with the usage of Marie de France, who considers herself the author of *contes*, not of lays (de Riquer, pp. 4–7); see the discussion of the lyric lay in Chapter 1, pp. 47–52 above.

tion for each? Its method of development is often through question and answer, the woman posing the question:

> "Sire, or me dites ensement
> S'il a tant de ioie en amors
> Con i'ai oi toz iors."
> (ll. 562–564)

> "Sir," fet ele, "or m'aprenez
> Se c'est voirs que i'ai oi dire
> Qu'amors abandonee est pire
> Que cele ou il a contredit."
> (ll. 680–683)

If the dilemma is resolved surprisingly easily—"choose a fourth lover," if it seems untrue to life, it may indicate the real character of *Lai du Conseil*: it is *poésie de salon* designed as reading for women, who wanted to see their dreams come true, at least in fiction (Barth, p. 826).

Lai de l'Ombre

In contrast, *Lai de l'Ombre*,[31] "une leçon de stratégie amoureuse,"[32] shows the influence of the *fabliau*. It is formally called a *lay* by its author Jean Renart (c. 1170–c. 1240), who wrote also the romance *L'Escoufle* and *Le Roman de la Rose ou de Guillaume de Dole*:[33]

> Or escoutez e icest conte
> Que ferai, s'aucun ne m'encombre,
> Et dirai ci, du Lai de l'Ombre
> (ll. 50–52)

---

[31] Jean Renart, *Le Lai de l'Ombre*, ed. John Orr (Edinburgh, 1948).
[32] Paris, "Le Lai de l'Ombre, publié par Joseph Bédier," *Romania*, xix (1890), 609–610.
[33] Orr, pp. xiv-xv.

Vilains est qui ses gas en fait
Quant ma courtoisie s'aoevre
A dire aucune plesant oeuvre
Au il n'a rampone ne lait.

(ll. 8–11)

Lai de l'Ombre tells how a resourceful knight makes a protesting lady his *amie*. He is so moved by her beauty that he asks her to pity him, but, since she is already married, she is offish. While she ponders his discomfort, she finds his ring on her finger and her suitor gone. Composing herself, she sends after him and then steps into the garden. He finds her still determined not to have his ring, but, confident of success, takes it back on condition that he may do whatever he wants with it. Then, as both watch her shadow on the water of a nearby well, he says that she will have it whom he loves next best. He drops the ring into the water. The lady is so impressed with this act of *courtoisie* that she can only pity him. In token of his success she gives him her own ring.

Renart gives this poem "something of the realism we associate with the fabliau," as well as its sustained interest (Orr, pp. xv–xvi). The plot of *Ombre* is well conceived. In 962 lines two lovers meet but remain apart until the knight devises an ingenious means of quieting his beloved one's fears. If, after her refusal, only her shadow can satisfy him, his love must be real; and he proves that it is by sacrificing the ring. Stylistically, his conquest is skillfully presented. Over one-half of the lines are devoted to dialogue: with the author in the far background the lovers dramatize the "lesson in the strategy of love."

LAI D'IGNAURE

Ombre and the other three didactic poems illustrate the application of *lay* to almost any short narrative poem of a serious nature. During the thirteenth century, however, *lay* could be applied to a dignified *conte à rire* as well, especially to avoid the connotation of *fabliau*, which suggested *vilenie*.[34] *Lai d'Ignaure*, which shows characteristics of both the didactic lay and the elevated fabliau, serves well to underline the conflict in nomenclature.[35]

Externally this poem recalls the Breton lay. It is short: 664 lines in octosyllabic couplets. Though written in a Franco-Picard dialect,[36] it tells a story set in Brittany, one "worth recalling":

> Pour chou, voel roumans coumenchier
> Une aventure molt estraigne
> Que, jadis, avint en Bretaigne
> D'un chevalier de grant poissanche,
> Ki bien doit estre en ramembranche.
> (ll. 14–18)

The double title found in certain of the lays comes up again:

> C'est la matere de cel lay
> Ichi le vous definerai.
> Franchois, Poitevin et Breton
> L'apielerent le Lay de Prison.

The "Lay of Ignaure," "of the Prisoner," based on the motif of the "eaten heart," takes place in ancient Brittany in the

---

[34] Bédier, *Les Fabliaux*, p. 35.

[35] *Le Lai d'Ignaure ou Lai du Prisonnier*, ed. Rita Le Jeune (Brussels, 1938), pp. 45–63.

[36] Le Jeune, pp. 18–20.

days of King Hoel. For over a year Ignaure secretly professes love to his neighbors' wives, but invites discovery by loving as many as twelve at the same time. As these twelve relax in a garden on the feast of St. John, they play a game of "confession": eleven reveal to a twelfth, acting as priest, their lover's name. When, to their mutual surprise, all say "Ignaure" they resolve to destroy their faithless lover. One of the twelve, accordingly, meets Ignaure in the same garden, where the eleven others await with knives. Their intended victim saves himself, however, by protesting that he loves all twelve equally. Angry, yet still infatuated, the ladies force him to confine his attention to one of their group—the one who played priest in the game. Love would be ideal, were the husbands to remain deceived, but one of them finds out and tells the eleven others. When they imprison Ignaure, their wives protest by refusing to eat for four days. At the end of their fast their first food turns out to be Ignaure's heart, which the irate husbands cut from their prisoner and disguised as a delicacy. Horrified upon learning what they have eaten, the twelve wives refuse to eat again and before dying compose a complaint in memory of their lover.

The poem is clear, as the author intended it to be:

> Sens est perdus, ki est couvers;
> Cis k'est moustres et descouvers
> Puet en auchum liu semenchier.
> (ll. 10–12)

That meaning is lost which is hidden; that which is made clear may instruct. In so remarking he at first may appear to echo Marie de France, who in lines 9–16 of the Prologue to her twelve lays points out a value to be derived from rereading an ancient text and finding its present meaning (above, pp. 13–44). The three lines quoted from *Ignaure*, however, seem to refer to the poet's choice of perfecting his writing until it is clear.

Elsewhere, *Lai d'Ignaure* shows the influence of the fabliau, as well as of the didactic lay. It opens with a statement of its purpose—to teach:

> Cors ki aimme ne doit repondre
> Ains doit auchun biel mot despondre
> U li autres puissent aprendre
> Et auchun biel example prendre.
>
> (ll. 1–4)

Although it teaches husbands how to handle unfaithful wives, and little more, it sometimes points out in its uncertain sympathy the force of ideal love. Ignaure, who finds himself loved by twelve women, and in return loves them, merely reverses the situation of *Lay du Conseil*. As the plot develops, love remains ideal, even to the very end, where Ignaure and the twelve wives continue to protest against human brutality. But the poem ends with the tone of a fabliau. The cynical revenge of the husbands is too prominent to be passed over easily. Occasionally there is humor: in verses 122–135 the women who confess to the priest show the poet's flair for the amusing.

The motif of the eaten heart would not belong exclusively to the *fabliau*, for it also appears in a setting of tragic love in the twelfth century *Lay of Guiron*, which is intended to be a lyric lay.[37] Ysolt

> En sa chambre se set un jor.
> E fait un lai pitus d'amour:
> Coment dan Guiron fu supris,

---

[37] Joseph Bédier, ed. *Tristan* (Paris, 1902–05), I, 295. As it occurs in *Tristan*, the lay is presented as the paraphrase of the lyric lay.

Pur l'amur de la dame ocis
Que il sur tute rien ama,
E coment li cuens puis dona
Le cuer Guiron a sa moillier
Par engin un jor a mangier,
E la dolur que la dame out
Quant la mort de sun ami sout.
La dame chante dulcement,
La voiz acorde a l'estrument;
Les mainz sunt beles, li lais bons,
Dulce la voiz, e bas li tons.
(ll. 833–846)

The difference between the two treatments of the same motif is that here the poet suppresses the painful details and gives a consistent impression without cynicism, humor or any of the unresolved conflicts of the longer poem.

III. THE ELEVATED FABLIAU

Five examples survive: *Lai de l'Épervier, Lai d'Aristote, Lai du Cor, Lai du Mantel* and *Lai de Nabaret.* They usually identify themselves as lays, are short and are intended to provoke laughter. Why they should be considered in the tradition of the Breton lay will become apparent.

Lai de l'Épervier

That the author of *Épervier* (232 verses; octosyllabic couplets) is familiar with the Breton lay can be established with certainty.[38] In his prologue he calls his story an aventure: though it is short, it is substantial enough to be recalled and, like Marie's lays, is fresh:

[38] G. Paris, "Le Lai de l'Espervier," *Romania,* vii (1878), 1–21.

94

> Une aventure molt petite
> Qui n'a mie este sovent dite
> Ai oi dire, tot por voir,
> Que je vos voil ramentevoir
>   (ll. 1–4)

In the epilogue he distinguishes his poem from the typical narrative lay: probably in mock-seriousness, he makes no claim to have heard the lyric version of the same *aventure*, which turns out to be an amusing, if trifling, escape from a deceived husband's anger:

> Cest aventure si fu voire:
> Avoir le doit on en memoire;
> Tot ensi avint, ce dit l'on:
> Le lays de l'espervier a non,
> Qui tres bien fait a remembrer.
> Le conte en ai oi conter,
> Mes onques n'en oi la note
> En harpe fere ne en rote.
>   (ll. 225–232)

Two knights are such close friends that they share everything, even their pleasures, until on the advice of one the other marries. His beautiful wife is devoted, but shows an almost fatal affection for his friend. When in time this grows, the envious husband asks his friend to leave. One day, however, while the husband is away hunting, the friend attempts to see the lady. First he hides his squire in her bedchamber and then takes his pleasure until her husband returns. As the husband comes into the bedchamber, the friend rushes out, according to plan, with a drawn sword. The husband, thinking that he is being attacked, forgets momentarily his guilty wife. The wife then explains everything by saying that the knight but for her would have killed his squire, who during a hunt had prematurely released his sparrowhawk and had then taken refuge from his master's anger and hidden in her bedchamber. The squire, still in hiding, comes out at the psychological moment and convinces the husband of his wife's fidelity.

Lai d'Aristote

The author of *Lai d'Aristote*[39] (645 lines; octosyllabic couplets) expects that his poem will not be confused with "low poetry":

> Ja vilains mot n'entreprendrai
> E oeure, n'en dit que je face;
> Quar vilonie si defface
> Tot riens et tolt sa savor
> Ne ja ne me ferai trovar
> De nule riens en mon vivant
> Ou vilains moz voist arrivant,
> Ainz dirai de droit examplere
> Chose qui puist valoir et plere;
> C'est en leu de fruit et d'espece.
> (ll. 50–59)

He fails to mention the Bretons: perhaps only a copyist appends "Chi fine li lai d'Aristote" (l. 645), yet if its chief note is dignity, *lai* is well applied. This story by Henri d'Andeli[40] tells how love entered the life of Alexander the Great and Aristotle, and perhaps stands as a protest by the Christian priesthood against Aristotle, who, though a pagan, enjoyed a position of honor in thirteenth-century France.[41]

---

[39] Henri d'Andeli, *Le Lai d'Aristote*, ed. Alexandre Héron (Rouen, 1901).
[40] Paris, "Oeuvres de Henri d'Andeli," *Romania*, xi (1882), 137–138.
[41] G. Sarton, "Aristotle and Phyllis," *Isis*, xiv (1930), 8–19.

The story should be familiar. During his conquests Alexander the Great falls in love with an Indian houri, but is embarrassed by Aristotle's remark that she is unworthy. On learning Aristotle's criticism of her, she causes Aristotle himself to become infatuated and to play an amorous game of horse and rider. As she rides him side-saddle, Alexander the Great watches from a hidden vantage point and enjoys the performance. Then, coming forward, he taunts Aristotle, but is firmly answered by Aristotle's observation: even he, even the great Aristotle, is made abject by love.

LAI DU COR

This poem and *Épervier* are mentioned first in this section because they show best how close some examples of the fabliau are to the Breton lay. They are not the earliest examples of the form. Written in couplets, *Lai du Cor* has been said to date from 1150–75.[42] It calls itself a lay (l. 575), is 586 lines long and has an Arthurian setting. Its purpose is to amuse: during Easter at Caerleon a messenger presents King Arthur with a magical drinking horn from King Mangons of Moraine. Only husbands of faithful wives may drink from it without spilling its contents. As the ladies listen, including the Queen, they bow their heads in anticipation of embarrassment. When the wine spills, King Arthur, who is first to try, grows angry and, after hearing the Queen's protests, insists that every noble present submit to the test and share his shame. He pardons the Queen only when almost everyone tries the test and fails. Carados alone remains.

[42] Robert Biket, *Le Lai du Cor*, ed. Heinrich Dorner (Strasbourg, 1907). For a discussion of this dating, see Warnke, *Die Lais der Marie de France*, p. xxxviii; and S. Hofer, "Bemerkungen zur Beurteilung des Horn—und Mantellai," *RF* LXV (1953), 38 ff.

When he drinks from the horn he spills nothing and receives the drinking horn as a reward.

CONTE DU MANTEL

The Arthurian setting is preserved in a similar fabliau, *Conte du Mantel* (922 lines; octosyllabic couplets), usually referred to as a *conte* rather than a *lay*: as in other poems of this section the tone of the fabliau is unmistakable. Before a full court at Pentecost Arthur is restless because there is no new adventure to hear. Just then a handsome youth brings from fairyland a magic mantle which detects unfaithfulness in a wife. If it fits her she has been faithful; if it is too large or too small, she has not been. Led by the Queen, the women of the court try it on, but all fail except the *amie* of Caradoc.

A nineteenth-century attempt to assign *Conte du Mantel* to Marie de France at least does credit to the skill with which the test scene is managed.[43] As his beloved confidently prepared to try on the mantle, Caradoc grows uneasy:

> "Ma douce amie,
> Por Dieu ne l'afublez vos mie
> Si vos vos dotez de neiant!
> Quar je ne voudreie saveir
> Vostre mesfait par nul aveir:
> Mieus en vueil je estre en doutance
> Par tot le reiaume de France
> N'en voudreie je estre cert;
> Quar qui sa bone amie pert
> Mout a perdue, ce m'est avis.
> Mieus voudreie estre mors que vis
> Se vos veisse ou renc assise
> O l'amie Gauvain est mise."
>   (ll. 805–817)

---

[43] Robert Biket, *Le Lai du Cor*, ed. Fredrik Wulff (Paris, 1888), p. 355.

Kay the seneschal tries to quiet him:

> "Et cilqui pert sa desleial
> Dont ne deit il estre mout liez?
> Vos serez, ja mout carociez,
> Se vos l'amez tant bonement.
> Vez en la seir plus de cent
> Que l'en cuidout jehui matin
> Plus esmerees que or fin;
> Or les poez totes veeir
> Por lor mesfaizou renc seeir."
> (ll. 820–828)

The lady, who can afford to be calmer than Caradoc, then tries on the mantle, which fits.

LAI DE NABARET

The fifth and last example of the elevated fabliau shows a greater familiarity with the external features of the Breton lay than does either *Cor* or *Mantel*. *Lai de Nabaret* (48 lines; octosyllabic couplets) opens and closes characteristically:[44]

> en Bretaigne fu li laiz fet
> ke nus apellum Nabaret
>
> cil ki de lais tindrent l'escole,
> de Nabarez un lai noterent
> e de sun nun li lai nomerent.
> (ll. 1–5)

In making fun of the jealous husband it stirs up more than mild amusement: Nabaret, a landed knight, marries a lady

---

[44] "Le Lai de Nabaret," in *Charlemagne, An Anglo-Norman Poem of the Twelfth Century*, ed. Francisque Michel (London, 1836), pp. 90–91. Gertrude Schoepperle, "The Old French Lai de Nabaret," *Romanic Review*, XIII (1922), 285–291, explains the point of the story, which is contained in the word *geruns*.

of beauty and rank. When she devotes too much time to her dress and appearance, Nabaret grows angry, sends for her relatives and asks them to speak to her. They find her obstinate but witty. She tells them that her husband should have his beard braided like a patriarch: only then can a jealous, old-fashioned husband take vengeance on a wife who wants to follow the styles.

IV. BRETON LAY APPLIED TO NON-BRETON MATERIAL

During the thirteenth century, imitations of the Breton lay, certain didactic poems and, finally, elevated fabliaux came to be designated by the term *lai*; it was a simple step to apply the term to narrative forms other than the Breton lay.[45] After the success of Marie de France it was equally simple and advantageous to call any short narrative poem of a serious nature a Breton lay regardless of its source. Whether this step was taken to any degree is beyond proof. We cannot determine very easily which stories the Bretons did not tell. Yet we have lays which are plainly Germanic in their matter. The Anglo-Norman *Lai d'Haveloc*,[46] calling itself a Breton lay, might at one time have been rendered by Breton minstrels, but it is probable that this poem developed first in some other form and was afterwards "converted" into a narrative Breton lay. The present section of this chapter,

[45] Hoops, *Der Begriff 'Romance' in der frühmittelenglischer und frühenglischer Literatur*, pp. 1–46, accounts for the parallel development of romance.

[46] Alexander Bell, ed. *Le Lai d'Haveloc and Gaimar's Haveloc Episode* (Manchester, 1925). The *Lai* is independent of the later *Haveloc*, written in Middle English, p. 38. See also by the same author "Gaimar's Early 'Danish' Kings," *PMLA*, lxv (1950), 601–640. F. P. Magoun, Jr., "Norman History in the 'Lay of the Beach,'" *MLN*, lvii (1942), 11–16, discusses an historical lay preserved in the ON. *Strengleikar*, but not called a *Breton Lay*.

which deals with the *Lai d'Haveloc*, will attempt to show how the Breton lay as a form became a conventional means of appealing to a larger audience without telling necessarily a story of Breton origin.

LAI D'HAVELOC

Haveloc (1112 lines; octosyllabic couplets) includes the typical prologue and epilogue:

> L'aventure d'un riche rei
> E de plusurs altres baruns
> Dunt jo vus nomerai les nuns,
> Assez briefment la vus dirai.
> Aveloc fu cest reis nomez
> E cuaron rest apellez.
> Pur co vus voil de lui cunter
> E s'aventure remembrer
> K'un lai en firent li Bretun
> Si l'apellerent de sun nun
> E Aveloc e Cuarant.
> (ll. 12–22)

> Li ancien en remembrance
> Firent un lai de sa victoire
> Ki tuz jorz mes seit en memoire.
> (ll. 1110–12)

During Arthur's conquest of Denmark, Gunter, King of the Danes, is treacherously killed by Odulf, who, on taking over the throne, threatens the surviving Queen and her two-year old son Haveloc. Before Odulf can harm them, however, they escape by sea with the help of Grim, a faithful retainer, only to encounter pirates, who kill the Queen. With Haveloc and others, Grim reaches Grimsby (in Lincolnshire) and there raises Haveloc as Cuaran his son. Years later, on Grim's encouragement, Haveloc seeks his fortune at court and serves Edelsi, King of Lincoln and Rutland, as well as of all the lands extending south to Surrey which belonged to his deceased brother-in-law, Achebrit. Since neither Haveloc nor Edelsi recognizes his rank, Haveloc is employed as a scullion and is soon renowned as the greatest wrestler of the land. Ironically, he marries Princess Argentille, daughter of deceased Achebrit and ward of scheming Edelsi: thus Edelsi satisfies the letter of a promise to her deceased father by selecting for her husband the strongest man in the land, yet a menial. During their first night together Argentille notices a flame issuing from Haveloc's mouth and with the help of a hermit identifies this as a sign of royalty; Kelloc, now the only survivor of Grim's family, confirms this identification by recalling Haveloc's escape from Denmark as an infant. Determined now to enjoy his heritage, Haveloc with Argentille returns to Denmark and, helped by Sigar Estal, a supporter of the long-deceased Gunter, kills the usurper and occupies the throne. Since Argentille also has been deprived of her heritage, Haveloc invades England, meets Edelsi in battle and recovers the lands which belonged to her father. Thereafter he and Argentille live in peace as king and queen.

The source of the *Lai d'Haveloc* is Geoffrey Gaimar's account of Haveloc in his *Estoire des Engleis*, "since no other source could explain the great number of similar passages and the overwhelming number of almost identical lines."[47] The *Lai*, therefore, could not have been written before around 1150 and might date from 1201, when Grimsby was incorpo-

---

[47] Edith Fahnestock, A *Study of the Sources and Composition of the Old French Lai d'Haveloc* (New York, 1915), p. 109. Bell's independent research leads him to the same conclusion, pp. 43 ff.

rated.[48] At this time the lays of Marie de France were circulating in Norman England: only a familiarity with these, especially *Guigemar*, *Les Dous Amanz* and *Eliduc*, could account for the scenes, characters and tone in *Haveloc* which recall Marie de France.[49] Verbal similarities are abundant, of which the following are typical.[50]

> La verité t'en cunterai (*Lai*, l. 600)
> La verité vus conterai (*Guigemar*, l. 313)
>
> De ren ne vus en mentirai (*Lai*, l. 756)
> De rien ne vous en mentirai (*Guigemar*, l. 314)
>
> Volenters devreit l'om oir/E recunter e retenir
> (*Lai*, ll. 1–2)
> Volentiers devroit on oir/Cos quist boine a retenir
> (*Guigemar*, ll. 1–2)
> Terme lur mist, jor lur noma (*Lai*, l. 303)
> Terme di dune e nume jur (*Eliduc*, l. 698)

One would agree in part that "the 'Bretonizing' in the *Lai d'Haveloc* is the effort of one man to give Breton coloring to a finished literary product, in order to make it conform to a certain ideal which he had in mind—the type of lay which Marie de France composed. He introduced the allusions arbitrarily, and they cannot be considered as giving trustworthy information regarding either the Bretons or their lays."[51] But in emphasis this poem is far from the "type of poem which Marie de France composed." Although like *Les Dous Amanz* it is a local legend, centered around Grimsby,[52]

---

[48] Bell, *Le Lai d'Haveloc*, p. 28.
[49] Fahnestock, pp. 129–136.
[50] Bell, *Le Lai d'Haveloc*, pp. 26 and 51–53.
[51] Fahnestock, p. 128.
[52] French, *Essays on King Horn*, p. 17, uses local legend loosely to include other lays, especially by Marie de France: "*The Two Lovers* is told to explain

this similarity is negligible, as are others which might be mentioned. In its treatment of love and adventure, which are the essence of the Breton lay, *Haveloc* is far removed from the poems of Marie de France.

From the text one perceives that not only Courtly Love, but Marie's softened version of it nowhere appears. Haveloc's marriage to Argentille is one of convenience—for Edelsi. The most important happening during their wedding night is the discovery of Haveloc's flame. The bliss which the royal couple enjoy at the end of the poem is passed over quickly. Similarly love among the background characters hardly ennobles as it should. Grim's life is simple and drab. His character in fact is conceived outside the courtly tradition; on reaching Grimsby he becomes a fisherman and Haveloc a scullion; the poet allows his sympathy to follow his characters.

Physical prowess, like love, is transformed. On its lowest level it becomes an exhibition of Haveloc's strength in wrestling as the prince becomes Edelsi's tool. When he wars in Denmark and England, he is seeking adventure neither for its own sake nor to impress Argentille, but to regain land rightly his. The motivation is that of the epic: the hero bears the destiny of his people, like Aeneas or Charlemagne.

The *Lai d'Haveloc*, according to the present interpretation, is simply an English legend composed apart from the tradition of the Breton lay except in such external details as have been noted. "The Norman invaders had early appropriated to themselves the traditions and legends of their adopted coun-

the name of a mountain; *Equitan* is located at Nantes; *Doon* involves several English towns; *Yonec* has its scene near Chepstow. Although now and then a modern commentator may not take these localizations very seriously, they are rather numerous to disregard."

try"[53]—and this is one of them. Why love and adventure find little place in *Haveloc* may be clear, if not in the source of the poem, certainly in the context of Anglo-Norman literature considered as a whole:

It must be admitted, in conclusion, that while courtoisie is undoubtedly present in Anglo-Norman literature, it is hardly, for the most part, the courtoisie of the Troubadors or of the French courtois writers, but something more pedestrian. [It is possible to find a reason for this neglect.] . . . the modified form in which courtoisie presents itself would seem to point to the fact that already in the England of the twelfth and thirteenth centuries with its curiously mixed populations, there was beginning to show itself that sense of concrete reality apparently so typical of modern times.[54]

V. LAI DU LECHEOR: A *REINTERPRETATION*

Jadis a saint Pantelion,
Ce nos racontent li Breton,
Soloient granz genz assembler
Por la feste au saint honorer,
Les plus nobles et les plus beles   5
Du pais, dames et puceles,
Qui dont estoient el pais;
N'i avoit dame de nul pris
Qui n'i venist a icel jor;
Molt estoient de riche ator   10

. . . .

Chascuns i metoit son pooir

[53] R. M. Wilson, *Early Middle English Literature* (London, 1939), p. 76.
[54] C. B. West, *Courtoisie in Anglo-Norman Literature* (Oxford, 1938), pp. 168–169.

En lui vestir et atorner.

. . . .

La estoient tenu li plet,   15
Et la erent conté li fet
Des amors et des drueries
Et des nobles chevaleries;
Ce que l'an estoit avenu
Tot ert oi et retenu: 20
Lor aventure racontoient
Et li autre les escoutoient.
Tote la meillor retenoient
Et recordoient et disoient;
Sovent ert dite et racontée,   25
Tant que de touz estoit loée;
Un lai en fesoient entr'eus,
Ce fu la costume d'iceus;
Cil a qui l'aventure estoit
Son non meismes i metoit: 30
Apres lui ert li lais nomez,
Sachoiz ce est la veritez;
Puis estoit li lais maintenuz
Tant que partout estoit seuz;
Car cil qui savoient de note   35
En viele, en harpe et en rote
Fors de la terre le portoient
Es roiaumes ou il aloient.
A la feste dont je vos di,
Ou li Breton venoient si,   40
En un grant mont fu l'asemblée
Por ce que miex fust escoutée.
Molt i ot clers et chevaliers,
Et plusors genz d'autres mestiers;
Dames i ot nobles et beles,   45
Et meschines et damoiseles.
Quant du mostier furent parti,

Au leu qu-il orent establi
Conmunement sont assemblé;
Chascuns a son fet reconté;   50
S'aventure disoit chascuns,
Avant venoient uns et uns.
Dont aloient apareillant
Lequel il metroient avant.
Huit dames sistrent d'une part,   55
Si disoient de lor esgart;
Sages erent et ensaingnies,
Franches, cortoises et proisies:
C'estoit de Bretaigne la flors
Et la proesce et la valors.   60
L'une parla premiérement,
Et dit molt afichiement:
"Dames, car me donnez conseil
D'une rien dont molt me merveil:
Molt oi ces chevaliers parler   65
De tornoier et de joster,
D'aventures, de drueries,
Et de requerre lor amies:
D'icelui ne tienent nul plet   69
Por qui li grant bien sont tuit fet.
Par cui sont li bon chevalier?
Por qoi aimment a tornoier?
Por qui s'atornent li danzel?
Por qui se vestent de novel?
Por qui envoient lor joieaus,   75
Lor treceors et lor aneaus?
Por qui sont franc et debonere?
Por qoi se gardent de mal fere?
Por qoi aimment le donoier,
Et l'acoler et l'embracier?   80
Savez i vos nule achoison
Fors sol por une chose non?

Ja n'avra nus tant donoie
Ne biau parle ne biau proie,
Ainz qu'il s'em puisse departir,   85
A ce ne veille revertir;
D'ice vienent les granz doucors
Por coi sont fetes les honors;
Maint homme i sont si amendé
Et mis em pris et em bonté,   90
Qui ne vausissent un bouton
Se par l'entente du con non.
La moie foi vos em plevis,
Nule fame n'a si bel vis
Por qu'ele eust le con perdu,   95
Ja mes eust ami ne dru.
Quant tuit li bien sont fet por lui,
Nu metons mie sor autrui:
Faisons du con le lai novel;
Si l'orront tel cui ert molt bel.   100
Conmant qui miex savra noter:
Ja verrez toz vers nos torner."
Les set li ont acreanté,
Dient que molt a bien parlé:
Le lai commencent aitant,   105
Chascune i mist et son et chant,
Et douces notes a haut ton:
Le lai firent cortois et bon.
Tuit cil qui a la feste estoient
Le lai lessiérent qu'il faisoient,   110
Vers les dames se sont torné,
Si ont lor fet forment loé:
Ensemble o eles le lai firent,
Quant la bone matire oirent;
Et as clers et as chevaliers   115
Fu li laiz maintenuz et chiers;
Molt fu amez, molt fu joiz,

Encore n'est il mie haiz.
D'icest lai dient li plusor
Que c'est le lai du lecheor;   120
Ne voil pas dire le droit non,
C'on nu me tort a mesprison.
Selonc le conte que j'oi
Vos ai le lai einsint feni.

Although there is agreement that *Lai du Lecheor* offers at least a "cynical analysis of sentiment in men,"[55] the precise literary form of this short poem has been disputed. Often taken for a fabliau, it includes in its 124 verses a prologue resembling that of a Breton lay, then a lay-within-a-lay—relating how the *Lay of the Lecher* was composed—and finally an epilogue. (a) Each year on the feast of St. Pantaleon the most distinguished of the Breton nobility assemble in their best attire to honor the saint. In the presence of ladies and clerics, each knight relates any amorous adventure which happened to him during the year previous. From this adventure a lay is then composed in communal fashion and named after the person taking part in it. Then the lay, which relates only the truth, is carried abroad by minstrels, who render it with harp, viol and rote in every land. (b) One particular year the Bretons, after leaving Church, assembled in accordance with their custom and took their places on a hillside so as to hear better. Then they came forward individually, told their adventures and tried to choose the best. During their judging, however, eight noble, courteous ladies sat apart, "de Bretaigne la flors." One of them asked, "Why do men

---

[55] Walter H. French, *Essays on King Horn*, p. 6. In this study references are made to the text of *Lai du Lecheor*, ed. Gaston Paris, *Romania*, VIII (1879), 64–66.

make much of us, go off on adventures, engage in tournaments, dress extravagantly and appear noble and pleasant?" Her answer was, "For one thing, not for our beauty, but for the enjoyment of the *membrum pudendum*." She and the seven others then composed a lay in communal fashion, "courtois et bon," on the subject of what attracts knights to ladies. When the others on the hillside heard the singing, they stopped the competition and at once joined in. (c) The lyric lay which the entire group of Bretons composed is known as the "Lay of the Lecher." In the present narrative lay it is not recalled by its alternate title because the author finds it difficult to use so undignified a word; he does not want to be misjudged.

In the third edition of Karl Warnke's *Die Lais der Marie de France, Lai du Lecheor* is simply listed with anonymous Old French Breton lays (p. xxxvii), but nothing is said of its distinctive contents, probably because Warnke like others was satisfied to accept Gaston Paris' statement denying that the poem explains how narrative lays were first derived; "L'introduction de ce lai est fort curieuse pour la manière dont on se representait au XIIe siècle la production de la poésie traditionnelle bretonne: naturellement il ne faut pas lui accorder d'autre importance" (p. 64). With this interpretation J. D. Bruce agrees:

> This so-called *lai* is merely a cynical joke on the true source of inspiration in chivalry—too gross for repetition. I cannot take seriously, either, its introduction—as G. Paris and Warnke have done—which tells us that on St. Pantelion's day people used to assemble in honor of the saint and the men would recount adventures of love and knighthood, whilst the ladies listened to them. The adventure

110

which pleased them most was turned into a lay by the company. This, however, is evidently a piquant invention, and nothing more, to introduce with mock seriousness the vulgar joke that follows. There is no reason to imagine that anyone in France or elsewhere ever imagined that Breton lays really came into existence in this manner.[56]

Lucien Foulet, however, is attracted less by the vulgar joke in the poem than by the anonymous author's mock serious-ness and, without detailing reasons, finds in the "badinage ingénieux" a trace of literary satire.[57] This, it can be shown, becomes more striking with a reexamination of the opening passage, which has been badly misread.

To know why the feast of St. Pantaleon should become the occasion for composing a Breton lay, communal style, is vital for an understanding of the poem. Foulet sees in the saint's name only a "facétie de plus" (p. 54); and Ernest Brugger concludes that the saint's feast, coming in July, "passt sehr gut für einer der Hoffeste; denn diese fallen fast alle in die schöne Jahreszeit."[58] Neither points out that the feast of St. Pantaleon would be most suitable for a parodist of the Breton lay to mention in his setting, for, according to medieval tradition, this day was never to be desecrated, certainly not by vulgar storytelling. The medieval reader remembered only too well that, in contempt of custom and the pleas of his neighbors, a well-intentioned farmer had harvested a crop on this day and in consequence had suffered the wrath of heaven:

Vespertino vero tempore, dum jam revertit, quasi rebus consuluisset, statueret, ecce, in medio itinere fulgurei

---

[56] *The Evolution of Arthurian Romance from the Beginnings down to the Year 1300* (Göttingen and Baltimore, 1923), II, 183.

[57] "Marie de France et les lais bretons," 53–54.

[58] "Ueber die Bedeutung von Bretagne, Breton," 115, n. 45.

111

ignium globi, cum ingenti tonitruo in vehiculum redeuntis illati, illud cum messe ac jumentis concremarunt, ut nulla combustorum vestigia remanerent. Quae res dum praefatis accolis, qui ei divinam ultionem proficiscenti imprecati fuerant, divulgata innotuit, majori devotione circa beatum Pantaleonem profecerunt ejusque festivitatis celebritatem Dominicae diei aequalem habendam statuerunt.[59]

In the parody, when the Bretons compose a lay about "love," actually about lechery, on a feast day never to be desecrated, even by necessary manual labor, the parodist at once reaches the heights of irony; and his reader thinks of those feast days in the lays and longer romances when knightly heroes go off on adventures—of Pentecost, the day when Desiré, after a tiring search, discovers his *amie*; of the vigil of the Feast of St. John, when the prince in *Lai de l'Épine* lies awake at the Perilous Ford; of *Lai du Cor* and its setting at Easter; and of *Lai du Mantel*, also set at Pentecost. Recalling the setting of other narrative lays, the reader, to appreciate the parody, has only to "supply knowledge of the model. He must hold up the model, and the author [of the parody] will furnish him with a distorted reflection of it."[60]

The effect of rereading *Lai du Lecheor* as a parody is partly immediate and partly cumulative as one looks for such features of the Breton lay as might be expected in a satirical treatment of the form. Whereas, in the opening verses of *Guigemar*, Marie de France asks the reader to take on faith the accuracy of "Les contes que jo sai verais/dunt li Bretun unt fait les lais" (ll. 19–20), the reader of *Lai du Lecheor* is

[59] As related in *Acta Sanctorum quotquot Orbe Coluntur*, . . . (Bollandist Society of Brussels, 1643–1925), July, vi, 425, col. 2.

[60] David Worcester, *The Art of Satire* (Cambridge, Mass., 1940), p. 42.

privileged to follow the development of a lay from the time when the adventure is first related to the final release of a freshly composed lay to the waiting Breton storytellers. These, as it happens, are assembled on a hill, so that they can hear everything, good or bad, and repeat faithfully what they hear. No longer does the reader have to wish vainly for a source less vague than Marie's familiar one:

> Des lais pensai qu'oiz aveie.
> Ne dutai pas, bien le saveie,
> que pur remembrance les firent
> des aventures qu'il oïrent
> cil ki primes les comencierent
> e ki avant les enveierent.
> (Prologue: ll. 33–38)

In fact, by the beginning of the thirteenth century or thereabouts, when *Lai du Lecheor* was already written, the claim that the Breton lay originates in a narrative account of an adventure must have been accepted less as a conventional opening than as a tongue-in-cheek reminder that the story is old and bound to be good. Thus, the author of the playful but dignified *Lai de l'Épervier*, plainly a fabliau, but introduced as a Breton lay, playfully asserts that he has heard only the old *conte* version of the lay:

> Cest aventure si fu voire:
> Avoir le doit on en memoire;
> Tot ensi avint, ce dit l'on:
> Le lays de l'espervier a non,
> Qui tres bien fait a remembrer.
> Le conte en ai oi conter,
> Mes onques n'en oi la note
> En harpe fere ne en rote.
> (ll. 225–232)

113

The double title given to Breton lays also affords in *Lai du Lecheor* an amusing opportunity for a thrust. In Marie de France this stylistic device occurs more than once, especially if a translation of the first title is vital for an understanding of the text:

> Bisclavret a nun et Bretan,
> Garulf l'apelent li Norman.
> > (*Bisclavret*, ll. 3–4)

> Laustic a nun, ceo m'est vis,
> si l'apelent en lur pais;
> ceo est russignol en Franceis
> e *nihtegale* en dreit Engleis.
> > (*Laustic*, ll. 3–6)

> 'Le Chaitivel' l'apele hum,
> e si i a plusurs de cels
> ki l'apelent 'Les Quatre Doels.'
> > (*Chaitivel*, ll. 6–8)

> 'Gotelef' l'apelent Engleis,
> 'Chievrefueil' le nument Franceis.
> > (*Chievrefueil*, ll. 115–116)

Realizing, however, the extreme danger of spelling out the first title and feeling that "the lay of the lecher" goes as far as propriety allows, the parodist ends briefly, "ne voil pas dire le droit non,/C'on nu me tort a mesprison." To say more would be to lose the advantage of both a euphemism and the carefully planned brevity which not only characterizes his work throughout but also recalls the comparable brevity and narrative simplicity of the twelve narrative lays of Marie de France and the anonymous lays which followed under her inspiration.

It is possible also to tell whether the parody applies to the treatment of love in the narrative lays alone, and not elsewhere in courtly romance. No one will deny that *Lai du Lecheor* is a "cynical analysis of sentiment in men," but to stop here and ignore the parodist's conscious attempt to copy stylistic features of the Breton lay is to miss the obvious in his "gentle" but dignified misrepresentation. Yet he must have had in mind certain anonymous narrative lays more than the so-called twelve originals. The latter, one would agree, present love seriously and inoffensively as "le sentiment naturel, naïf et spontané, . . . exaltant les courages, poussant aux exploits héroiques et aux sacrifices sublimes, mais aussi aux crimes les plus abominables."[61] Although Marie de France is amused in *Chaitivel* by the casuistry of love, she differs from writers following the tradition of Courtly Love when she tolerates adulterous love in only one instance, when the woman has been forced into marriage with an ill-natured husband.[62]

The specific narrative lays which the parodist contemplates must then be found among the later anonymous lays. While in their treatment of love *Desiré, Graelent, Guingamor, Doon, Melion, Épine* and *Tydorel* would be only slightly less orthodox than the poems of Marie de France, certain others, *Épervier, Aristote, Cor, Mantel,* as fabliaux should, treat the physical side of human love simply to provoke laughter. In *Épervier,* for example, emphasis falls on the skillful escape of an adulterer from an angry husband's revenge, and love as a "sentiment naturel" gives way to what the paro-

---

[61] Hoepffner, *Aux origines de la nouvelle française,* p. 20. For a fuller discussion see Schiött, *L'amour et les amoureux dans les lais de Marie de France.*
[62] Hoepffner, ibid.

Lay de la croyz
Lay des hermins
Vithel penmeyn
Merlin le suuage
Lelays alic̃s
Amis amer
Belylle
Beu desconu
Bisclaueret
Beu desire
La cotidre
Doun
Eygnor
Frene
Gorum
Glitor
Glou degloucests
Lay de puceles̃
Rey mabun
Rey haueloch
Lay de amurs
Laumual
Le ieuene rey
Mil de Mereth
Le numper
Veyn le fiz urien
Tidorel
Tristram
La Loune
Vinerun
Vespris
Luelan Lychlez
Eliduc
Le rey march
Le rey arthur
Le rey nytun

Glygis
Le eir deleycests̃
Lay deuent
Le rey barnagoy̌s̃
Van delmer
Cadewelan le ueyl
Le rey aluered
Lau diduc
Le rey pepyn
Le rey richard
Le rey heremon
Laurnut
Anyle egalerun
Le rey aaron
Le cạy cyuel
Ranbaud defrise
Nobaret
La pleinte vavayn
Ley del engleis
Cheurefoil
Milun
Vygamer
Le hauthoil
Karleyn
Yonech
Ysanbras len veyse
La pleynte meliaduc
Fluriun
Le beau bretun
Coscra
Lay sent brandan

dist would be satisfied to consider mere lechery. *Cor* and *Mantel* could also be mentioned, as probably could others now lost, to lengthen the list of fabliaux framed as Breton lays but lacking their dignified treatment of human love. These, rather than the twelve poems of Marie de France, suggest themselves as the parodist's target.

Other poems of the time framed as Breton lays treat love differently: (1) short didactic poems about love, *Lai du Trot, Oiselet, Conseil* and *Ombre*, and (2) the so-called historical lays, of which OF *Lai d'Haveloc* is representative, although, judging from titles in the recently noted Shrewsbury MS. VII, f. 200—*Rey Mabun, Le Ray March, Le Rey Pepyn, Le Rey Richard, Le Rey Aaron*[63]—there were other examples now lost. In neither of these "derivatives" of the Breton lay, which merely trade on the popularity of the original form, is human love reduced, as it is in *Lai du Lecheor*, to its lowest physical level. Love in the didactic lays is the same force as that which ennobles the great romances. If *Haveloc* really is representative, it may also be concluded that the historical lays, which treat love only incidentally and are concerned more with glorifying an epic-like hero, cannot be intended in the parody. By a process of exclusion, when these two derivative forms are considered and rejected, only "elevated" examples of fabliaux framed as Breton lays remain; and, in these, love does add up to lechery.

Such fabliaux appeared when changes in emphasis were occurring within the Breton lay. These were what the Breton lay had become, the *terminus ad quem*, after the discovery, by imitators of Marie de France, of a solid advantage in call-

[63] Brereton, 40–45.

ing any short poem a Breton lay, regardless of its contents. Although didactic and historical lays must have developed concurrently with such fabliaux, they deviate less from the original narrative lay from the standpoint of seriousness and so offer smaller opportunity to the parodist, who, we may be sure, is attacking the Breton lay in its *present* state and in its weakest examples. "The irony of revolt," according to Professor Lowes, "lies in the inability of the new to remain the new for more than a fleeting moment. The less commonplace it is, the more eagerly it is seized upon, and the more swiftly and surely worn trite. The cliché is merely the sometime novel, that has been loved not wisely but too well."[64] By the time *Lai du Lecheor* was written, the Breton lay was no longer new. In its meaner examples physical love is represented outside marriage at an hour when the Church was pronouncing on this very topic.[65] Still not the least of the reasons for the parody may be stylistic, to include the conventional prologue and epilogue with their sober and repeated assertions—now worn thin and demanding the parodist's "proof"—that the story is true and is based on an actual adventure. The parodist's attack is as much to be expected as a contemporary's, which in *Lai d'Ignaure* finds it effective to write, not *oscurement*, but directly:

> Sens est perdus, ki est couvers;
> Cis k'est moustres et descouvers
> Puet en auchum liu semenchier.
> (ll. 10–12)

[64] John Livingston Lowes, *Convention and Revolt in Poetry* (Boston and New York, 1919), pp. 145–146.

[65] For a discussion of the attitude of the Church toward Courtly Love, see Alexander J. Denomy, *The Heresy of Courtly Love* (New York, 1947), pp. 33–40.

THE DEVELOPMENT OF THE BRETON LAY

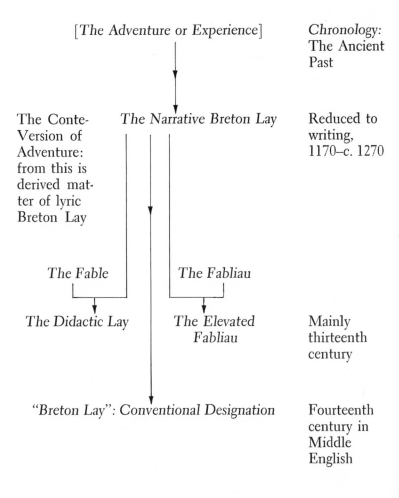

[*The Adventure or Experience*]

Chronology:
The Ancient
Past

The Conte-
Version of
Adventure:
from this is
derived mat-
ter of lyric
Breton Lay

The Narrative Breton Lay

Reduced to
writing,
1170–c. 1270

The Fable

The Fabliau

The Didactic Lay

*The Elevated
Fabliau*

Mainly
thirteenth
century

"Breton Lay": Conventional Designation

Fourteenth
century in
Middle
English

3

The Middle English Breton
Lay in Octosyllabic Couplets

About the year 1200 French literature came to dominate the whole of Christendom, especially in the matter of stories; not only sending abroad the French tales of Charlemagne and Roland, but imparting plots, scenery and so forth, from many lands, Wales and Brittany, Greece and further east, and giving new French forms to them, which were admired and, as far as possible, borrowed by foreign nations, according to their several tastes and abilities. The English took a large share in this trade. Generally speaking their taste was easily satisfied. What they wanted was adventure; slaughter of Saracens, fights with dragons and giants, rightful heirs getting their own again, innocent princesses championed against their felon adversaries. . . .[1]

[1] W. P. Ker, "Metrical Romances, 1200–1500," *The Cambridge History of English Literature* (Cambridge, 1908), I, 281–282. For a survey see Derek Pearsall, "The Development of Middle English Romance," *MS*, XXVII (1965), 91–117. Helaine Newstead, "Romances," in J. Burke Severs, ed. *A Manual of*

SINCE THE DEVELOPMENT of the Breton lay in thirteenth- and fourteenth-century England parallels that of the long romance, this characterization is acceptable with one qualification: the Breton lay does not usually have to be "sent abroad," but merely translated into English. Almost from the very start adventure in the sense in which W. P. Ker uses the word supersedes love as its leading motive; earlier, *Lai d'Haveloc* showed how the external features of the form could be advantageously applied to heroic legend almost devoid of love. In the following chapters the Middle English examples illustrate this preference for adventure. But this adventure is not the *action collective* of the *chanson de geste* in which warriors fight out of love for God and country;[2] the precise influence of the *chanson de geste* on the Breton lay would be difficult to establish. Rather, it is the adventure of twelfth-century romance unaccompanied by the usually inseparable element of love;[3] risks are taken by the hero as an individual, both for their own sake and for the advantage of a good story.

In the history of the Breton lay this change of emphasis amounts to a retrogression and tends to reduce the lay to a folktale. Hypothetically, this is what Marie de France starts with before she imparts a courtly idea and makes each lay an effective expression of ideal conduct. As her original intent is ignored or misunderstood, however, the Breton lay in the

the *Writings in Middle English 1050–1500*, Fascicule 1 (New Haven, 1967), pp. 11–16 and 199–205.

[2] E. Hoepffner, "La chanson de geste et les débuts du roman courtois," *Mélanges de linguistique et de littérature offerts à M. Jeanroy* (Paris, 1928), p. 437.

[3] Charles Sears Baldwin, *An Introduction to English Medieval Literature* (New York, 1922), p. 64. For a discussion of the *chanson de geste* and the romance, See Everett, "A Characterization of English Medieval Romances," p: 118.

hands of Middle English imitators and redactors loses its full measure of *courtoisie* but retains such elements of the original as would appeal to a new audience. Earlier in this study I examined the narrative lay for emotional passages suggestive of the lyric lay; the examination now centers around what is left of the love-adventure formula. Significantly, the rise of an English audience contributed to the change of emphasis.

During the first half of the thirteenth century, the Anglo-Norman nobility had their own language and literature, and the lower classes theirs; to say that "two literatures exist side by side and for essentially different classes of readers"[4] over-simplifies yet must contain some truth. Why interest in Anglo-Norman literature extends to the Breton lay can be explained as much by the composition of society at the time as by the richness of the Breton lay itself. The Anglo-Norman audience, in fact, was partly Breton.[5] The Conqueror, not forgetting his Breton allies after taking over the the new country, handed out lands in the north and west to Bretons, whose descendants continued to preserve their heritage in later centuries: "Les Bretons, toujours fort attachés aux croyances de leur ancêtres et à leurs anciennes traditions, ne les oubliaient point dans leur nouvelle patrie. . . ."[6] That other Anglo-Normans not of Breton descent appreciated the Breton lay is clear from the dedications of Marie de France, who sought out for honor no less a person than a king of England.

It should not be thought, however, that during the thirteenth century the Breton lay belonged exclusively to one class. In fact, Anglo-Norman as a language "appears to have

[4] Wilson, *Early Middle English Literature*, pp. 12–13.
[5] Ahlström, "Marie de France et les Lais narratifs," pp. 20–21.
[6] P. 21; also Francis, "Marie de France et sons Temps," pp. 76–97.

been used among all classes, save the very poorest; some of
the French literature of the time was addressed more particularly to the middle classes."[7] The author of the Middle English
Owl and the Nightingale,[8] written as early as the reign of King
John when Anglo-Norman was still the language of the court,
is probably familiar with the poetry of Marie de France. When
the owl taunts the nightingale by reminding her that

> þe louerd þat sone underȝat,
> liim & grine wel eiwat,
> sette & leide þe for to lacche,
> (ll. 1055–57)

the lines recall in *Laustic*

> Il n'ot vaslet en sa maisun,
> ne face engin, reiz u lacun,
> puis les metent par le vergier.
> N'i ot coldre ne chastaignier
> u il ne metent laz u glu.
> (ll. 95–99)

As the thirteenth century advanced, however, and English
became the language of the cultivated class as well, the Breton
lay became available in translation to any user of English,
regardless of rank.

The fact of translation has been advanced as the reason for
the prolonged vogue of the Breton lay, extending from 1170
to after 1400.[9] Although in Continental France the form was

[7] Kathleen Lambley, *The Teaching and Cultivation of the French Language
in England during Tudor and Stuart Times*, Publications of the University of
Manchester, French Series, No. III (Manchester, 1920), pp. 7–8. Legge, *Anglo-
Norman Literature and Its Background*, pp. 5–6.

[8] *The Owl and the Nightingale*, ed. J. W. H. Atkins (Cambridge, 1922).

[9] Lucien Foulet, "Le Prologue du *Franklin's Tale* et les Lais bretons,"
ZfRPh, xxx (1906), 707. The delayed vogue of other forms derived from
French literature is familiar: see Helen E. Sandison, *The Chanson d'Aventure
in Middle English* (Bryn Mawr, 1913), pp. 22–23.

probably dying by 1250, it lived on in England for over a hundred years. Why, can be understood less in terms of geographical and cultural insularity than through a phenomenon attending the change of language. When English was substituted for French as the language of the cultivated class, any Breton lay in favor at the time was translated into English and given life as a new poem. Translation often amounted to modernization. It is not until the fourteenth century, however, that the effect of modernization becomes clear, for the Breton lay of that period is extant in two of the three poetic styles. Although there are no examples in the alliterative lines of the Northwest Midlands, some occur in the popular tail-rhyme stanza and in the octosyllabic couplet, which Chaucer and Gower were later to use. *Sir Launfal, the Erl of Toulous, Emare* and *Sir Gowther,* in the East Midland tail-rhyme stanza, constitute one group, while *Lai le Freine, Sir Landeval* (and the related *Sir Lambewell* and *Sir Lamwell), Sir Orfeo* and *Sir Degare,* the other group; all vary slightly the four-stress couplet of the original. Although these few poems offer but limited evidence, "it is difficult to believe that this is all that were ever composed."[10] As a Breton lay Chaucer's *Franklin's Tale,* in decasyllabic couplets, is unique and will be considered separately.

Versification appears to be a prominent area of difference between extant Breton lays in Middle English and, therefore, a convenient starting point for this section. Historically, the octosyllabic couplet of the fourteenth century is not exclusively French in origin. If it were, it might show consistently "a rigid syllabic symmetry, regular rhyme in couplets, caesura almost in the middle, and a fully classical elision of final vowels

---

[10] Wilson, "More Lost Literature in Old and Middle English," pp. 25–26.

before initial sounds in the next word."[11] These came mainly with Gower, if at all. Although the French influence on versification throughout the period is great, it builds on the four-stress alliterative line of Old English poetry; "it was natural that the eight-syllabled French line should therefore be the first to establish itself, as a line of four dissyllabic feet."[12] Generalization to this point is easy enough, but, approaching individual poems, one is hampered by certain preconceptions which classical prosody has left, as well as by a tendency to "exaggerated formalism" which neither Middle English poets nor scribes ever intended.[13] Except for an isolated work like the *Owl and the Nightingale*, literature before Gower is slow to accept the regularity of the French couplet; in any of the poems to be considered here, lines varying from six to ten syllables in length will be clear enough indication.

I. LAI LE FREINE

The Middle English Breton lays derived from Marie de France will be examined before *Sir Orfeo* and *Sir Degare*, which have no single extant source in French. Since *Lai le Freine* is closer to its sources than the *Lanval* poems in couplets, its value is great for purposes of a detailed study. This section will consider briefly the manuscript and date of *Lai le Freine* and in detail such departures from its sources as illuminate the trans-

---

[11] George Saintsbury, *A History of English Prosody from the Twelfth Century to the Present Day* (London, 1906), I, 57. See also L. E. Kastner, *A History of French Versification* (Oxford, 1903), p. 140.

[12] Enid Hamer, *The Metres of English Poetry* (London, 1930), pp. 24–26.

[13] Paull Franklin Baum, *The Principles of English Versification* (Cambridge, Mass., 1926), p. vii. A more recent expression of dissatisfaction with the state of ME prosody studies is found *passim* in French, *Essays on King Horn*.

lator's understanding of the Breton lay.[14]

Lai le Freine is preserved on folios 261ª and 262ª of *Auchinleck Manuscript* W. 4. I in Advocates' Library, Edinburgh. Lines 121 through 133 are missing, and the story breaks off abruptly after line 340. The date of the manuscript is early fourteenth century; the date of the poem itself is no earlier than the middle of the thirteenth century and no later than 1330–40, when the manuscript was prepared. Its dialect is close to Chaucer's. In spite of its distinctive style there is no evidence to connect it with the author of *Sir Orfeo*.[15]

It is customary to say that *Lai le Freine* is "in the same tradition as the original"[16]—in octosyllabic couplets, regardless of the objection that few lines count out exactly eight syllables. No real value derives from classifying the lines according to sixteen types, which exhaust the possible combinations of accented and unaccented syllable.[17] When the expression *octosyllabic* or short couplets is used, it must stand for something far less than the regularity of the corresponding French couplet. The evidence hardly supports "chopping up the lines into 'feet,' as in Latin prosody, which really deals with 'short' and 'long' syllables" (p. xxix).

If the conventional reduction to foot, line and stanza be conceivable, the versification of *Lai le Freine* shows frequent liberties. The movement of the poem is generally iambic, but

[14] Manuscript and date are discussed by Margaret Wattie in her edition of the poem, pp. vii ff. Ed. also by T. C. Rumble (Detroit, 1965), pp. 81–94.

[15] Hibbard, *Mediaeval Romance in England*, p. 294.

[16] See Theo Stemmler, "Die mittelenglischen Bearbeitungen zweier Lais der Marie de France," *Anglia*, LXXX (1962), 243–263, for analysis of artistic changes wrought by the English translator; my own study is concerned with changes in genre features.

[17] Walter W. Skeat, ed. *The Lay of Havelok the Dane* (Oxford, 1902), pp. xxviii–xxix.

occasionally the initial unaccented syllable is dropped from a line:

> riche men in her best liif   (l. 31)
> Sone þerafter bifel a cas   (l. 83)

Ordinarily each line has four accented syllables except for a rare short line:

> Anon fer sche aliȝt   (l. 205)
> & a pel him about   (l. 216)

Unaccented syllables vary from two to an extreme of six per line:

> In þe west cuntre woned tvay kniȝte   (l. 29)

The couplet itself shows a similar variety. Although there are no examples of enjambement extending the sense from one line or couplet into the next without any grammatical pause, yet as many as four types of couplet can be distinguished, in addition to the common end-stopped couplet, of which there are 48 examples.

(1) The two lines of the couplet can be grammatically independent of each other and of adjacent couplets (12 examples):
> "Is his leudi deliuerd wiþ sounde?"
> "Ȝa, sir, yþonked be God þe stounde."
> (ll. 50–51)

(2) The first verse can be grammatically independent, but the second belongs with the following verses (five examples):
> "Madam, what rede ȝe of þis þing?
> Today riȝt in þe morning,

sone after þe first stounde,
a litel maidenchild ich founde
in þe holwe assche þerout,
& a pel him about.

(ll. 211–216)

(3) The first verse of the couplet can belong grammatically with the preceding passage; the second
verse is independent (two examples):
"Go," hye seyd, "on heiȝing,
& feche it hider Y pray þe.
It is welcom to God & to me."

(ll. 220–222)

(4) The first verse of the couplet can belong grammatically with the preceding passage; the second
verse, with the following passage (three examples):
þe maide toke þe child hir mide
& stale oway in an euentide,
& passed ouer a wild heþ.
þurch feld & þurch wode hye geþ
al þe winterlong niȝt.

(ll. 145–149)

The versification of Lai le Freine is distinguished in two
other respects. For every two masculine rhymes there is one
feminine, which offers variety. As in French verse, alliteration,
frowned on by Geoffrey of Vinsauf,[18] slips in unnoticed.[19]
According to the foregoing identifications there are numerous
examples of metrical variation in Lai le Freine; how these
examples operate, of course, remains for study in the future.

Certain other differences between this poem and its original

[18] E. Faral, Les Arts póetiques du XIIe et du XIIIe Siècle (Paris, 1924),
p. 256.
[19] Ll. 17, 46 and 317.

point directly to the translator's understanding of the Breton lay as a form. *Lai le Fraisne* opens simply:

> Le lai del Fraisne vus dirai
> sulunc le cunte que jeo sai.
> (*Le Fraisne*, ll. 1–2)

The Middle English version, on the other hand, contains an elaborate prologue which in three divisions describes the genre of *Lai le Freine:*

(1) We redeþ oft & findeþ ywriȝte
& þis clerkes wele it wite,
layes þat ben in harping
ben yfounde in ferli þing.

(2) Sum beþe of wer & sum of wo,
& sum of ioie & mirþe also,
& sum of trecherie & of gile,
of old auentures þat fel while;
& sum of bourdes & ribaudy,
& mani þer beþ of fairy.
Of al þinges þat men seþ,
mest of loue for soþ þai beþ.

(3) In Breteyne bi hold time
þis layes were wrouȝt, so seiþ þis rime.
When kinges miȝt our yhere
of ani meruailes þat þer were,
þai token an harp in gle & game,
& maked a lay & gaf it name.
Now of þis auentours þat weren yfalle
y can tel sum ac nouȝt alle.
(*Lai le Freine*, ll. 1–20)

In lines 1–4, the narrator describes the Breton lay as it is known in writing to clerks and rendered musically with harp.

Its chief subject is love in a variety of forms (ll. 5–12). The lay was composed in ancient Brittany and carried abroad, a record of an adventure preserved in the rhymed source, which belongs in the more recent past (ll. 13–20).[20]

This description in *Lai le Freine* leaves a question unanswered: was a single "text" of each lay made to serve both modes of presentation, musical-vocal and through reading? Modern scholarship has circulated a somewhat standard, but also ambiguous, definition to explain the term *Breton lay* as it applies to the Middle English poems under study: these are so named from their "evident dependence on Breton *lais*— short poems of romantic content intended to be sung, represented best in the *lais* of Marie de France" (Wells, pp. 124–125). Marie's disinclination to render a lyric lay, however, is clearly expressed in her short prologue, which somehow became lost to the fourteenth century: "I shall relate the lay (*lai*) of Freine / According to the tale (*conte*) which I know." Her paired terms *lai* and *conte* distinguish one from the other, but this distinction is not necessarily adhered to by the English poet or composer of the long prologue. Further that the English writer rejected the two-line prologue may indicate that (a) it was too weak an opening or (b) the reconstructed prologue was intended to introduce an entire collection of lays which are no longer extant, if they were written at all.[21]

Even more remarkable than the fact of a synthetic prologue in *Lai le Freine* is the appearance of the same prologue, practically *verbatim*, in *Sir Orfeo*, which also dates from the early

---

[20] In "Zum Lai le Freine," *Englische Studien*, x (1887), 41, Julius Zupitza notes that lines 13–18 are a synthesis of borrowed phrasing and ideas which he traces to the narrative lays of Marie de France.

[21] Brugger, "Ueber die Bedeutung von Bretagne, Breton," p. 154, n. 103.

fourteenth century. The resemblance of one passage to the other is so nearly complete that any explanation of the fact other than through borrowing is impossible:

> We redyn ofte and fynde ywryte,
> As clerkes don us wyte,
> þe layes þat ben of harpyng
> Ben yfounde of frely þing.
> Sum ben of wele and sum of wo,
> And sum of joy and merþe also,
> Sum of trechery and sum of gyle,
> And sum of happes, þat fallen by whyle,
> Sum of bourdys and sum of rybaudry,
> And sum þer ben of þe feyre.
> Off alle þing þat men may se,
> Moost o lowe forsoþe þey be.
> In Brytain þis layes arne ywryte,
> Furst yfounde and forþe ygete,
> Of aventures þat fillen by dayes
> Wherof Brytouns made her layes,
> When þey myght owher heryn
> Of aventures þat þer weryn,
> þey toke her harpys wiþ game,
> Maden layes and ȝaf it name.
> Of aventures, þat han befalle,
> Y can sum tell but nought alle.
> Herken, lordyngs, þat ben trewe,
> And y wol ȝou telle of Sir Orphewe.
>
> (*Sir Orfeo*, ll. 1–24)

In which of the two lays, then, did the prologue first occur? Since *Lai le Fraisne* of Marie de France, which is the source of the Middle English poem, has its own prologue of two lines, it could not have come from this poem. It very likely came from the lost *Lai d'Orphéy* and was later passed on in the process of translation to *Sir Orfeo*.[22] Thereafter it was added to *Lai le Freine*, whose author was first a translator and on occasion a borrower. The evidence, however, is hardly conclusive enough to invalidate a second interpretation.[23] Accordingly, the English author of *Lai le Freine*, who is more than a mere translator, prepared the prologue, and this was later copied by a rival. For his prologue, on study, is so unlike the typical synthetic prologue of *Tydorel* and *Doon* that it can hardly be the work of the French author who wrote *Lai d'Orphéy*; it must have been written first in English. Secondly, not only in his prologue, but also in the rest of *Lai le Freine* he presents evidence to show that he knows the lays of Marie de France; the author of *Sir Orfeo*, except for his prologue, seems to know nothing at all of her work. The second interpretation, which is more complicated than the first, is also less compelling, but certainly unanswerable.

Except, then, for its prologue, which bears no relation to *Lai le Fraisne*, the Middle English poem is seldom far from its source. The few significant differences in plot and style which do occur are limited to deliberate alterations of the plot and to additions and omissions.

a. *Alteration of details:*	*Fraisne:*	*Freine:*
The setting is changed from Brittany to the "west cuntre" (=England, 239)	3	29
A midwife rather than "celes ki en chambre" is instructed to kill the child.	95	115

[22] Lucien Foulet, "The Prologue of *Sir Orfeo*," *MLN*, xxi (1906), 46–50. This view was earlier expressed by George Lyman Kittredge, "Sir Orfeo," *AJPh*, vii (1886), 176, n. 2.

[23] Gabrielle Guillaume, "The Prologues of the *Lay le Freine* and *Sir Orfeo*," *MLN*, xxxvi (1921), 458–464.

a. *Alteration of details:*

	Fraisne:	Freine:
Gurun lives in the west of England and not in Dol.	253	251
Gurun's intention to have Freine as as his mistress is made explicit. The source only suggests the relationship.		272
The clergyman who dissolves the marriage is a bishop instead of an archbishop.	371	339
The abbess explains to Freine as an adolescent that she is a foundling; in the source this explanation comes later, with less regard for its effect on characterization.	305–312	214–250

b. *Additions to the story:*

	Fraisne:	Freine:
The mother of the twin boys is described as "milde" and contrasts with her neighbor, who is jealous and spiteful.		33
The English version particularizes adultery by making it *in bour.*		70–72
The neighboring knight curses his wife and asks God to punish her with a "wers auentour" if she ever bears a child.		77–82
The messenger, who is present during the jealous wife's display of feeling, is "sore aschamed."		73
During the maid's flight with the infant Freine, the poet gives an idea of the passage of time, dramatizes	135–150	145–162

and intensifies the difficulties, and
adds atmosphere:

Þe maide toke þe child hir mide
& stale oway in an euentide,
& passed ouer a wild heþ
Þurch feld and þurch wode hye geþ
al þe winterlong niȝt,—
þe weder was clere, þe mone was liȝt,—
so þat hye com bi a forest side;
sche wex al weri & gan abide.
Sone after sche gan herk
cokkes crowe & houndes berk.
Sche arose & þider wold.
Ner & nere sche gan bihold.
Walles & hous fele hye seiȝe,
a chirche wiþ stepel fair & heiȝe.
Þan nas þer noiþer strete no toun,
bot an hous of religioun,
an ordre of nonnes wele ydiȝt
to seruy God boþe day & niȝt.

La dameisele prist l'enfant;
de la chambre s'en ist a tant.
La nuit quant tut fu aseri,
fors de la vile s'en eissi.
en un grant chemin est entree
ke en la forest l'a menee.
Par mi le bois sa veie tint.
Od tut l'enfant ultre s'en vint;
unques del grant chemin n'eissi.
Bien loinz sur destre aveit oi
chiens abaier e cos chanter:
iluec purra vile trover.
Cele part vet a grant espleit,
u la noise des chiens oeit.

En une vile riche e bele
est entree la dameisele.

The English adds the description of   180–182
the dawn:

Wiþ þat it gan to dawe liȝt.
Þe foules vp and song on bou,
and acremen ȝede to þe plou.

The duties of the porter are enlarged   188
to include his putting "forþ bokes &
al redi diȝt."

Translates *freyne* as meaning "ash"   231–234
in the language of the French.

As Guiron pleads with Freine to leave   297
the abbey with him, the English poet
says that she *trusts* him.

c. *Omissions:*   *Fraisne:*   *Freine:*
When the jealous wife bears twin   68
daughters, the English poet omits saying that her neighbor is now avenged.

The English omits the reference to
Freine's courtly breeding:

Franche esteit e de bone esteit   245–252

He omits Gurun's "casual" meeting   259–260
with Freine. In going to the abbey
Gurun "bad his men sigge verrament
he schuld toward a turnament." In
the French he stops by on his way
from the tournament.

When Gurun is urged to take a wife   332–334
the reason is omitted from the English version: to have an heir and so
to prevent the possibility of civil
disorder.

Stylistically, the author of *Lai le Freine* departs on occasion
from his text. He five times substitutes direct for indirect
discourse;[24] twice he reverses this process.[25] He avoids needless
repetition, especially of "dous enfanz."[26] He translates literally
"aveir lur fraternité" to mean "to become a brother of a religious group," which the text may not support.[27]

In ways proper to each, other medieval genres treat materials
found in *Lai le Freine*: the birth of twins, the husband with
two wives, and the return of the lost daughter.[28] The closest
analogue is *Galeran de Bretagne*, a romance of 8000 lines,
derived partly from *Lai le Fraisne* and showing the expan-
siveness of a longer work.[29] Of greater interest, however, as a
literary form is the analogue *Fair Annie*, No. 62 in Child's
collection of ballads.[30] It raises the question of the relationship
between the Breton lay and the ballad of tradition. In this

[24] *Freine*, ll. 39–42, 49–54, 116–118, 211–224 and 279–284.

[25] *Fraisne*, ll. 45–48 and 197–202.

[26] Guillaume, "The Prologue of *Lai le Freine* and *Sir Orfeo*," pp. 461–462.

[27] *Freine*, l. 282.

[28] Wattie, pp. xvii–xix. A discussion of analogues by Reinhold Köhler and
Johannes Bolté, is included in the introduction to Warnke's edition of the
Lais, pp. cvi–cxxi. See Ferguson, pp. 1–24, and Gerald Bordman, *Motif-Index
of the English Metrical Romances*, FFC No. 190, vol. lxxix (Helsinki, 1963),
read with F. L. Utley, "Arthurian Romance and International Folktale
Method," *RPh*, xvii (1964), 596–607.

[29] Edited by A. Boucherie (Montpellier, 1888).

[30] *English and Scottish Popular Ballads*, ed. Helen Child Sargent and George
Lyman Kittredge (Boston, 1904), pp. 117–121.

instance both poems tell the same story, but differ in presentation. The Breton lay tells it directly and with complete detail; the ballad of tradition, by reference to something already known. Differences could be multiplied to include stanza, method of development, audience and the like: for the two forms are distinct. The ballad "would seem to have its own laws, independent of all forms of narrative poetry in extant medieval English. . . ."[31] It belongs to no one time, place or author; the narrative lay of Marie de France and later is a local form of known authorship: if unnamed today, the author of *Lai le Freine* can at least be accurately placed in time and nationality.

The changes in *Lai le Freine* which are noted above lead directly to the question of how they came about in the process of translation and modernization. First, the Middle English short couplet was the closest available metre to that of *Lai le Fraisne* and so was preferred. Then, the change from the introductory two lines of *Lai le Fraisne* to an omnibus prologue suggests that the fourteenth century needed to be reminded at length of the Breton lay and its tradition: certainly the original two lines are inadequate for this purpose. In the story itself the setting is changed from Brittany to the western part of England, which was long familiar as Celtic in tradition and brought the story closer to home. Stylistically, *Lai le Freine* here and there improves on the original by frequent translation into more concrete language, and by the addition of the two colorful descriptions, which are to be credited to the inventiveness of the translator. Last, but not least significant, the omission of any reference to Freine's courtly breeding (ll. 245–252) suggests that the translator thought little of the passage in

[31] Ker, "Metrical Romances, 1200–1500," pp. 299–300.

question and of its emphasis on courtly conduct and *courtoisie*. He wanted simply a readable story which would suit an audience of more than one class and found it in *Lai le Freine*.

II. THE LANVAL POEMS IN COUPLETS

Since the translations of *Lanval* are written in more than one Middle English prosodic style, they are more difficult to study than the single translation of *Lai le Fraisne*. Five examples in octosyllabic couplets consitute a group, called the "Short Version." *Sir Launfal* or *Launfal Miles* of Thomas Chestre, in tail-rhyme stanzas, represents a different style and belongs with related poems in the last chapter.

The manuscripts of the Short Version, however, can hardly be studied apart from *Sir Launfal*.[32] They include two complete versions and three fragments:

Two Complete:

> R. *Sir Landavall*. MS. Rawlinson C. 86 in the Bodleian Library, fol. 119b–128. The date of the second part of the MS., which includes *Landavall*, is 1480–1508. There are 535 verses in couplets.
> P. *Sir Lambewell*. The Bishop Percy MS., now British Museum MS. Additional 27879, fol. 29b–33b, written about 1650. 632 verses.

Three Fragments:

> H. *Sir Lamwell*. The so-called Halliwell Fragment, preserved in Bodleian Malone 941[33] and consisting of

[32] George Lyman Kittredge, "Sir Launfal," *AJPh*, x (1889), 1–5.
[33] Wells, *A Manual of the Writings in Middle English, 1050–1400*, fourth supplement (New Haven, 1929), p. 1262. But see, based on Wells, the new Severs, ed. *Manual*, Fascicule 1, for treatment of the Breton lays, by Mortimer J. Donovan, pp. 133–143 and 292–297.

nine printed leaves, eight of which belong to *Sir Lamwell*. The fragment may be part of John Kynge's edition, licensed in 1557–58.

D. *Sir Lamwell*. The Douce Fragment, consisting of one printed leaf and 61 lines, was called Douce II, 95, and is now Douce Fragments e.40.[34]

F. *Sir Lamwell*. Cambridge University Library MS. Kk. 5, 30, f.11, dated around 1612.[35] This fragment consists of 90 lines.

Launfal Miles, the long version, is available in one manuscript:

C. *Launfal Miles*. British Museum MS. Cotton Caligula Aii, ff. 35b–42b, dated from the first half of the fifteenth century. The poem contains 1044 verses.

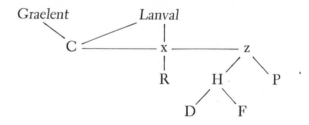

The manuscript tradition as elaborated above is reasonably detailed, but not quite satisfactory.[36] The existence of x as the first Middle English translation of *Lanval* is established by the general similarity of C and the Short Version and by

[34] Wells, p. 1262.

[35] Julius Zupitza, "Zum Sir Launfal" *Archiv*, LXXXVIII (1892), 69–70, revises Kittredge's dating (1460–70).

[36] The basic study is Anton Kolls, *Zur Lanvalsage* (Berlin, 1886). It precedes Kittredge's article based on R and Rudolf Zimmermann's critical edition, *Sir Landeval* (Königsberg, 1900), which is close to Kittredge in working out lineage. Zimmermann differs from Kittredge in believing that the author of C used Marie, but, having x at his disposal, referred to it chiefly as a convenience.

the presence in these of lines not found in the source; there is no reason for supposing two or more translators working independently.[37] R, H and P present little difficulty: they are, "on the whole identical not only in contents, but in phraseology and rhymes. They follow the narrative of Marie step by step, often rendering her words literally, and seldom departing farther from them than the liberty of a translator allows" (p. 5). Why a missing version z is necessary in the sub-group P and H becomes clear from errors which P, H and their descendants share (pp. 9–12). The relationship, however, of C with both Lanval and the anonymous Graelent cannot be clarified before the relationship of these two old French poems, which at present requires further study.[38]

In a comparison of the Short Version with Lanval, R seems to recommend itself for study before P, which also is complete.[39] Certainly R is closer to the first Middle English translation of Lanval and so to the Old French original. P can serve to indicate the changes which followed with later development of the poem. This section will present, then, a comparison first of R with M and, where necessary, P with R. If the fragmentary H, D and F contribute significant changes in the form of the Breton lay, they will be mentioned.

Sir Landavall dates from the first half or third of the fourteenth century,[40] the same period as produced Lai le Freine, and originates in the South (Wells, p. 133). Since it is a translation of Lanval, it should be associated with the same

[37] Kittredge, "Sir Launfal," p. 5.

[38] Stokoe, "The Sources of Sir Launfal: Lanval and Graelent," p. 392.

[39] The quotations from R in the following pages are taken from Kittredge's printing of the poem, pp. 21–32. For a study of artistic changes in the short version see Stemmler, pp. 243–263.

[40] Zimmermann, pp. 27–28.

group of analogues as the latter,[41] the chief of which is
Graelent. In external features, it sometimes resembles *Lai le
Freine*, showing comparable deviations from its source.

Its versification, first, is close to that of *Lai le Freine*.[42] The
octosyllabic couplets are far less regular than those of *Lanval*
and show a lack of restraint not found in the Old French:

> "Now commyth my loue, now commyth my swete;
> Now commyth she my bale shalle bette.
> Now I haue her seyne with myne ee,
> I ne reke when that I dye."
>
> (ll. 454–457)

> "Par fei," fel il, "ceo est m'amie!
> Or ne m'est guaires ki m'ocie,
> s'ele nen a merci de mei:
> kar guariz sui, quant jeo la vei."
>
> (ll. 613–616)

But the effect is monotony more often than in *Lai le Freine*.
Of the 265 complete couplets,[43] at least 70 are one-sentence
long and sometimes occur in solid and unvaried blocs:

> The mauntelle for hete downe she dede
> Right to hir gyrdille stede.
> She was white as lely in May
> Or snowe that fallith in wynterday.
> Blossom on briere ne no floure
> Was not like to her coloure.
> The rede rose whan it is newe
> To her rud is not of hewe.
> Her heire shone as gold wire;
> No man can telle her atyre.

---

[41] See Reinhold Köhler's notes in Warnke's edition of the *Lais*, pp. cxxx–cxl.
[42] Zimmermann, pp. 20–23, has a section on versification.
[43] Single unrhyming lines: 17, 24, 26, 215 and 216.

"Landavale," she seide, "myn hert swete,
For thy Loue now I swete."
(ll. 101–112)[44]

Internal rhyme is found occasionally:

With hym there was a bachiler,
A yonge knyght of mushe myght
(ll. 17–18)[45]

A greater number of alliterating phrases distinguish *Sir Landavall* from *Lai le Freine*. While many passages show a possibly unintentional repetition of initial consonants, eleven contain fixed alliterating phrases,[46] such as

With ruddy rede as rose coloure   (l. 60)
Ientylle and iolyffe as birde on boweh   (l. 430)

If a detailed comparison were made between R and P, few differences in versification, especially in rhymes, would be noted:

(R)
Sothly by Arthurys day
Was Bretayne yn grete nobyle,
For yn thys tyme a grete whyle
He soiourned at Carlile.
He had with hym a meyne there,
As he had ellys where,
Of the rounde table the knyghtes alle,
With myrth and ioye yn hys halle.
(ll. 1–8)

---

[44] See also ll. 101–112, 163–170, 189–200, 209–216, 390–397 and 446–451.
[45] Also ll. 116, 181, 220, 313 and 411. See Zimmermann, p. 21.
[46] Noted in J. P. Oakden, *Alliterative Poetry in Middle English* (Manchester, 1935), pp. 312–343.

(P)
Doughty in King Arthures dayes
When Brittaine was holden in noblenesse,
and in his time a long while
he soiourned in merry Carlile.
With him he had many an heire
as he had else many a whide where;
Of his round table they were knightes all,
& the had much mirth in bower & hall

(ll. 1–8)

Apart from versification other differences distinguish the Short Version from *Lanval*. These are limited to significant alterations of detail in the plot, additions thereto and omissions.

a. *Alterations of detail:*

	Lanval:	R:	P:
In R Lanval meets the *fée* during the warm part of the day and finds her unclothed. In P it is evening.		34–36	55
Instead of stopping with an embrace Lanval and the *fée* spend a night together.	185–188	145–149	179–184
Instead of Arthur's *baruns*, twelve knights are chosen to judge Lanval's case.	503	289–313	330–351
The trial scene is shortened.	417 f.	324 f.	

b. *Additions to the story:*

| Before Lanval leaves Arthur's court for the country, he bids | — | — | 28–50 |

farewell to the knights Huon,
Gaion, Kay, Perceval, Agrau-
aine, Garrett, Griffin, Iron-
side, in an epic list of names.

On his return to court he joins the knights in a dance outside Guinevere's bower. The description of the dance, with its special formation of ladies and knights, is added.	—	201–208	237–246
Lanval's soliloquy as he realizes that in revealing his love he will lose his beloved.	—	314–315	309–312

c. *Omissions:*

R and P omit the four-line prologue of *Lanval*: L'aventure d'un altre lai, cum ele avint, vus conterai. Fuz fu d'un mult gentil vassal; en Bretanz l'apelent Lanval.	1–4	—	—
R and P omit reference to Lanval's courtly qualities (except his *largesse*).	21–28	—	—
R and P fail to translate "mes sis chevals tremble forment" and so miss the implication that Lanval is near fairyland.	46	—	—
They fail to translate the line "pur vus vinc jeo fors de	283–285	—	—

ma tere," in which the *fée* indicates that she is from another land.

Although many differences can be cited between the Short
Version and *Lanval*, the most significant are the few omissions. Without the typical prologue of the original, R and P
both become simply a short romance with an Arthurian setting. In their own day they were never called a *lay*, or a *Breton
lay*, and became such only in modern literary history. In R
and P, the chivalric framework which Marie de France gave
Lanval is partly destroyed. Although Lanval's *largesse*, vital
to the story, is prominent, his *valur*, *bealté*, noble birth and
pruesce go unmentioned. His love for the *fée*, in the pavilion
scene, is more sensual than Marie de France would allow. The
P-version alone adds the list of knights to whom Lanval says
farewell on leaving court for the first time, but this enumera-
tion may merely attempt to trade on famous names. In two
passages the Short Version conspicuously loses the sense of
otherworldliness found in the original. It fails to note that
Lanval's horse trembles on approaching fairyland, nor does it
include the passage in which the *fée* says that she comes from
another land. Stylistically, the octosyllabic couplets of the
Short Version lack variety and, unlike those of *Lai le Freine*,
favor alliteration and internal rhyme. This poem, in general,
does not intend to advertise itself as a Breton lay and departs
further from its original than does *Lai le Freine*.

III. SIR ORFEO

Unlike *Lai le Freine* and the *Lanval* poems in couplets,
neither *Sir Orfeo* nor *Sir Degare* has an extant original in

Old French. One can be assumed, however, for *Sir Orfeo*.[47]
Of the many references to Orpheus and Eurydice in medieval
literature,[48] two specify a *Lai d'Orphéy*, which may in fact be
the source of the Middle English poem. The first of these
is found in *Lai de l'Épine* and tells how the king of Brittany
and his knights hear a lyric version of the story:

> Le lais escoutient d'Aielis,
> Que uns irois sone en sa rote;
> Mout doucement le chante et note.
> Après celi d'autre commenche,
> Nus d'iaus ni noise ne ni tenche;
> Le lai lor sonne d'Orphéy
>   (ll. 180–185)

The same reference, again to a lyric lay, appears in *Floire et
Blanceflor*:[49]

>   grant com un uilains:
> Une harpe tint en sa mains,
> Et harpe le lai d'Orphéy:
> Onques nus hom plus n'en oi
> Et le montee et l'avalee.

How different *Sir Orfeo* is from the missing *Lai d'Orphéy* is
uncertain; but the development of *Sir Orfeo* as a Breton lay
can be traced with fair accuracy, even without the advantage of a French original, for a classical version of the story,

---

[47] See Kittredge, "Sir Orfeo," pp. 181–182. F. Lindner, reviewing Zielke's
Sir Orfeo in *Englische Studien*, v (1881–82), 166–170, concludes, especially
from the form of *Orfeo* as a name, that there is "eine indirekte italienische
Quelle" for the English poem; but he is alone in this claim.

[48] Zielke, *Sir Orfeo*, pp. 130 ff. Zielke's text is used throughout this study.
See notes on the text by F. Holthausen, "Zu Mittelenglischen Romanzen,"
Anglia, XLII (1918), 425–429.

[49] Ed. E. du Méril (Paris, 1856), p. 231.

known to have circulated in the Middle Ages, offers excellent material for this study.[50]

Sir Orfeo is preserved in three manuscripts.[51] The oldest, Auchinleck W 4 I, Advocates' Library, Edinburgh, dated 1330–40, lacks the familiar prologue, verses 1–22. Both Ashmole 61, Oxford University, prepared in the fifteenth century, and Harleian 3810 of the British Museum, dated from the early fifteenth century, contain the prologue. The original dialect of the poem is thought to be North Northamptonshire.[52] Like *Lai le Freine*, included also in the Auchinleck MS, *Sir Orfeo* shows an irregular couplet, distinguished, however, by a far larger number of alliterating phrases, 29 by count.[53]

The story of *Sir Orfeo*—the myth of Orpheus and Eurydice, but ending happily—derives ultimately from a classical version read during the Middle Ages in the *Metamorphoses*, Books X and XI, as well as in Boethius. The following is a summary of the myth as it is related in the *Metamorphoses*:[54] here Orpheus is denied a second chance to rescue Eurydice. Hymen is present at Orpheus' marriage to Eurydice, but the omens are far from propitious. His torch sputters, smokes and fails to ignite. While Eurydice is walking in the grass, she

[50] Douglas Bush, *Mythology and the Renaissance Tradition in English Poetry* (Minneapolis, 1932), p. 14, n. 8. C. Bullock-Davies, "Classical Threads in Orfeo," *MLR*, LVI (1961), 161–166.

[51] See Wells, p. 128. All three are printed in A. J. Bliss, ed. *Sir Orfeo* (Oxford, 1954). Rumble, pp. 207–226, prints Ashmole 61.

[52] Mary S. Serjeantson, "The Dialects of the Westmidlands in Middle English," *RES*, III (1927), 330–331.

[53] Oakden, *Alliterative Poetry in Middle English*, pp. 312–343.

[54] *Ovid: Metamorphoses*, tr. Frank J. Miller, LCL (London and New York, 1928). The *Metamorphoses*, of course, was read with medieval appartus (*accessus*, glosses, etc.)

is bitten in the ankle by a serpent and dies. Orpheus, heart-broken, descends into the Underworld and to the music of his lyre requests that Eurydice's fate be rewoven, so that his love for her may continue in the Upper World. The gods are moved to pity by his playing and grant his request on condition that he shall not turn his eyes in her direction during the ascent. As Eurydice limps along behind him, however, Orpheus, eager for one look, turns around and instantly loses her. He is refused a second chance to return to the Underworld and for seven days sits on the bank of the Styx in rags and without appetite for food. Complaining of the gods, he travels to Rhodope and Haemus and there for three years rejects the love of women. Inconsolable, he plays his lyre, and plays so well that the beasts, trees and stones listen. Still scorning love, he is finally stoned by the women of the Cicones, who then scatter his limbs about. His head and lyre float down the Hebrus river and reach the shore of Lesbos, near the city of Methymna; and his shade in due time is united with Eurydice's in the Underworld, where they remain. In the early sixth century Boethius included the myth in the *De Consolatione Philosophiae* to illustrate a moral: happy the man untied by earthly bonds:[55]

> Felix qui potuit boni
> Fontem uisere lucidum,

[55] *The Theological Tractates and the Consolation of Philosophy*, LCL (London and New York, 1918), Book III, Metrum XII. Pre-Christian Greece produced also an Orpheus story with a happy ending. Although Hermesianax of Colophon, born c. 300 B.C., includes in his *Leontion* an elegy of Orpheus and Agriope, which ends without tragedy, this version has never been related to the late medieval *Sir Orfeo*: Otto Kern, *Orpheus* (Berlin, 1920), p. 24, and Ulrich von Wilamovitz-Moellendorff, *Der Glaube der Hellenen* (Berlin, 1932), II, 195–196, discuss the Greek version.

Sir Orfeo is not to be considered a literary influence on Henryson's poem.

Felix qui potuit grauis
Terrae soluere uincula.

At first sight, *Sir Orfeo*, in 602 verses, simply expands the myth and gives it a happy ending; the substance of the myth is ever present.

Orfeo, stalwart king of Thrace, descendant of Pluto and Juno, and a great harper as well, lives happily with his queen, Herodis. On a May morning, when Herodis goes into the orchard with her women to enjoy the spring, she falls asleep under a tree and later awakens in great distress, scratching her face and tearing her clothes. When Orfeo hurries to her bedside and assures her that he will stand by her always, whatever happens, she replies that she must leave her beloved Orfeo. She then explains what happened during her troubled sleep. The king of the fairies, accompanied by a hundred knights and a hundred damsels, all on white horses, took her to his palace and bringing her back to the orchard instructed her to be there on the following day, when he would take her to his kingdom again and there she would remain. Since Orfeo would rather lose his life than his queen, he next day surrounds her in the orchard with ten thousand knights. But she is whisked away at the appointed time despite their numbers. Orfeo is so grief-stricken that he gives his kingdom to his steward with orders for a parliament to choose a successor on news of his death. Then, clothed only in a pilgrim's robe

See G. Gregory Smith, *The Poems of Robert Henryson*, STS (Edinburgh and London, 1914), I, lii: "Henryson's Orpheus, as might be expected from the poet's general cast of mind, has nothing in common with the romantic type. But, while it reproduces the classical story with fair accuracy, it superimposes on the plain narrative a philosophical purpose."

150

and taking with him his harp for solace, he enters the forest alone and for ten years lives in the open. In good weather he plays his harp and charms the wildlife in the forest; occasionally he sees the king of the fairies out hunting with a large retinue, but never discovers where they go when they leave his sight. One day, as he watches sixty ladies hunting with falcons, he is quick to notice Herodis among them; and she sees him. Without speaking they look sorrowfully at each other until she is drawn off by the other ladies. This time Orfeo follows and behind them enters a cave which leads out onto the plain of fairyland. There he sees a richly built castle and knocking at the gate is received as a minstrel. Inside he notices people in various postures, just as they were when brought in by the fairies, and among them Herodis, under the same tree. By playing expertly, he passes for a harper and so is allowed by the king of the fairies to choose his own reward. When Orfeo asks for Herodis, the king hesitates—she is so beautiful and Orfeo so pale and emaciated—but yields as Orfeo reminds him of his promise. Orfeo and Herodis return to Thrace, stopping outside the city, where Herodis remains and Orfeo assumes beggar's clothes. Disguised as a needy minstrel, he tests his steward and finds him hospitable to minstrels. When invited into the castle to eat, he plays his harp, which the steward soon recognizes. Then Orfeo makes up an explanation of how he got it: it belonged to the missing king who was killed in the forest. On hearing this report, the steward faints. Immediately Orfeo knows the steward to be true and, after identifying himself, says that the steward will be next in succession. Amid joy and music Orfeo is crowned a second time, and he and his queen continue their interrupted life of happiness.

Modern study, however, reveals that *Sir Orfeo* results from the fusion of the classical myth and an independent tale, probably Celtic, relating the abduction and rescue of a queen.[56] During the Middle Ages, various "waifs and strays from the ancient authors were floating about,"[57] and associated themselves with similar stories from India, Arabia and Celtic England and France. Although no exact source can be found for the Celtic elements in the poem, analogous passages are not uncommon and have been carefully recorded.[58] The tale resulting from such fusion can be assumed to resemble in content *Sir Orfeo*. Whether the tales named so far can account for the many Celtic elements singly or in combination remains a trying question (for a review of evidence see Bliss, *Sir Orfeo*, pp. xxxi–xli). The ballad *King Orfeo*[59] "is something new, and . . . something which it is futile to compare with its original, except for the material in it. Its efficient and formal causes are elsewhere."[60]

Why a tale about Orpheus circulated during the Middle

---

[56] Loomis, *Arthurian Tradition & Chrétien de Troyes*, p. 39, cites *Sir Orfeo* as an example of contamination resulting "when two or more distinct stories are welded into one indissoluble unit." See also my "Herodis in the Auchinleck Sir Orfeo," *MÆ*, xxvii (1958), 162–165.

[57] Edward Kennard Rand, *Ovid and His Influence* (Boston, 1925), pp. 116–117.

[58] For a discussion of Celtic and other sources see Kittredge's article already referred to; Gertrude Schoepperle Loomis, *Tristan and Isolt* (London and Frankfort, 1913), ii, 541–544; Howard R. Patch, *The Other World According to Descriptions in Medieval Literature*, Smith College Studies in Modern Languages, New Series (Cambridge, Mass., 1950); basic research is found in Roger Sherman Loomis, "Sir Orfeo and Walter Map's *De Nugis*," *MLN*, li (1936), 28–30; the most recent literary treatment of sources is J. Burke Severs, "The Antecedents of *Sir Orfeo*" in Mac E. Leach, ed. *Studies in Medieval Literature in Honor of Professor Albert Croll Baugh* (Philadelphia, 1961), pp. 187 ff.

[59] *English and Scottish Popular Ballads*, p. 37.

[60] Ker, *Form and Style in Poetry*, pp. 34–35.

Ages is not hard to discover. Apart from the beauty of the story, *Sir Orfeo* also puts the minstrel in a favorable light and so contributes to his stature in society.[61] A king becomes a minstrel:

> [Orfeo] loved for to harpe
> And layde þereon his wittes scharpe,
> He learnyd to, þer noþing was
> A better harper in no plas.
>
> (ll. 37–40)

At his court other minstrels are welcome, as they should be.[62] Although apparently unnecessary, this defense of minstrelsy in the fourteenth century was politic and vital, for real opposition was offered by Church and state, which found in their art, not an opportunity for recreation, but an occasion for sin and sedition respectively.[63]

Very simply, the tale from which *Sir Orfeo* developed contains a defense of minstrelsy. It must have attracted, among others, Breton minstrels, who saw in it both beauty and a means of securing their position. From this point, however, the development of the hypothetical tale is long but explainable. After the tale had begun to circulate, Breton minstrels

---

[61] Alois Brandl, "Spielmannsverhaltnisse in frühmittelenglischer Zeit," *Sitzungsberichte der Königlich preussischen Akademie der Wissenschaft,* XL (1910), 892, calls *Sir Orfeo* "das Loblied eines feinen Minstrels auf seinen eigenen Stand."

[62] Ll. 33–34, 515–516, 427–432 and 447–450.

[63] E. K. Chambers, *The Mediaeval Stage* (Oxford, 1903), I, 38–41: "The canon law, as modified by Gratian, treats as applicable to minstrels the pronouncements of fathers and councils against *scenici* and adds to them others more recent, in which the clergy who attended *spectacula*, or in any way by word or deed play the *joculator*, are uncompromisingly condemned. This temper of the Church did not fail to find expression in Post-Conquest England. The Council of Oxford in 1222 adopted for this country the restatement of the traditional rule by the Lateran Council of 1215 . . . ."

153

gave it new form when they rendered it as a lyric lay to the accompaniment of harp and rote. Even when the prologue of *Sir Orfeo* is ignored, since it may have been written for either *Lai le Freine* or this poem, still the epilogue is authentic and mentions a musical version which in the absence of evidence to the contrary must be considered:

> Harpours in Bretaine after þan
> Herd, hou þis mervaile bigan,
> And made herof a lay of gode likeing
> And nempned it after þe king:
> Þat lay Orfeo is yhote,
> Gode is þe lay, swete is þe note.
> (ll. 595–600)

Certain lines, furthermore, suggest a lyric version of the same story as is told in the extant narrative lay:[64] we can at once agree that Orfeo's lament, followed by Herodis' reply, retains an emotional intensity really striking in narrative poetry:

> "O lef liif, what is te?
> Þat ever ʒete hast ben so stille
> And now gredest wonderschille!
> · Þi body, þat was so white yoore,
> Wiþ þine nailes is al totore!
> Alas þi rode, þat was so red,
> Is as wan as þou were ded!
> And also þi fingres smale
> Beþ al blodi and al pale!
> Allas! þi lovesum eyʒen to
> Lokeþ so man doþ on his fo!
> A dame, ich biseche merci!
> Lete ben al þis reweful cri,

---

[64] French, *Essays on King Horn*, p. 16. The existence of a lyric version is hypothetical. See Chapter I, in which a lyric version is suggested for two of the original twelve lays. On the artistry of this passage see F. Carpinelli, "Sir Orfeo," *Explicator*, xix (1960), item 13.

And tel me, what þe is and hou,
And what þing may þe help now!"
(ll. 100–114)

Still later, when the Old French narrative lay was enjoying
its vogue (probably during the thirteenth century) a writer
told a courtly audience the contents of the lyric lay, added
elements of *courtoisie*, but omitted any Christian references
or coloring. Assuming that *Sir Orfeo* is a fairly close translation, one would agree that "there is nothing wrong in the
descriptions of it as a 'Breton lay,' for it is wholly such a
tale as the Bretons, and many other people, might have told
without any suggestion from Greek or Latin";[65] but to say
that *Sir Orfeo* "is an utterly different thing from the rambling
tales of chivalry" misleads. As a narrative lay retelling in
simplified form the contents of a lyric lay, *Sir Orfeo* certainly
should not ramble; but it does come close to the romances
of chivalry by representing life ideally and investing it with
the various elements associated with *courtoisie*.

Orfeo himself, generous, courteous, royal, is represented as
a courtly figure:

Orfeo was a king,
In his time an heiȝe lording,

[65] Ker, "Metrical Romances, 1200–1500," p. 295. The French version of
Sir Orfeo must have lacked the following instance of direct address found in
the "intrusive" prologue of the English translation:
Of aventures, þat han befalle,
Y can sum telle, but nought all.
Herken, lordyngs, þat ben trewe,
And y wol ȝou telle of Sir Orphewe.
During translation, or after, two "English" elements came into the story: the
mention of a parliament (ll. 213–215) and the lines, omitted by Zielke,
For Winchester was cleped þo
Traciens wiþouten no.
(following Auchinleck MS. 48)

155

> A stalworþ man and hardi bo,
> Large, curteys he was also.
> His fader was comen of king Pluto,
> And his moder of king Juno,
> Þat sum time were as godes yhold
> For aventours, þat þai dede and told.
> (ll. 25–32)

His queen is a woman of esteem and beauty:

> He had wiþ him a quen of priis,
> Þat was ycleped dame Herodis,
> Þe fairest levedi for þe nones
> Þat miȝt gon on bodi and bones
> Ful of loue and of godenisse
> Ac no man may telle hir fairnise.
> (ll. 49–54)

Her appreciation of Spring (ll. 61–66) indicates a feeling for beauty such as the villain in *Lai d'Oiselet* lacks. When she is taken away, Orfeo loses the ennobling force of her love, and life has no meaning until her rescue:

> "O lef liif, what is te?
> Þat ever ȝete has ben so stille
> And now gredest wonderstille!
> (ll. 100–102)

When he leaves for the forest, he depends on the *fidélité* of his steward, who will rule in his place (ll. 202–216). The king of the fairies enjoys hunting and, surrounded by retainers and living in a rich castle, is represented as a feudal leader.[66]

In three scenes of sharp dramatic action a courtly ideal conflicts with a lesser motive. First, after performing on the harp, Orfeo asks for his promised reward. When he chooses

[66] Ll. 289–290 and 356–372.

Herodis, the king of the fairies hesitates: to give her to an ugly harper offends his sensibilities; not to do so reflects on his largesse and good faith. Since he is idealistic, he gives her up.[67] In disguise, Orfeo later tests his steward and finds him hospitable to minstrels and faithful to his king (ll. 513–516, 532). The story ends happily, as it should, and love is ideally satisfied. Although it is always love within marriage, in its effect it is like the exalting, overpowering force known as Courtly Love: Orfeo undertakes the rescue only out of love for Herodis.

Although the changes made in the lost *Lai d'Orphéy* during translation into Middle English will doubtless remain unknown, they must have been few. *Sir Orfeo* retains many characteristics of a courtly narrative lay and suggests as well its origin in a tale which developed from the fusion of a classical myth and a Celtic story. If the classical myth were less well defined, *Sir Orfeo* as a Breton lay would still be subject to suspicion; but the Celtic contribution is clear: the visit to fairyland and the happy ending. Although the defense of minstrelsy made in *Sir Orfeo* is continually prominent, emphasis falls first on the essentials of courtly literature—the greatness of love, and such ideal qualities of character as *largesse*, *fidélité* and a buoyant trust in the future. The only advantage of proof which *Lai le Freine* and *Landaval* have over *Sir Orfeo* as examples of the Breton lay in Middle Eng-

[67] Ll. 447 ff. For a discussion of *largesse* see Marion Parker Whitney, "Queen of Mediaeval Virtues: Largesse," *Vassar Mediaeval Studies* (New Haven, 1923). See also French and Hale, p. 337, note to line 367: "The whole scene may be rationalized, and the minstrel's words are reduced from a threat to persuasion. Bards were once greatly feared, because their verses and lampoons were supposed to bring bad luck." To see in Orfeo's act only a threat causes the text to lose in dramatic value: the king of the fairies has a decision to make, but not under compulsion.

157

lish is that their originals in Old French still exist and belong to Marie de France; if the lost *Lai d'Orphéy* were suddenly to reappear, it would probably not differ from any of the twelve original Breton lays as an example of courtly refinement. Since, however, it lacks their Christian context, it would be listed with the "anonymous" lays considered in Chapter 2, not written by Marie de France, but inspired by her.

IV. SIR DEGARE

Sir Degare, the fourth and last example of the Middle English Breton lay in octosyllabic couplets, survives in black-letter prints as well as in the following manuscripts:[68]

Auchinleck MS in the Advocates' Library, Edinburgh, ff. 78ª–84ᵇ, contains 1065 lines and is incomplete. It is dated 1330–40.[69]

Egerton 2862 in the British Museum, dating from the end of the 14th century. Ff. 95 and 97 give two fragments totalling 161 lines.

Cambridge University Library Ff. ii.38, c. 1450, an incomplete version in 602 lines, ff. 257ᵇ–261ᵇ.

---

[68] A detailed study of the texts appears in George Patterson Faust, *Sir Degare, A Study of the Texts and Narrative Structure*. Princeton Studies in English No. 11 (Princeton, 1935), pp. 3–39, and in Muriel Bothwell Carr, "Sire Degarre," *A Middle English Metrical Romance edited from MS. and Black Letter Texts, with introductory chapters on filiation of texts and phonology*, University of Chicago dissertation, summarized in *University of Chicago Abstracts of Theses*, Humanistic Series II (1923–24), pp. 369–378.

[69] For a description of the Auchinleck MS. see E. Kölbing, "Vier Romanzenhandschriften," *Englische Studien*, vii (1884), 178–191. The text used in this study is that of the Auchinleck MS., the oldest, as printed by French and Hale, pp. 285–320. Gustave Schleich, *Sire Degarre*, Englische Textbibliothek No. 19 (Heidelberg, 1929) presents a critical edition.

158

Rawlinson F. 34 in Bodleian Library, 15th century. Ff. 10ᵇ–17ᵇ contain 989 lines and are complete, ed. Rumble, pp. 45–78.

Douce 261 in Bodleian Library, dated 1564. Ff. 8–14 give four fragments of 350 lines.

Additional 27879 (Percy Folio) in the British Museum, dated c. 1650. Ff. 183ᵇ–198ᵃ, give a complete version in 900 lines.

A sixteenth century version is found in three black-letter prints:

Wynkyn de Worde's print in the J. Pierpont Morgan Library, New York, dated possibly 1502–34, includes 18 leaves of 995 lines and is complete.

Wyllyam Copland's print, C21, c66, in the British Museum, dated possibly 1548–68; 16 leaves and 993 lines; complete.

John King's print; S. Selden d. 45 (3) in the Bodleian Library, dated 1560; contains 16 leaves and 993 lines.

The account is substantially the same in each of the above.

The King of Brittany, a widower undefeated at jousting, successfully keeps his only daughter and heir from marriage by requiring any suitor to unhorse him. On the anniversary of his wife's death, he sets out to visit her grave and while travelling loses his daughter, who with two attendants wanders in the forest and finally onto a heath. There in the warm forenoon, while her attendants nap, she gathers flowers, listens to the birds and suddenly meets a knight from fairyland, who by force makes her his mistress. Then he predicts that she will bear him a son, for whose defense he leaves a broken sword; he retains its missing point so that in years to come he can identify its bearer as his son. Returning finally to her castle, the princess fears that she will be accused of incest, for she has been near no man except her father. When her son is born, she has him abandoned outside a cave, where a hermit finds him, together with money, a pair of gloves and a note asking that the infant be nurtured and instructed to recognize as his mother whatever woman the gloves fit. The boy, christened Degare, for ten years lives away with the hermit's sister and then returns to study under the hermit himself. In another ten years he is old enough to be told about the note and, armed with only a staff, begins the search for his parents. While wandering in the forest, he rescues an old earl from the attacks of a dragon, which he kills, and then goes on to the earl's castle. There he finds that the gloves fit none of the women present and before leaving is knighted and given a horse, armor and an attendant. From a group of people returning from a parliament, he learns that their king has offered his daughter and heritage to whoever can unhorse him. After trying and succeeding, Degare marries the king's daughter, whom he identifies, by means of the gloves, as his own mother. He learns about his parentage and receives from her the broken sword which his father years earlier left behind. Continuing his search for his father and coming upon a castle in the middle of a river, he enters, warms himself before the fire, and is ignored by four huntresses, who are followed into the hall by a dwarf. At supper, Degare sits before the lady of the castle and falls in love with her. In her chamber later on, he sits down on her bed and, while she plays the harp, falls asleep. Awakening next day he shows his prowess by defeating in combat her hostile neighbor and rejected suitor, who has killed off all the men of her castle. When the lady offers as his reward both her land and her love, Degare accepts and promises to return after a year of adventure. After riding westward he meets a knight and is accused of poaching his deer. He protests and finally fights with the knight, who, from the sword without a tip, recognizes Degare as his lost son. Before Degare himself is married, he returns to Brittany, where his father and mother are united.

Sir Degare is a Sohrab and Rustum story and more besides.[70] It recalls two Breton lays already considered, *Milun* and *Doon*,[71] which also relate a combat between father and son. Although the poet's primary purpose is to tell but one story, he includes elements of two others. In the first, a jealous father, for any of several reasons, sets before his daughter's suitors an impossible task; herein the opening of *Sir Degare* resembles that of *Les Dous Amanz*, in which a Norman king requires any suitor to carry the princess up a difficult hill with the reward of a bride for anyone who succeeds. The other type of story tells of the lover who unwittingly marries his own mother: *Sir Degare*, in this respect, comes close to the Legend of Gregory, of which no examples are to be found among the Breton lays so far considered.

There are known sources for only isolated passages in *Sir Degare*. Although the handsome knight whom the princess meets in the forest recalls the knight in *Yonec* and *Tydorel*

---

[70] For a discussion of sources and analogues see Clark Harris Slover, " 'Sire Degarre': A Study of a Mediaeval Hack Writer's Methods," *The University of Texas Bulletin* (Studies in English, No. 11), 1930, pp. 5–23; Faust, *Sir Degare*, pp. 41–87.

[71] M. A. Potter, *Sohrab and Rustum*, Grimm Library No. 14 (London, 1902), pp. 46–48. Smithers, pp. 75 ff., "Type III."

and possibly the king of the fairies in *Sir Orfeo,* who carries off Herodis, these and other similarities have not been advanced as anything more than analogues. There seems to be agreement, however, that *Sir Degare,* from the birth of the child to its discovery by the hermit, borrows from the Middle English *Lai le Freine.*[72] When Degare unhorses the King of Brittany, he is promised, "King ȝow schalt ben after me," just as the steward in *Sir Orfeo* is told, "ȝou shust be king after miday."[73] The description of the dragon in *Sir Degare* may draw from *Beues of Hamtoun* (Faust, p. 30).

Sir Degare has certain features of the Breton lay. Although it lacks the familiar prologue and epilogue, it is set in Brittany:

> In Litel Bretaygne was a kyng
> Of gret poer in alle þing,
> Stif in armes vnder sscheld,
> And mochel idouted in þe feld
> (ll. 7–10)

The life which the author represents is generally that of the nobility. Details which suggest fairyland—the handsome knight, the castle in the river—suggest as well the nonrealistic type of Breton lay, such as *Guigemar, Lanval* and *Yonec* of Marie de France.[74] *Sir Degare,* by romance standards, is short: the *Auchinleck* text contains 993 lines. Degare's name is formally derived to explain the title:[75]

> He hit nemnede Degarre.
> Degarre nowt elles ne is

[72] Slover, p. 17, n. 21, and Faust, pp. 9–13.

[73] *Sir Degare,* l. 603; *Sir Orfeo,* l. 570.

[74] P. J. Heather, "Colour Symbolism IV," *Folk-Lore,* LX (1949), 322, discusses color symbolism in *Sir Degare.*

[75] As in *Lai le Fraisne* (ll. 28–30), *Bisclavret* (ll. 3–4), *Laustic* (ll. 5–6), *Chievrefueil* (ll. 115–116).

> But þing þat not neuer whar it is,
> Oþer þing þat is negȝ forlorn also;
> Forþi þe schild he nemnede þous þo.
>
> (ll. 252–256)

The verse-form is the octosyllabic couplet, "the finer points" of which the author neglects.[76] Like other courtly poems in couplets this one was intended to be read aloud or privately, but not in the manner of the tail-rhyme romances; the following instance of direct address, lacking in the Auchinleck MS, seems intrusive:[77]

> Lysteneþ, lordinges, gent and fre!
> Ich wille ȝou telle of Sire Degarre

Usually the "auentures bi niȝt and dai" are skillfully told, the most notable exception being the awkward assignment of two values to the gloves which Sir Degare uses to identify his mother: these are both a recognition and a marriage test.[78] An occasional inelegance produces humor, rather uncommon in a Breton lay:

> And Sire Degarre so þriste him þan
> Þat, maugre whoso grouchche bigan,
> Out of þe sadel he him cast,
> Tail over top, riȝt ate last.
>
> (ll. 573–576)

The presence of these features indicates that an original of *Sir Degare* might be expected in Old French. Whether one existed is uncertain. "A translator's misunderstanding best

---

[76] Faust, p. 86; Schleich, pp. 41–42.

[77] Schleich, p. 56. There are 66 alliterative expressions in *Sir Degare*; Oakden, *Alliterative Poetry in Middle English*, pp. 312–343.

[78] Slover, pp. 19 ff.

163

accounts for the eight lines which alone confuse the glove plot. Evidence on the whole seems to favor a French original for *Sir Degare*, but needs more searching examination than it has yet received."[79] Other evidence is available pointing to the possibility of a translation: the hero's name, suggesting Old French *esgaré*; the typically Breton chestnut tree under which the princess' attendants rest.[80] Although there is mention of the florin, used in England only from 1343, still the Auchinleck MS. was prepared around 1330–40, which is so close to the critical year of 1343 that the point is inconclusive (1. 285).

There is evidence, on the other hand, pointing to an "English element" in the poem. Although the parliament which the king of Brittany convenes is as English as its counterpart in *Sir Orfeo*,[81] it may in both instances be only a translator's interpolation and nothing else:

> "Sire," he seide, "varraiment,
> We come frameward a parlement.
> Þe King a gret conseil made
> For nedes þat he to don hade."
> (ll. 431–434)

A more convincing "English" passage can certainly be found. When Sir Degare meets his father in single combat, he sees him as

> a douȝti kniȝt
> Vpon a stede, god and liȝt,
> In armes þat were riche and sur,

---

[79] Muriel Bothwell Carr, review of George Patterson Faust, *Sir Degare*, in *MLN*, LIII (1938), 155.

[80] L. 72; Schleich, pp. 54–55.

[81] Kittredge, "Sir Orfeo," pp. 185–186; "The English element is seen in the parliament which is to appoint a new king if Orfeo does not come back."

Wiȝ þe sscheld of asur
And þre bor-heuedes þerin,
Wel ipainted wiȝ gold fin.
(ll. 992–997)

Although a shield charged with three boars' heads may sig-
nify only a ferocious warrior, the combination of its details
is too striking in *Sir Degare* to pass unnoticed: (1) a shield
with an azure field, (2) three boars' heads, (3) in gold.[82] The
description, as it happens, fits perfectly the traditional coat
of arms of the Gordon family and recalls an incident during
the Barons' War involving a Gordon.[83]

---

[82] Degare's shield, 1018–21, on the other hand, mentions charges, but omits
the field. E. Kölbing, "Zu Chaucer's Sir Thopas," *Englische Studien* XI (1887–
88), 506–507, briefly calls attention to other shields in later literature:

(1) *Libeaus Desconus*, ed. Max Kaluza, Altenglische Bibliothek No. 5
(Leipsig, 1890):

> His scheld was asur fin,
> Þre bores heddes þer inne,
>   As blak as bronde y-brennt
> Þe bordure of ermine,
> Nas non so queint of gin
>   From Carlile into Kent (ll. 1657–62)

(2) *Sir Thopas*:

> His sheeld was al of gold so reed,
> And therinne was a bores heed,
> A charbuncle by his syde (ll. 869–871)

(3) *Octavian*, ed. Gregor Sarrazin (Heilbronn, 1885)

> Þe helm was queynte kest;
> A borys heed stood on þe crest.
> Whan Florent was all redy drest
>   In hys armure
> Hys fomen myȝte of hym be agast
>   We mowe be sure (ll. 1033–38)

[83] John W. Papsworth and A. W. Morant, ed., *An Alphabetical Dictionary
of Coats of Arms Belonging to Families in Great Britain and Ireland Forming
an Ordinary of British Armorials* (London, 1874), II, 924. A clear reproduction
of the Gordon coat of arms is found in *Scalachronica, The Reigns of Edward I,
Edward II and Edward III as Recorded by Sir Thomas Gray*, tr. Sir Herbert
Maxwell (Glasgow, 1907), facing p. 72.

In 1266, Sir Adam de Gordon (d. 1306), or Gurdon, sided with Simon de Montfort and, with others of the disinherited, ravaged Berkshire, Buckinghamshire and Hampshire.[84] When Lord Edward marched against the group he faced Sir Adam in single combat, wounded him seriously and then took him to Windsor Castle.[85] This is the historical version of the incident. According to tradition, however, the combat was interrupted when Lord Edward, recognizing the valor of his Scottish opponent, suddenly and dramatically restored him to his position of trust. The elements of the tradition are: (1) a single combat, (2) between two great warriors, (3) the interruption and (4) the happy ending; all are present in *Sir Degare*.

During the early fourteenth century, when the Auchinleck MS was prepared, this tradition must have been strong. It is related, in fact, in the ballad "Prince Edwarde and Adam Gordon,"[86] which preserves the happy ending. As Lord Edward fights, he stops to say:

[84] *DNB*, "Adam Gurdon," VIII, 795–796.

[85] *DNB*, "Edward I," VII, 436.

[86] Printed "for the first time" in the second edition of Thomas Evans' *Old Ballads, historical and narrative* (London, 1784) and reprinted in *The House of Gordon*, ed. John Malcolm Bullock, The New Spalding Club (Aberdeen, 1907), II, 523–528. Substantially the same account of the combat is given in Nicholas Trivet, *Annales Sex Regum Angliae*, ed. Thomas Hog (London, 1845), p. 269: "Cujus vires et probitatem ex fama cognitas cupiens Edwardus experiri, cum in manu forti supervenisset eidem se ad pugnam paranti, praecepit suis, ne quis inter eos impediret singulare certamen. Congressi itaque mutuos ictus ingeminant; parique sorte, neutro cedente alteri, diutius dimicant. Delectatus tandem Edwardus militis virtute et animo, inter pugnandum consulit ei ut se redderet, vitam pollicens et fortunam. Cui miles adquiescens, abjectis armis se illico reddidit, quem eadem nocte Gildfordiam Edwardus transmisit, reginae matri cum recommendatione supplici praesentandum, quem postea hereditati restitutum, Edwardus semper carum habuit atque fidem."

> Adam, thy valour charms my soule,
> I ever love the brave;
> And tho I feare not thy dread sword
> Thy honoure I would save.
>
> (ll. 85–88)

He offers friendship or continued combat:

> Nowe, Adam, take thy lasting choice,
> Thy prince awaits thy word:
> Accept, brave man, my smile or frowne,
> My friendship or my sword.
>
> (ll. 109–112)

The ballad, suggested here as an analogue of *Sir Degare*, recalls vividly an incident which must have remained well known after the Barons' War. When Sir Adam de Gordon honorably gives up and the combat ends happily, he provides the author of *Sir Degare* with an allusion suitable for the climax of the Sohrab and Rustum scene. The shield of the Gordons is retained to color the narrative and preserve memories of Sir Adam and his royal opponent.

The full significance of *Sir Degare*, lines 992–997, is at once apparent in a text lacking datable references. Since no "French original" is extant, and no clues point unmistakably to the existence of such a work, beyond the assumption that Middle English romance is derivative, these lines corroborate the fact of a strong English element. Once this assumption is made, and the poem is reconsidered in the light of known borrowings from such English works of the same period as *Lai le Freine*, *Sir Orfeo* and *Beues of Hamtoun*, *Sir Degare* can be thought of as coming not so much from one "original," let alone French, as from more than one, perhaps several. Accordingly, there is no English translator, but a composer, who

167

wrote during the early fourteenth century, when the Breton lay was in vogue in Middle English. The real test of this assumption is whether or not his representation of courtly ideals is consistent with that of the Breton lay as written by Marie de France and her early imitators. If it is inconsistent, if the composer betrays a "desire to present the manners and life of his own time" rather than "true love, its loyalty, endurance, trials and rewards,"[87] then the assumption will have a basis.

The characters of *Sir Degare* are usually represented in accordance with accepted formulas as courtly; one can see why this poem proved attractive to Professor Baugh in his study of poetic improvisation worked out by means of formulas (*Speculum*, XLII [1967], 1–31). A king of great strength has a daughter whose breeding and beauty are known in every country. The knight from fairyland is

> Gentil, ʒong, and iolif man;
> A robe of scarlet he hadde vpon;
> His visage was fair, his bodi ech weies;
> Of countenance riʒt curteis;
> Wel farende legges, fot and honde:
> Þer nas non in al þe kynges londe
> More apert man þan was he.
> (ll. 89–95)

When Degare greets the four huntresses and the dwarf, but receives no reply, he shows dramatically that he expects one as a common courtesy;[88] later at dinner he deports himself

[87] Warren, "Notes on the Roman d'Aventure," p. 346.
[88] Ll. 795–812. See Henri Dupin, *La Courtoisie au Moyen Âge* (Paris, 1931), pp. 18–24.

correctly before his hostess.[89] These passages are faithful to courtly convention, but another passage is not and may be considered a bourgeois intrusion. The hermit's sister is married to an urban merchant, who is described as "riche":

> Þa hermite þat was holi of lif
> Hadde a soster þat was a wif;
> A riche marchaunt of þat countré
> Hadde hire ispoused into þat cité.
> (ll. 257–260)

When the hermit sends her his foundling, he forwards as well the silver:

> To hire þat schild he sente þo
> Bi his knaue, and þe silver also.
> (ll. 261–262)

This she keeps without compunctions and in spite of her husband's wealth.

"True love," in fact, receives less prominence in *Sir Degare* than knightly prowess, which is plainly the substance of the story:

> Kniȝtus þat werey sometme in lande
> Ferli fele wolde fonde,
> And sechen auentures bi niȝt and dai,
> Hou he miȝt here strengthe asai;
> So dede a knyȝt, Sire Degarre:
> Ich wille ȝou telle wat man was he.
> (ll. 1–6)

At 20, Degare begins searching for his parents, armed only

---

[89] Ll. 819–822. William Edward Mead, *The Medieval Feast* (Boston and New York, 1931), pp. 130, 137, 138 and 151, discusses the etiquette of the banquet hall.

with a staff. He first achieves the status of knight when he investigates a noise in the valley, rescues the earl from the dragon, and is generously rewarded with armor, palfrey, squire and knighthood (ll. 333–414). Thereafter, as he uses "his armes als he wel can" (l. 424), his adventure is usually motivated by a desire to find his parents. When he unhorses the king of Brittany, however, and wins as a bride his own mother and later when he defends the lady of the castle out of love for her, he is temporarily distracted from his primary mission and plays the "aunterous kniȝt, / For to seche werre and fiȝt" (ll. 1106–07).

In fact, love in *Sir Degare* is either lacking or treated mechanically. The ravishing of the princess can hardly be explained as love, although the knight from fairyland claims to love her for a time:

> Þou best mi lemman ar þou go,
> Weþer þe likeþ wel or wo.
> (ll. 105–106)

Degare marries the princess of Brittany by special arrangement with her father; neither of the "lovers" has seen the other before (ll. 583–590). When he enters the castle in the river, however, he experiences the impact of love for the first time:

> At þe soper litel at he,
> But biheld þe leuedi fre,
> And seȝ as feir a wimman
> As he heuere loked an,
> Þat al his herte and his þout
> Hire to loue was ibrout.
> (ll. 823–828)

Entering later her chamber, he sits on her bed with an attendant at her feet, while the lady entertains on the harp. She plays so beautifully that Sir Degare falls asleep and apologizes next morning for not having stayed awake. Although his love may be technically "pure," it stops short of full development and for present purposes is insignificant[90] and explainable possibly through analogues,[91] but not completely by the text itself. In fact, Degare's love appears real only when he returns at the end of a year and, like his parents, is married in a few brief lines. Compared with Milun's love for the princess, Degare's fails to motivate his every action and so to unify the poem. The reason may be that the composer of *Sir Degare*, yielding to "hooly chirches feith," saw love not as the ennobling force of twelfth-century romance, but as an emotion leading directly to sanctification in matrimony. Contrasting sharply with pagan *Sir Orfeo*, *Sir Degare* remains Christian throughout.

In courtly content, then, *Sir Degare* resembles the twelve original lays only superficially. It remains a Sohrab and Rustum story without any consistent reference to an ideal of *courtoisie* and with well-contrived sensationalism as its objective. Although adventure is usually related to Degare's primary mission of finding his parents, it sometimes appears without this context. Love, usually subordinate to prowess, is unlike the subdued *amour courtois* of Marie de France and receives

---

[90] *Andreae Capellani de Amore Libri Tres*, ed. Amadeu Pagès (Castelló de la Plana, 1930), pp. 105–106: "Et purus quidem amor est, qui omnimoda dilectionis affectione duorum amantium corda coniungit. Hic autem in mentis contemplatione cordisque constitit affectu, procedit autem usque ad oris osculum lacertique amplexum et verecundum amantis nudae contactum, extremo praetermisso solatio; nam illud pure amare volentibus exercere non licet."

[91] Faust, pp. 73 ff.

so little prominence as to be a negligible factor in the motivation of the poem. Finally, a small detail, the introduction of the hermit's sister, "riche" and apparently in every way estimable, betrays a bourgeois sympathy uncommon in the Breton lay. If *Sir Degare* is a Breton lay, it should be so called with the following qualification, based primarily on a study of its motifs: "As an imitation, and as that alone, can it be placed in the same category with the poems of Marie de France."[92]

It has the setting in Brittany (England in the Rawlinson MS.), the atmosphere of supernaturalism—not a necessary characteristic of the form—and certain other external features, but it lacks the content of the Breton lay. Since, further, it includes borrowings from contemporary English literature, a safe view is that it represents the work of an English composer drawing widely from whatever materials are at hand, sometimes failing to understand them, and writing at a late date, when *courtoisie* was losing its meaning. His poem, copied in the Auchinleck MS. by the same scribe who copied *Lai le Freine* and *Sir Orfeo*,[93] could not have existed in its present form before 1266, the date of Lord Edward's single combat, and probably should be associated, in composition as well as transcription, with the early vogue of the English Breton lay, which is centered around the Auchinleck MS. during the first half of the fourteenth century.

[92] Faust, pp. 85–86.
[93] Laura Hibbard Loomis, "Chaucer and the Breton Lays of the Auchinleck MS," *SP*, xxxviii (1941), 14–15.

4

Chaucer and the Franklin's Tale

I. FROM THE AUCHINLECK MS. TO CHAUCER

THAT THE MIDDLE English Breton lay enjoyed a certain vogue between 1330–40, date of the Auchinleck MS., and the 1390's is evidenced by the Franklin's Tale, for this shows Chaucer's definite knowledge of the form.[1] Whether Chaucer derived this knowledge from one olde bok or several will be discussed below (pp. 179–183). Although there are five fourteenth-century manuscripts in French containing Breton lays, the only English one extant from this period of 70-odd years is Egerton 2862, which preserves fragments of Sir Degare.[2] There

---

[1] F. N. Robinson, ed. The Works of Geoffrey Chaucer, 2nd ed. (Cambridge, Mass., 1957), p. xxix, dates the so-called "Marriage Group" between 1393–1400. The manuscripts in which the Franklin's Tale has come down are described in John M. Manly and Edith Rickert, The Text of the Canterbury Tales (Chicago, 1940), vi, 573–671.

[2] Laura Hibbard Loomis, "Chaucer and the Breton Lays of the Auchinleck MS," SP, xxxviii (1941), 15–16. When Mrs. Loomis contends that Chaucer's knowledge of the Breton lay derives from the Auchinleck collection, she

are numerous manuscripts, especially of Breton lays in tail-rhyme stanzas, written or copied during the fifteenth century. It seems unwise at this point, however, to conclude from the scarcity of manuscripts that the vogue of the Middle English Breton lay tapered off before Chaucer; to accept such an assumption would presuppose a fifteenth-century revival of the form—not impossible, but unnecessary.[3] Rather it is safer to assume that the popularity dating from 1330–40 must have been continuous, although perhaps thin at any one point. Some allowance, certainly, has to be made for lost examples of the form; according to its original numbering, the Auchinleck MS. lacks fourteen of its original poems, some of which might have been close in form to *Lai le Freine*, *Sir Orfeo* and *Sir Degare*.[4]

develops an idea expressed earlier by Lucien Foulet in "Le Prologue du Franklin's Tale et les Lais bretons," 698–711. Foulet, however, specifies that it was probably *Sir Orfeo* which gave Chaucer the idea of composing a Breton lay—with an added prologue and "a little dexterity," a Breton lay could be made from any *conte*—and that Chaucer did not know Marie de France except perhaps in isolated translations of some of her lays. See also Mrs. Loomis, "Chaucer and the Auchinleck MS: 'Thopas' and 'Guy of Warwick,'" *Essays and Studies in Honor of Carleton Brown* (New York, 1940), pp. 115 ff. Recent research includes: Bliss, *Sir Orfeo*, pp. xlvi ff.; Peter N. Heydon, "Chaucer and the *Sir Orfeo* Prologue of the Auchinleck MS.," *Papers of the Michigan Academy of Science, Arts, and Letters*, LI (1966), 529–545.

[3] Loomis, "Chaucer and the Breton Lays of the Auchinleck MS," 16: "If the lays had been currently popular, we should, indeed, be at a loss to explain why Chaucer so deliberately emphasized the ancient air of his own Breton lay, or the noble but old-fashioned tastes of the white-bearded Franklin. Chaucer's archaistic emphasis, however, agrees with the manuscripts in suggesting that between 1350–1400 the Breton lay type was somewhat out of date and fashion." On the other hand, it would seem that the Breton lay of Chaucer's time had an "ancient air," not because its early fourteenth-century vogue had ended, but because, very simply, the form was set in the past—in this instance, in the Roman past of Brittany. Therein lay its *antiquity*.

[4] Loomis, "Chaucer and the Breton Lays of the Auchinleck MS," 14.

174

Whether the *Franklin's Tale* revives an "old" literary type, for some decades disused, or, more probably, continues an uninterrupted tradition, it, like other works by Chaucer, reflects a definite knowledge of literary form.[5] It is written for a sophisticated audience and belongs to the poetry which "at the end of the fourteenth century grows unmistakably to a head, a culmination—whatever one may choose to call it; it is refined to the utmost, in grace and elegance it becomes equal to anything in French."[6] When the Franklin has the opportunity to speak, he speaks *gentilly* and makes *gentilesse* the burden of his tale. Whatever the character of the poems preserved in the Auchinleck MS., the *Franklin's Tale* aspires to be reading for the noblest, and its teller, "a member of that class of gentry which was already old in the fourteenth century and which has never felt the lack of any higher title than gentlemen,"[7] is firmly aware of his status and the obligation which it brings.

Specific features of the Breton lay are found in this tale of *gentilesse*. Short, with a twenty-line prologue, the *Franklin's Tale* reaches a total of 916 lines. A more characteristic feature than length, however, is the prologue itself, which proclaims the following story a Breton lay:

> Thise olde gentil Britouns in hir dayes
> Of diverse aventures maden layes,
> Rymed in hir firste Briton tonge;
> Which layes with hir instrumentz they songe,

[5] Warren Wells, "Chaucer as a Literary Critic," *MLN*, xxxix (1924), 264, discusses form in Chaucer from the easily identified tragedies in the *Monk's Tale* to the sermon, fable and fabliau.

[6] Ker, *Form and Style in Poetry*, p. 54.

[7] Gordon Hall Gerould, "The Social Status of Chaucer's Franklin," *PMLA*, xli (1926), 278–279.

Or elles redden hem for hir pleasaunce,
And oon of hem have I in remembrance,
Which I shal seyn with good wyl as I kan.
(ll. V [F] 709–715)

Brittany is given as the setting, "Armorik," but not of the same vague period as Marie de France conceived, not *al tens ancienur*,[8] when Bretons

Jadis suleient par pruësce
par curteise e par noblësce
des aventures que oeient,
ki a plusurs genz aveneient,
faire les lais pur remembrance,
qu'un nes meist en ubliance.
(*Equitan*, ll. 3–8)

What is remarkable is that "Chaucer took much pains to put the story back in Roman times, and in doing so showed an historical imagination rare in the Middle Ages outside Italy."[9] *Arveragus* and *Aurelius* as names are given a Latin form: Aurelius prays to Apollo and mentions Neptune; and the Franklin ridicules un-Christian belief as "nat worth a flye,"[10] without noticing that the university at Orleans, whence it issued, developed in Christian times.

Alongside these prominent features, however, there are others which distinguish immediately the *Franklin's Tale* from earlier Breton lays in couplets. Two features are worth mentioning at this point. Instead of octosyllabic couplets, Chaucer's are couplets of ten syllables, which are noted in the

[8] *Guigemar*, l. 26.
[9] J. S. P. Tatlock, *The Scene of the Franklin's Tale Visited*, Chaucer Society Publications, Second Series, No. 51 (London, 1914), p. 20.
[10] V (F) 1132.

Canterbury Tales for the first time in English literature.[11]
Apart from Chaucer's superior skill in versification, they present a slower movement and impart a greater dignity than the short couplet:

> Thise olde gentil Britouns in hir dayes
> Of diverse aventures maden layes,
> Rymed in hir firste Briton tonge

The contrast with the short couplet is marked:

> In Breteyne bi hold time
> Þis layes were wrouȝt, so seiþ þis rime.
> When kings miȝt ouryhere
> Of ani meruailes þat þer were,
> Þat taken an harp in gle & game,
> & maked a lay & ȝaf it name.
> (*Lai le Freine*, ll. 13–18)

The second departure is that Chaucer enriches his text immeasurably with rhetorical devices, contrary to the Franklin's profession in the prologue to the tale:

> But, sires, by cause I am a burel man,
> At my bigynnyng first I yow biseche,
> Have me excused of my rude speche.
> I lerned nevere rethorik, certayn;
> Thyng that I speke, it moot be bare and pleyn.
> (ll. V. [F] 716–720)

Of the rhetorical passages, Dorigen's complaint[12] stands out because of its twenty-three *exempla*, which will be discussed below (pp. 187–188) with the rhetorical aspects of the *Franklin's Tale*.

---

[11] Hamer, *The Metres of English Poetry*, pp. 44–45.
[12] V (F) 1367 ff. See my article "The *Anticlaudian* and Three Passages in the *Franklin's Tale*," *JEGP*, LVI (1957), 53–55.

The story of the *Franklin's Tale* is familiar; it treats love ideally. The marriage of Arveragus, a Breton knight of great courtesy, and Dorigen, his wife, is happy because neither is the other's superior, and both as equals are motivated by true love. When Arveragus leaves for England to seek fame, Dorigen grows unhappy despite the suggestion of friends that during his absence she seek their company. At a dance she rejects a love-sick squire named Aurelius with the playful answer that he may have her love if he can remove the rocks just off the Breton seacoast. Desperate, he vainly asks Apollo to cover them with a flood and, in his distress, remains bedridden for two years. With his brother's help, however, he makes an agreement with a magician of Orleans to have the rocks removed in return for one thousand pounds; but, when they actually disappear from view, Dorigen is faced with the necessity of keeping her word: she has a choice between dishonor and self-inflicted death. During her third day of indecision, when Arveragus returns from England, he determines the cause of her grief and, distressed himself, insists that she both keep her word as the most important duty in the world and, despite his own feelings and hers, satisfy Aurelius. On her way to the trysting place she happens on Aurelius and mentions her husband's reluctance to see the agreement broken; Aurelius is so moved by this show of liberality, as well as by Dorigen's distress, that he allows her to return home untouched. Left owing the magician the thousand pounds, Aurelius can pay only one-half and so asks for time. When the magician demands why and learns of Arveragus' generosity and his wife's distress, he is moved to cancel the entire debt. The reader is left with a question: which of the characters shows the greatest nobility?

178

Since the sources of the *Franklin's Tale* have been carefully investigated, one can tell with some assurance that the poem is not a true Breton lay but rather an imitation, probably without a French original, for only the twelve Breton lays of Marie de France can be called, strictly, "true" lays. Chaucer's methods as an imitator and his success call for separate sections.

II. THE SOURCES OF THE FRANKLIN'S TALE

Although the possibility of a single source was entertained for a time, present scholarship considers the *Franklin's Tale* a fourteenth-century imitation of the Breton lay, prepared, in fact, from available materials and given the appearance of the twelfth-century French form.[13] In this respect it recalls *Lai d'Haveloc*, to date the most carefully examined imitation of a Breton lay (above pp. 101–105). The significance of *Lai d'Haveloc* at this point is that it shows clearly how an imitation was prepared, even as early as the thirteenth century, from materials not necessarily Breton in origin. Since, in fact, there is more than one source for the *Franklin's Tale*, and a separate one for the prologue, it may be advisable to consider first the prologue.

[13] Germaine Dempster and J. S. P. Tatlock, "The Franklin's Tale," *Sources and Analogues of Chaucer's Canterbury Tales*, ed. W. F. Bryan and Germaine Dempster (Chicago, 1941), p. 376. Earlier, when a lost Celtic folktale was considered the source, William Henry Schofield, "Chaucer's *Franklin's Tale*," *PMLA*, xvi (1901) 444–449, allowed, however, for "certain parts of the *Franklin's Tale* which we can affirm with some confidence first became connected with the story in his [Chaucer's] hands. Of these the following may be mentioned: 1, the discussion of the cause of evil in the world, à *propos* of the existence of the dangerous rocks on the Breton coast; 2, the abundant references to astrology; 3, the 'pleynt' of Aurelius to Apollo, 'Lord Phebus' (303–351); and 4, Dorigen's 'Compleynt to Fortune'...."

The prologue can be satisfactorily traced. Its first nine lines contain a body of ideas common enough in the introductory and concluding lines of *French* Breton lays, but found in no single example.[14] (*Lai du Lecheor* contains all except one, that the Bretons composed in their own language, but, because it is not a lay at all, but a daring parody, it could hardly have been Chaucer's source for a serious poem.) Since all nine ideas, however, are present in the prologue of the Auchinleck *Lai le Freine* and also, probably, in the lost prologue of *Sir Orfeo*, the presumption is that Chaucer read in the Auchinleck MS. as he did before writing *Sir Thopas*,[15] and knew about the Breton lay chiefly through this source; then he set to work composing his prologue after the model before him.[16]

A question asked in the study of the English *Lai le Freine* (129–131 above) applies here: did a user of this now tradi-

[14] Loomis, "Chaucer and the Breton Lays of the Auchinleck MS," 17–24: "No. 1, the lays were made by Britouns; No. 2, the *Britouns* were *gentil;* No. 3, they lived in old days; No. 4, they composed in their own language; No. 5, the lays were in rhyme; No. 6, the lays were sung; No. 7, they were accompanied by musical instruments; No. 8, they were written down; No. 9, they were on divers subjects."

[15] Laura Hibbard Loomis, "Sir Thopas," *Sources and Analogues of Chaucer's Canterbury Tales,* pp. 489–490.

[16] Loomis, "Chaucer and the Breton Lays of the Auchinleck MS," 23–24, discusses the probability of Chaucer's having seen the Auchinleck MS: "In a text by a London scribe, in a manuscript far more probably accessible to the poet than any French text of the lays, in one compact and comprehensible statement, instead of a series of scattered and in one instance contradictory observations, we find here a complete explanation of Chaucer's ideas and a close verbal anticipation of one of his couplets. Though we cannot deny the possibility that he had read the old French lays with their various references to the type, as, most assuredly, the author of the *Freine-Orfeo Prologue* had done, the balance of reasonable probability inclines against the supposition that within some fifty years two English poets should have extracted from their reading in the French lays precisely the same ideas and even the same words, the same rime, to describe them."

tional prologue inherit an ambiguity, namely, that his lay was (or was not) read and sung from a single "text" suited to both kinds of presentation? In the lays of Marie de France the pairing of *conte* and *lai* (or *narrative lay* and *lyric lay*, respectively) provides a workable distinction known to Chaucer possibly no more than to the composer (or translator) of the English *Lai le Freine*, who, late in the history of the genre (1330–40), could pass on without question the claim that his poem *depends on a lyric form intended to be sung and represented best in the lays of Marie de France:* so runs a modern interpretation of the prologue common to *Lai le Freine, Sir Orfeo* and now to the *Franklin's Tale.* In the last named, we are told, the Bretons sang or read their lays—whether from a single text is not made clear.

Like the prologue which introduces it, the story itself of the *Franklin's Tale* is taken from literature available to Chaucer. It is "highly possible"[17] that it comes from Boc-

---

[17] Bryan and Dempster, p. 376. Pio Rajna, "Le Origini della novella da Frankeleyn nei *Canterbury Tales* del Chaucer," *Romania,* xxxii (1903), 235–244, counters Schofield's source in a Breton folktale and in detail establishes that Chaucer drew mainly from the *Filocolo.* After Rajna only one significant study has sided with Schofield: Hubertis Maurice Cummings, *The Indebtedness of Chaucer's Works to the Italian Works of Boccaccio,* University of Cincinnati Studies, Series II, Volume x (Part 2), pp. 196–197, concludes that the burden of proof rests with those who say that "Chaucer did not use a Breton lay, or that Chaucer used the *Filocolo* in the F.T." When Cummings fails, however, to consider the probability of free borrowing and, secondly, the conventional fourteenth century ascription of *Breton lay* to any poem having at least the necessary external features, he naturally rejects any doubt cast upon Chaucer's prologue and its profession, and cannot understand "why Chaucer should attempt the feat of writing a pseudo-Breton lay in an age when Englishmen were still translating genuine lays." Tatlock, *The Scene of the Franklin's Tale Visited,* p. 58, at about the same time as Cummings finds it "hard to doubt that Chaucer drew at least in part from Menedon's story; it would be almost over-temperate to call this a highly acceptable hypothesis."

caccio's *Filocolo*. Thus Menedon's story of the enchanted garden in the Questioni d'Amore episode comes closer to Chaucer's version than the comparable story told in the *Decameron*, X, 5, which also has been mentioned. Tarolfo, a Spanish knight, secretly falls in love with the wife of another knight, but is rejected with the glib assurance that he may enjoy her love only if he can provide her in January with a garden such as one would expect in May. Undaunted, Tarolfo tries to provide the garden and, approaching Tebano, a Thessalian wretch, promises one-half his wealth in return for the successful performance of his magic. When it works, Tarolfo takes the surprised lady to the garden, where she pleads for time until her absent husband returns. She sadly goes home to her husband, describes her plight, but is reassured when he tells her above all to keep her word. When Tarolfo learns of her husband's generosity, he is too ashamed to demand his promised reward. Likewise Tebano is moved to refuse his fee, one-half of Tarolfo's money. The story ends with the question: which of the three is the noblest?

Additions in the *Franklin's Tale*, however, are many: the new setting, the comments on mastery in marriage, Dorigen's complaint, as well as others less conspicuous. Not the least of these involves the personal names—Arveragus, Dorigen and Aurelius. When the *Franklin's Tale* was first examined, the royal pair were associated with King Arviragus and his queen Genuissa in Geoffrey of Monmouth's *Historia Regum Britanniae*.[18] Genuissa is the daughter of Claudius, who on leaving Roman Britain entrusts to his son-in-law the government of the island. When Arviragus usurps power, he is opposed by a large Roman Army and forced to make peace. This account

---

· [18] Schofield, "Chaucer's *Franklin's Tale*," pp. 405–417.

in Geoffrey of Monmouth, however, omits any clear reference to the happy marriage of Arviragus and Genuissa and to Arviragus' promise to Claudius that he will be faithful to his father-in-law and leader—both of which are related in Layamon's *Brut* in an analogous account of the same incident.[19] In view of the limited evidence, it seems safe to call both accounts analogues, suggesting that Chaucer read a comparable source from which he derived the personal names. It has been suggested also that the completely different task which Aurelius has to perform to win Dorigen's love recalls Book VII, Chapters 10–12, of Geoffrey's *Historia*, in which Merlin carries from Ireland the rocks of the Dance of the Giants; but, again, there is occasion for doubt.[20] Indications that Chaucer borrowed freely are common and have been pointed out so carefully that the possibility of a "single source" for the *Franklin's Tale* grows more remote with time and continued investigation.[21]

III. THE FRANKLIN'S TALE *AS A BRETON LAY*

Certain "external features" of the Breton lay, it has been noted, are present in the *Franklin's Tale*. They include the

---

[19] Jerome Archer, "On Chaucer's Source for 'Arviragus' in the *Franklin's Tale*," *PMLA*, lxv (1950), 318–322.

[20] Tatlock, *The Scene of the Franklin's Tale Visited*, p. 69.

[21] John Livingston Lowes, "The *Franklin's Tale*, the *Teseide*, and the *Filocolo*," *MP*, xv (1918), 138: "Lines 901–1037 of the *Franklin's Tale*, then—barring the conversation in lines 960–1010, which has to do with the situation peculiar to this particular story—are a free working over of definite suggestions drawn from the third and fourth Books of the *Teseide*." Lowes goes on to assert, pp. 139–141, that Machaut's *Dit dou Lyon*, ll. 2040–24 and 2066–76, are the immediate source for the *Franklin's Tale*, ll. 767–770 and 771–778, on the necessity of freedom in love.

"typical" prologue, setting in Brittany, a specific length and metrical form. Chaucer, however, correctly conceives as the essence of the Breton lay, not these features, but that idealism associated with *courtoisie* in the poems which have been previously considered. In the link between the *Squire's Tale* and the *Franklin's Tale*, he causes the Franklin to praise the discretion of the Squire and to wish that his own son had some of it; instead his son

> . . . hath lever talken with a page
> Than to comune with any gentil wight
> Where he myghte lerne gentillesse aright.
> (ll. V [F] 692–694)

After his praise of *gentilesse*, the Franklin goes on to his tale, which emphasizes that nobility of character in one person sympathetically produces the same in those around him. The model character in the tale is Arveragus, who demonstrates his individuality as a knight, servant of love and understanding husband. Dorigen serves as the woman to be loved; and Aurelius, youthful and impulsive, as the second lover of Chaucer's Courtly Love situation.

"Ideal love, with its concomitant of fidelity to troth is the theme" of the *Franklin's Tale*.[22] As practiced by Arveragus, love is self-sacrificing and recalls both *Lai le Fraisne*, in which Fraisne voluntarily gives up a lover whom she dearly wants, and *Eliduc*, in which a wife sacrifices to another woman a husband whom she would see happy at any cost. In Aurelius, love is conventional Courtly Love, carried on outside marriage, but with misgivings which Chaucer is quick to express:

[22] William Henry Schofield, *Chivalry in English Literature*, Harvard Studies in Comparative Literature ii (Cambridge, Mass., 1912), p. 52.

The conduct of Aurelius is more conventional than that of Arveragus; indeed Aurelius is so conventional that he loses his individuality almost entirely, becoming a mere puppet, moved as it were, by the code of love. He had loved Dorigen best above all others for two years and more, never daring to reveal to her his unhappy state, and easing his pains by writing to her in secret.[23]

Chaucer, living possibly in a more orthodox age than the twelfth century, expresses only slightly stronger criticism of Courtly Love than does Marie de France. He represents love outside marriage, but with a corrective tone and a "proper" ending. In fact, Aurelius' suit is made to fail, while the married love of Dorigen and Arveragus prospers. It is based, not on the woman's superiority according to the rules of Courtly Love, but on "mutual love and forebearance, which are the guiding principles of the relations between husband and wife";[24] and at this point the *Franklin's Tale* momentarily loses its identity as a Breton lay and becomes a vehicle for the expression of Chaucer's own reflections on marriage: having presented through the Wife of Bath and the Clerk opposing views of the marital relationship, here he states positively an ideal of equality between husband and wife, which may not always be realized in life. Whether or not the "Marriage Group" remains for every reader an integrated unit within the *Canterbury Tales*, Chaucer in the *Franklin's Tale* firmly ends the debate which starts with the Wife of Bath and continues as far as the gentle, but equally determined, Franklin.

For a Breton lay, then, the treatment of love in the *Frank-*

---

[23] Agnes K. Getty, "Chaucer's Changing Conceptions of the Humble Lover," *PMLA*, xliv (1929), 213–214.

[24] George Lyman Kittredge, "Chaucer's Discussion of Marriage," *MP*, ix (1912), 32–33.

lin's Tale, is more expressive of the author's personality, and more individualized, than any comparable treatment of love after Marie de France and before the fourteenth century. Individuality is a mark of the *Franklin's Tale* and goes far in Chaucer's art. His versatility in the use of rhetoric has already been mentioned. As he saw it, the function of the poet is:

> one of finding means and methods of making the old seem new. He might therefore well begin his task of composition by choosing some familiar but attractive text —some tale, or poem, or oration, or treatise—or by making a patchwork of pieces selected from many sources. His problem would be that of renewing the expression and especially that of making it more beautiful—*ornatior* is the common term.[25]

The "means and methods" which he employs are the rhetorical colors. No one any longer takes the Franklin's prologue seriously—"I sleep nevere on the Mount of Pernaso"—where the Franklin disavows any interest in rhetoric.[26] In all, over seventy examples of figures of speech have been noted[27]— for a short poem, a number large enough to distinguish it at once from the anonymous lays, especially, for example, *Doon*. The effect is immediate—richness with a corresponding love

[25] John M. Manly, *Chaucer and the Rhetoricians*, [The British Academy] Warton Lectures on English Poetry, xvii (London, 1926), p. 10.

[26] Charles S. Baldwin, "Cicero on Parnassus," *PMLA*, xLii (1927), 106–112.

[27] Benjamin S. Harrison, "The Rhetorical Inconsistency of Chaucer's Franklin," *SP*, xxxii (1935), 56–57: "*Descriptio* 1 (1245–55), *Sententia* 13 (761– 86; 1479), *Contentio* 1 (792–3), *Interrogatio* 4 (803–5; 1165; 1550; 1621–2), *Transitio* 2 (814–5; 1099–1100), *Articulus* 3 (819; 933; 948), *Similitudo* 4 (829–31; 951–2; 1110; 1113–5), *Apostrophe* 3 (865–93; 1031–79; 1090–3), *Translatio* 4 (907; 1036; 1045; 1112), *Superlatio* 2 (911–2; 929–30), *Circuitio* 2 (1016–7; 1252), *Expolitio* 2 (1016–8; 1263–4), *Repetitio* 3 (1146–9; 1162–3; 1286–91), *Exclamatio* 1 (1355–1456), *Traductio* 1 (1091–2), *Compar* 1 (1604–5), *Exemplum* (1364–1456)."

of the "simplicity" set down in Chapter 1 as a characteristic of the narrative lay. Why Chaucer concealed his intention to adorn his poem is debatable: the Franklin's apology may be only conventional; or the tale may have been set aside and given to the Franklin, for whom he later wrote a special prologue; or the apology may be merely playful.[28]

The most striking rhetorical passage is Dorigen's complaint, in which "ensamples many oon / Of olde stories longe tyme agoon" are related of women similarly troubled. Consisting of twenty-three *exempla*, which come from St. Jerome's *Adversus Jovinianum*, the complaint attempts to show that even before Christianity pagans respected chastity and disapproved of second marriages. In this study, it is significant because it reveals something about Chaucer's methods—his use of Jerome as an "open book," from which he freely drew to ornament his work[29] and perhaps, if he saw *Sir Orfeo*, to present a "richer" complaint than Orfeo's, already quoted, "O lef liif." About the interpretation of Chaucer's purpose, little more can be said; "it is by no means certain that in his displays of learning Chaucer is not mocking or parodying others as well as relieving himself." Of course, the rhetoric of the complaint might recall the importance of the *aventure* in each of Marie's and later French lays. According to the thesis mentioned in Chapter 1, human experience is seen at first dimly as if controlled by Fortune, whose ways trouble the thoughtful, as they do

[28] Harrison, p. 60. See also Germaine Dempster, *Dramatic Irony in Chaucer*, Stanford University Publications, University Series, Language and Literature, Volume IV, Number 3 (Stanford University, 1932), for a discussion of irony in the *Franklin's Tale*, especially p. 63.

[29] Germaine Dempster, "Chaucer at Work on the Complaint in the Franklin's Tale," *MLN*, LII (1937), 16–23, and "A Further Note on Dorigen's Exempla," *MLN*, LIV (1939), 137–138.

[30] Saintsbury, *Cambridge History of English Literature*, II, 217.

Dorigen, until they are explicated with time (Eberwein, p. 27). Although it may be objected that Chaucer hardly needed prodding by earlier composers of lays and was interested in the meaning of Fortune or Providence almost instinctively, still the Franklin's Prologue early, in its second line, announces that Breton lays record *aventures*, "happenings" in the most basic sense of the word, even as this one will.

Although there are other marked, but accidental, differences between the *Franklin's Tale* and earlier examples of the Breton lay, these do not reflect on the success of Chaucer's imitation.[31] His purpose was to write a romance which would above all appeal to the imagination and take the reader into the remote past,[32] when man seemed more idealistic and moral than in the fourteenth century. A comparison with the *Filocolo* version stresses the change in setting, from the recent period to Chaucer's Roman Brittany. In the adaptation of his material Chaucer "medievalizes" Boccaccio, as he does *Il Filostrato*,[33] enhancing the idealism of the original and bringing together, like Chrétien de Troyes, the doctrinal and narrative elements of courtly romance. On the one hand, the French poet "combined, magnificently, the interest of the story and the interest of erotic doctrine and psychology."[34] Chaucer, on the other

---

[31] Walter Morris Hart, "The Franklin's Tale," *Haverford Essays Prepared by Some Former Pupils of Professor Francis B. Gummere* (Haverford, Pa., 1919), p. 215, "claims that the contrasts [which the *Franklin's Tale* affords with other lays] are more striking than the resemblances." Without specifying which lays, he goes on to say that the *Franklin's Tale* lacks their vivid background, their glamor of the past, their social setting, pseudo-historical, yet realistic in effect, their vivid characterization and their abhorrence of moralizing.

[32] Howard R. Patch, "Chaucer and Mediaeval Romance," *Essays in Memory of Barrett Wendell by His Assistants* (Cambridge, Mass., 1926), p. 100.

[33] C. S. Lewis, "What Chaucer Really Did to Il Filostrato," *Essays and Studies by Members of the English Association*, xvii (Oxford, 1932), p. 56.

[34] P. 58.

hand, stresses theme, sometimes to the prejudice of his story:

> The central motive of the story is essentially an apologue theme, a theme for a moral tale. But Chaucer was, as has been said, interested even more in its concrete than in its abstract possibilities, that is to say, in the characters and emotions of the persons concerned, and by virtue of this interest the story becomes something more than a mere apologue structure. This conflict of abstract and concrete interests, of two distinct literary types, accounts for most of the peculiarities of structure of the *Franklin's Tale.*[35]

If the *Franklin's Tale* is at all similar to the didactic lay exemplified by *Lai de l'Oiselet,* it would be partly because of the question posed by the Narrator, who leaves nothing to chance as he applauds the nobility of the characters in the action just ended. Surely, however, a recent study is right in reminding us not to mistake Chaucer's intention both to individualize his characters and not to use them as stock figures in the development of the Marriage Group.[36] Beginning with the passage on marriage (V[F] 744–805) we are led to discover that these lines relate not only to the three preceding tales, but also to "everything else which happens in the *Franklin's Tale*" (p. 385); and we are led to discover in one further area, characterization, reason for regarding this tale as possibly the most complex artistically of all the narrative lays.

---

[35] Hart, "The Franklin's Tale," p. 199.

[36] J. Burke Severs, "Appropriateness of Character to Plot in the 'Franklin's Tale,'" in *Studies in Language and Literature in Honour of Margaret Schlauch* (Warsaw, 1966), pp. 385–396.

5

The Middle English Breton
Lay in Tail-Rhyme Stanzas

I. INTRODUCTORY

THE MIDDLE ENGLISH Breton lay appears in the fourteenth century not only in couplets of eight and ten syllables—never in the alliterative line[1]—but also in the tail-rhyme stanza popularized by the Auchinleck manuscript, the "fountain-head of tail-rhyme romance."[2] Showing the same prosody and differing chiefly in length, it may be thought of as developing beside the longer romance, to which it is related. Whether

---

[1] James R. Hulbert, "Hypothesis concerning the Alliterative Revival," *MP*, xxviii (1931), 412. The style, the flow of the alliterative long lines indicate, however, that the poems were written for a cultivated audience; the vocabulary is unsuited to a popular audience; and the "material of the poems" fits courtly tastes. Smithers, pp. 88–91, explains the reference to lays in *Sir Gawaine and the Green Knight*, ll. 30–36 in which a *laye* (in present terms a narrative lay) is associated with alliterative verse.

[2] A. McI. Trounce, "The English Tail-Rhyme Romances," *MÆ*, i (1932), 92, lists from this manuscript *The King of Tars*, *Amis and Amiloun*, the stanzaic *Guy of Warwick*, *Reinbrun*, *Roland and Vernagu*, *Horn Childe*. Trounce's three articles constitute a long discussion of tail-rhyme romance and will be mentioned in this chapter frequently.

190

the frequent appearance of this stanza is a native development of the fourteenth century—"the extensive use of materials already in English may help to explain why French originals [of tail-rhyme romances] are often lacking"[3]—is uncertain; East Anglia, however, seems to be the center of the tradition.[4] The audience is noncourtly in the sense that its level of comprehension need not be high. Although one may agree in part that "it is the people of England, rather than the cultivated literary class, to whom this measure was dear,"[5] this judgment, for all that is known about the composition of medieval audiences, may be too exclusive to be true. Whatever its audience, the tail-rhyme stanza does not necessarily lack dignity; it is the stanza reserved for the Deus of the Towneley Plays:[6]

> Ego sum alpha et o
> I am the first, the last also

[3] Trounce, *MÆ*, I (1932), 97. See also pp. 98–99, where he finds common stylistic elements suggesting a "community of practice" and the fact of a tail-rhyme tradition.

[4] Trounce, *MÆ*, II (1933), 42 ff.

[5] Caroline Strong, "History and Relations of the Tail-Rhyme Strophe in Latin, French and English," *PMLA*, xv (1907), 414–415. See also Edith Rickert, ed., *The Romance of Emare Re-edited from the MS with Introduction, Notes and Glossary* (Chicago, 1907), who comments on *Emare* as an example of the tail-rhyme Breton lay: "The sentence structure and phrasing are uncommonly rough and careless, and no doubt often corrupted in transmission. The paratactic sentence prevails throughout, only the simplest clauses of time, place and comparison being subordinated. When transitional expressions are found, they are crude and abrupt. As in the ballads, speeches are introduced without mention of the speaker; and indirect discourse is changed to direct in the same passage without indication. The subject is very often repeated in different forms, in a manner suggesting the progression of an Old English sentence; while, on the other hand, it is omitted in lists of verbs where it is needed. The connection is extremely loose, *that* being often omitted; and sentences are regularly made up of several short clauses with different subjects. . . . Here again the character of a popular poem by a market-place minstrel is maintained" (Introduction, p. xxvii).

[6] Ed. George England with side notes and introduction by Alfred W. Pollard, EETS ES, LXXI (London, 1897).

Oone god in mageste;
Meruelus, of mught most,
Ffader, & son, & holy goost
On god in trinyte.

(ll. 1–6)

The tail-rhyme stanza in twelve lines, four accents on the couplet line and three on the tail, contrasts with the octosyllable couplet. It is primarily a lyrical form, but it is used to tell a story. We are told that the "difference between the narrative and lyric is often illusive and difficult to fix"; but if "the narrative poem gives much of the tone of the author's mind, if in listening to it one does not attend simply to the story, but is affected by the sentiment, then there is something lyric in the narrative, something besides the story."[7] If, as has been suggested,[8] the stanza developed historically when the two long lines of the ballad quatrain were doubled, its lyric quality may be better understood, even in these short quotations:

The king sits in Dunfermline town,
Sae merrily drinkin the wine:
'Where will I get a mariner,
Will sail this ship o mine?'

(*Sir Patrick Spens*: ll. 1–4)

As rose on rys her rode was red;
Þe her shon upon her hed
As gold wyre þat schynith briȝt.
Sche hadde a crounne upon her molde

---

[7] Ker, *Form and Style in Poetry*, p. 286.

[8] Hamer, *The Metres of English Poetry*, pp. 172–173. See also Strong, "History and Relations of the Tail-Rhyme Strophe in Latin, French and English," 373–374.

> Of riche stones and of golde,
>   Þat lofsom lemede liʒt.
>   (*Sir Launfal:* ll. 937–942)

The inherent weakness, however, of a lyric form used for a
narrative purpose is that monotony results after a few hundred
lines, the more so when the minstrel is unskilled: e.g. in *Sir
Thopas* (below pp. 198–199).

The success of the stanza often depends on the tail-line,
which serves many purposes and can be manipulated accordingly. It is first thought of as the vehicle for formula-like
expressions, references to source, statements of time and place
and the like, sometimes showing alliteration.[9] At times it may
complete the sentence begun in the preceding couplet as an
effective period:

> Þo seyde king Arthur þat was hende:
> Launfal, if you will from me wende,
>   Tak with þe greet spending.
>   (*Sir Launfal:* ll. 79–81)

Whatever its grammatical function, the tail-line is objection-
able only when it is a mere tag:

> Many a lord of Karlioun
> Þat day were ybore adoun,
>   Certayn, withouten ote.
>   (ll. 454–456)

The strategy, then, of the highly conventional and readily
assembled tail-rhyme stanza is to make the most of convention

---

[9] Though highly conventional in many respects, the tail-rhyme poem does
not have a distinctive vocabulary, according to A. R. Dunlap, "The Vocabulary
of the Middle English Romances in Tail-Rhyme Stanza," *Bulletin of the University of Delaware*, xxxvi, N.S., No. 3 (1941), 36.

without filling the all-important tail-line with expressions of no functional value.

This stanza is intended, of course, for a professional minstrel or reciter. No evidence shows that it might have been sung. "In the Middle Ages the masses of the people read by means of the ear rather than the eyes, by hearing others read or recite rather than reading to themselves."[10] The four Breton lays in tail-rhyme stanzas presuppose a minstrel and an audience which is frequently addressed:

1) *Sir Launfal:*

> Now herkeneþ how hit was.
>
> (l. 6)

> Þey wer wedded, as I you say,
> Upon a wytsonnenday
>   Before princes of moch pryde.
>   (ll. 49–51)

> To certayn day, I you pliȝt,
> Was twelf moneþ and fourteniȝt.
>   (ll. 817–818)

> Seþþe saw him in þis lond no man
> Ne no more of him telle I ne can.
>   (ll. 1036–37)

2) *The Erl of Tolous:*

> Leve Lords, y shall you tell
> Of a tale, some tyme befell
>   Far yn unkouthe led
> How a lady had gret myschef,
> And how sche covyrd of hur gref.
>   Y pray you, take hed.
>   (ll. 7–12)

---

[10] Crosby, "Oral Delivery in the Middle Ages," p. 88.

A warre wakenyd, as y you say,
  Betwen hym and a knyght.
                    (ll. 23–24)

Leve we now te emperour in thoght
                    (l. 163)

Moche god of them he hadd;
Y can not tell, so god me gladd.
                    (ll. 172–173)

Let we now the erl alloon,
And spek we of Dame Beulyboon,
  How sche was cast in care.
                    (ll. 478–480)

3) *Emare:*

Who-so wylle a stounde dwelle
Of mykylle myright y may ȝou telle,
  And mornyng þer a-monge
                    (ll. 19–21)

At þe mayden leue we,
And at þe lady fayr and fre,
  And speke we of þe emperour
                    (ll. 70–72)

For sothe, as y say þe.
                    (ll. 96, 144)

At þe emperour now leue we,
And of þe lady yn þe see,
  I shalle be-gynne to telle
                    (ll. 310–312)

I say ȝou for certayne
                    (l. 381)

Leue we at þe lady whyte as flour,

195

> And speke we of þe emperour,
> That fyrste þis tale of y-told
>> (ll. 946–948)

4) *Sir Gowther:*

> Bot y schall tell you of a warlocke greytt,
> What sorow at his modur hart he seyt
>> With his warcus wylde.
>>> (ll. 22–24)

> Hende, harkons yee!
>> (l. 117)

> Wytte you wyll, he wex full styron,
> And fell foke con he feyr.
>> (ll. 143–144)

In addressing his audience the minstrel follows conventions which recall the epic. He begins with a prayer or invocation, which by its seriousness calls the audience to attention and sets the tone for the lay that follows:

> Ihesu, þat ys kyng in trone,
> As þou shoope boþe sonne and mone,
>> And alle þat shalle dele and dyghte,
> Now lene vs grace such dedus to done,
> In þy blys þat we may wone,
>> Men calle hyt heuen lyghte;
> And þy modur Mary, heuyn qwene,
> Bere our arunde so bytwene,
>> That semely ys of syght,
> To þy sone þat ys so fre,
> In heuen wyth hym þat we may be,
>> That lord ys most of myght.
>>> (*Emare*, ll. 1–12)[11]

---

[11] See also *Sir Launfal*, ll. 1042–44; *The Erl of Tolous*, ll. 1–12; and *Sir Gowther*, ll. 1–12. But see the third person and other formalities of *Guigemar*, ll. 1–14: "Oez, seignur, que dit Marie."

In his first or second stanza, as in lines 1–7 of the *Aeneid*, he formally states his theme:

> Leve Lords, y shall you tell
> Of a tale, some tyme befell
> Far yn unkouthe led:
> How a lady had gret myschef,
> And how sche covyrd of hur gref.
> (*Erl of Tolous*, ll. 7–11)

> Of mykylle myrght y may ʒou telle,
> And mornyng þer a-mong;
> Of a lady fayr and fre,
> Her name was called Emare.
> (*Emare*, ll. 20–23)

> Bot y schall tell you of a warlocke greytt
> What sorow at his modur hart he seyt
> With his warcus wylde.
> (*Sir Gowther:* ll. 22–24)

The external characteristics, the development, weaknesses, audience and methods of presentation of the tail-rhyme stanza have been described briefly to identify the style of *Sir Launfal*, *The Erl of Tolous*, *Emare* and *Sir Gowther*. Something should follow now on the contents of the four poems, whose model in romance literature is, at least remotely, the Breton lay of Marie de France, written for a courtly audience. How close these popular "imitations" come to the idealism of the originals will be important to see. They may suggest that "the ideals of knighthood remained a simple individualist code of ethics in which honour and dishonour had the sharp contrasts of heraldic colours—like the blood upon the snow in *Gawayne*."[12] Love without adultery may remain the same

---

[12] Gervase Mathew, "Ideals of Knighthood in Late Fourteenth Century England," *Studies in Mediaeval History Presented to Frederick Maurice Powicke* (Oxford and New York, 1948), pp. 354–362.

overpowering, beneficial force. The sometimes aimless and unmotivated adventure of the sort found in *Sir Degare*, considered in Chapter 3, may reappear and indicate a change of emphasis, to the external aspects of chivalry from the internal, in a transformation of romance which was to continue into the fifteenth century:

> We can sympathize with these fifteenth-century authors who came into the field so late in the day, and who must have felt that all the best materials had been used. They could only take the French romances and give them an English form, sometimes by cutting out much introspection and conversation . . . , or by giving them a strongly didactic tone. Often, however, they took the easiest course and piled incident upon incident without much thought of structure . . . so that long, rambling narratives resulted which relied on picturesque incident or elaboration of detail for their many effects. In a few romances there is a great sense of narrative . . . or of dialogue . . . , but, on the whole, the romance was living in the past.[13]

By the time Chaucer wrote, the tail-rhyme romance must have been familiar enough to insure the success of his parody: *Sir Thopas*, in its own day, was at least a criticism of inferior romances in this stanza-form.[14] Chaucer recognizes the inappropriateness of intrusive bourgeois elements[15] and leaves the tale unfinished as proof that it may be unterminable. He knew well, of course, the importance of the tail-line and purposely leaves that line unemphatic in the following passages:

[13] H. S. Bennett, *Chaucer and the Fifteenth Century* (Oxford, 1947), p. 164.

[14] On this point there is disagreement, some of it needless. George Kitchin, *A Survey of Burlesque and Parody in English* (Edinburgh, 1931), p. 10, finds that "we must demur to the idea that Chaucer is more concerned to satirize the Flemings than to parody an outworn literary convention."

[15] Robinson, p. 738, notes to ll. 724–735, 738, 740 and 760.

> Yborn he was in fer countree,
> In Flaundres, al biyonde the see,
> At Poperyng, in the place.
>
> (ll. 718–720)

> Ful many a mayde, bright in bour,
> They moorne for hym paramour,
> When hem were bet to slepe
>
> (ll. 742–744)

> He priketh thurgh a fair forest,
> Therinne is many a wilde best,
> Ye, bothe bukke and hare
>
> (ll. 754–756)

> And there he swore on ale and breed
> How that the geaunt shal be deed,
> Betyde what bityde!
>
> (ll. 872–874)

The date of *Sir Thopas* is uncertain. If the poem was written around 1390, or slightly earlier, that date might mark the point of high interest in tail-rhyme romance.

The year 1390 falls within the period to which the four Breton lays in tail-rhyme stanzas are assigned. By present methods of dating, all appeared between 1350 and 1400, or shortly thereafter, and for present purposes become a species of romance. Before 1350 there were the *Auchinleck* Breton lays in octosyllabic couplets. Whether *Sir Launfal, The Erl of Tolous, Emare* and *Sir Gowther* constitute a separate development in the history of the Middle English Breton lay remains to be seen.[16]

---

[16] The dating of the four poems is approximate. See Trounce, *MÆ*, III (1934), 48. Later in this chapter more specific dating will be attempted for *The Erl of Tolous*.

II. SIR LAUNFAL

Of the four Breton lays which will be considered in this chapter, *Sir Launfal* alone has an extant original in Old French as well as an author who is named. Although its relations with other *Lanval* poems in Middle English at present require further study, *Sir Launfal* is believed to come, not directly from the Old French original, but from the "earliest English translation made," with help from the anonymous *Graelent* and *Lanval* of Marie de France.[17] A disadvantage faced in the study of this poem is the fact that it is found in only one manuscript, *Cotton Caligula Aii*, ff. 35^b–42^b.

Although the authorship of *Sir Launfal* is known, little can be said about Thomas Chestre, who signs his work:

> Thomas Chestre made þys tale
> Of þe noble knyȝt Syr Launfale,
> Good of chyualrye
> (ll. 1039–41)

He did not write around 1430, as was originally believed,[18] but between 1350 and 1400, probably in Essex.[19] There is no reason for thinking that he also wrote *Libeaus Desconus* and

---

[17] Kittredge, "Sir Launfal," p. 16; Zimmermann, *Sir Landeval,* p. 9; Stokoe, "The Source of *Sir Launfal: Lanval* and *Graelent,*" p. 392. Kittredge, pp. 5 ff., established that a Middle English version of *Lanval* is the basis of the poem: *Sir Launfal* is an "amalgamation of the Lai de Lanval with the anonymous Lai de Graelent, and contains in addition two long episodes drawn from the author's imagination, or from the common stock of mediaeval romances." B. K. Martin, " 'Sir Launfal' and the Folktale," *MÆ*, xxxv (1966), 199–210.

[18] *DNB*, iv, 206.

[19] Erna Fischer, *Die Lautbestand des südmittelenglischen Octovian, verglichen mit seinen Entsprechungen im Lybeaus Desconus und im Launfal,* Anglistische Forschungen LXIII (Heidelberg, 1927), p. 199. See *MED*, P & B p. 33.

Octovian, a theory of authorship which is now rejected.[20] All else about Thomas Chestre is left to deduction, which is sometimes sterile.[21]

When Thomas Chestre adapted the *Lanval* story to tail-rhyme romance, he lost the simplicity of the short couplet and instead produced a musical, sometimes jingling, contrast with the original.

> A Kardoeil surjurot li reis,
> Artur, li proz e li curteis,
> pur les Escoz e pur les Piz
> ki destrueient le pais;
> en la terre de Loengre entroënt
> e mult suvent le damajoent.
> > (ll. 5–10)

> Douȝty Artoure somwhyle
> Soiournede yn Kardeuyle,
> > *Wythe ioye and greet solas;*
> And kynȝtes þat wer profitable
> With Artour of þe Rounde Table
> *Neuere noon better þer nas*
> > (ll. 7–12)

---

[20] This theory, developed by Max Kaluza, "Thomas Chestre, Verfasser des Launfal, Libeaus Desconus und Octovian," *Englische Studien*, xviii (1893), 168–184, is no longer held. More recently it has been thought that *Sir Launfal* imitated *Lybeaus Desconus*: see Trounce, *MÆ*, ii (1933), 199 ff.; but this point is questioned by Dorothy Everett, "Chestre's *Launfal* and *Lybeaus Desconus*," *MÆ*, vii (1938), 29–49.

[21] Trounce, *MÆ*, ii (1933), 108: "I picture Chestre as a man with some talent for narrative but little for poetry, who desired to take a hand in the popular and profitable business of composing a tail-rhyme poem. He had a good story, which he filled out and improved in some ways; but in giving it a poetical dress he was successful only here and there. Like the amateur in poetry everywhere, he was proud of his lucubration and signed it." See Stemmler, pp. 263 ff.

If the italicized tail-lines are omitted, there is little difference between the French and English versions. Once retained, the tail-lines not only produce a different rhythm, but also help expand the 664 lines of *Lanval* to a new total of 1044. In comparison with the simplified story which Marie de France tells, the result is a complex of separate stanzas each with a unity and emotional appeal of its own. The price of this change is the loss of the essential simplicity characterizing the first Breton lays.

Sir Launfal, in fact, is not presented as a Breton lay—simply as a *lay*. In the following lines, the term means at least a "short narrative poem":

> Be douȝty Artours dawes
> þat helde Engelond in good lawes,
> þer fell a wondyr cas
> Of a ley þat was ysette
> þat hyȝt Launval and hatte ȝette
> (ll. 1–5)

The *wondyr cas* (l. 3) must be the *aventure* or fortunate experience narrated in *Sir Launfal*. This poem the composer designates a *tale* (l. 1039), one developed at least in part from a *romance* (l. 741), which means the medieval genre or, like Marie's *romanz*, a work written in the French vernacular (Bliss, *Sir Launfal*, p. 97). We list the various terms for genre to prepare for the same set of terms in the three other lays in tail-rhyme stanzas according to a usage which may prove meaningful. The courtly qualities, of course, which *Lanval* possesses change little in this version: Launfal's *largesse* remains prominent, and, if anything, is heightened. Two relatively long additions to the plot, however, reveal a departure from the more or less brief rendering of a tale:

(1) *The Tournament at Caerleon* (ll. 433–492): Rescued from poverty by his *amie*, Launfal goes to Caerleon and there displays great *largesse*. He is welcomed by the lords of the city, who sponsor a tournament in his honor. When Launfal engages and promptly unhorses the rich constable of Caerleon, Gifre, Launfal's attendant, runs off with the riderless horse and arouses the antagonism of all present. Seeing the advantage taken of the constable, the Earl of Chester angrily rides against Launfal, but is similarly unhorsed. Then a group of Welsh knights ride up only to suffer defeat at Launfal's hands. His reputation established, Launfal holds a feast which lasts for two weeks.

(2) *The Fight with Valentine* (ll. 505–612): After the tournament at Caerleon, Launfal is challenged to a joust by Valentine, a Lombard knight fifteen feet tall. Encouraged by his *amie*, he embarks, reaches Italy and prepares for the engagement. He is embarrassed, however, by his opponent's skill until finally he sinks a fatal blow, which is so mighty that it kills both rider and mount. When the lords of Italy in turn offer a challenge, Launfal checks their jealousy by taking them on singly and laying each of them low.

These additions serve one of two purposes. They either are needed for characterization or to satisfy a fourteenth-century interest in spectacle. Since Launfal's prowess is adequately developed in *Lanval* and in the earlier English translations, the first possibility is immediately ruled out. The very nature, however, of the interpolated incidents supports the second possibility, that Thomas Chestre is here cultivating seekers after adventure, no matter how incredible, or how tall Launfal's opponent. With these additions he sacrifices continuity and straightforwardness. His *Sir Launfal* may be thought of not as a lay, but as a romance—in miniature, fitting in with the tail-rhyme literature of the fourteenth century and preserving more than a suggestion of the original.

III. THE ERL OF TOLOUS

Sir Launfal does not call itself a Breton lay, but *The Erl of Tolous*, *Emare* and *Sir Gowther* either do or claim a Breton lay as their source. The last three poems have other similarities, some superficial. All are anonymous. All concern a historical incident, real or imagined, happening in a real world; in one, *Sir Gowther*, there is a supernatural character. In none is the story set in Brittany. All three preserve variously the idealism of the original Breton lay; *The Erl of Tolous* comes closest in this respect and will be considered first.

Not the earliest in date of composition, it has been placed in the fourteen hundreds.[22] Four manuscripts survive, from the fifteenth and sixteenth century:[23]

A. Cambridge University *F* f. *II* 38, f. 63ᵃ–70ᵇ.
B. Bodleian Ashmole 45, f. 3ᵃ–31ᵇ, the only complete text.
C. Lincoln Cathedral Library A.5, or Thornton f. 114ᵇ–122ᵃ.
D. Bodleian Ashmole 61, f. 27ᵃ–38ᵇ.[24]

The Emperor of Germany, who is terrorizing Western Europe by seizing vast lands at will, rejects the plea of his

---

[22] Gustav Lüdtke, ed., *The Erl of Tolous and the Emperes of Almayn*, Sammlung englischer Denkmäler in Kritischen Ausgaben, III (Berlin, 1881), p. 42. All quotations are from Lüdtke's edition. Ed. Rumble, pp. 135–177.

[23] Lüdtke, pp. 1–30. See also *MED*, P & B, p. 40.

[24] Lüdtke, pp. 31–44, describes MSS.

beautiful wife, Dame Beulyboon, that he restore to Sir Barnard, the Earl of Toulouse, everything that he has taken from him. In his anger he raises an army, meets Sir Barnard in battle, is soundly defeated and loses his stoutest followers, including the faithful Sir Tralabas. Humiliated but unmoved by the injustice of his quarrel, he plans to fast until he defeats his enemy. Sir Barnard, meanwhile, counting the faithful Sir Tralabas among his prisoners, learns from him about Dame Beulyboon's beauty and promises freedom on condition that Sir Tralabas arrange a meeting with her. The two knights set out for Germany, Sir Barnard disguised as a hermit, and presently reach the court of the Emperor. When Sir Tralabas informs Dame Beulyboon that a mortal enemy is present in disguise, he is reminded of his agreement with Sir Barnard, which she insists that he keep. Accordingly, Sir Barnard enters the chapel next morning still disguised as a hermit and there enjoys a look at the beautiful lady. Understanding his disguise, she gives him alms and, as a love token, a ring from her finger. Next day Sir Barnard departs for Toulouse, leaving Sir Tralabas, as he thinks, still faithful to the agreement, but the latter with two henchmen overtakes him on the road and attempts a murder. This fails so badly that Sir Barnard kills the attackers and escapes to his own castle. Back in Germany, the Emperor, about to go abroad, appoints two knights to protect Dame Beulyboon. Since the two are her undeclared lovers, they quickly exchange confidences and agree to a plan for enjoying her. One of them will be surprised by the other when alone with her in her chamber. If she refuses the wishes of either thereafter, the discoverer will inform the Emperor of her "infidelity." The plot miscarries as Dame Beulyboon is firm and completely faithful to her husband. When the two knights fear that she will tell all and endanger their lives, they plot again, this time with the help of a young knight, her official carver, who is anxious in every way possible to please her. They pretend that they are planning a game for her amusement, and at night the young knight is hidden naked behind a curtain in her chamber and is to come out only on their instructions. Dame Beulyboon, suspecting nothing, retires for the night. Time passes slowly, and, just as the young knight begins to fear that he has been forgotten, the two conspirators raise a cry that some one has lain with Dame Beulyboon. Leading rescuers to her chamber, they discover the youth behind the curtain, stab him without questioning and accuse Dame Beulyboon of infidelity. At the very same hour the Emperor, still abroad, dreams that two boars have attacked his wife and, hurrying home, to his grief finds her charged with adultery. At a special council, however, she is stoutly defended by an old knight, who, doubting the accusers' testimony, proposes an alternate way of deciding her case: combat between the two accusers and a volunteer champion. Sir Barnard, still her admirer, hears about the challenge and is escorted to Germany by a horse-dealer, stopping off at an abbey one mile from the Emperor's court. There he learns from the abbot, who is Beulyboon's uncle and confessor, that she has committed no sin except to give a certain Sir Barnard a ring. To satisfy his own mind, Sir Barnard poses as a monk and on the day appointed for her execution determines from her confession her complete innocence. Immediately he challenges and subdues her accusers in a trial by champion, by which she is publicly exonerated. Elated over his wife's innocence, the Emperor accepts Sir Barnard as a friend. Three years later, when the

Emperor dies, Sir Barnard takes his place and marries Dame Beulyboon.

The Erl of Tolous is based on a ninth-century incident which soon became legendary.[25] Bernard I, count of Barcelona and Toulouse, was made prime minister with the connivance of Empress Judith, second wife of Louis le Débonnaire, who used him to forward plans for her son Karl. The two conspirators of the poem are identified with Hugo, Count of Tours, and Matfrid, Count of Orleans. The Empress was accused of adultery with Bernard and at an assembly in 831 cleared herself when, according to law, no accuser appeared. Although Bernard was *ipso facto* exonerated, he asked the privilege of a duel with any accuser, but, none coming, never fought.

If the legend spread outward from a center around Toulouse, an Old French original for *The Erl of Tolous* is to be expected. Although analogues are numerous, no poem designated a Breton lay and telling the same legend survives in that language. To compare the author's references to his source might be confusing, since he refers to a *tale, story, romance* and *lay of Bretayne*:

> Leve Lords, y schall you tell
> Of a tale, some tyme befell
> Far yn unkouthe led
> (ll. 7–9)

> He examyned hur, wytterly,
> As hyt seys in the story
> (ll. 1069–70)

[25] Lüdtke, pp. 72–166, discusses in detail the origin and development of the legend.

Togedur lovely can they kyss,
Therof all men had gret blyss,
The romaunse tellys soo.
(ll. 1201–03)

Yn Rome thys gest cronyculyd ys,
A lay of Bretayn callyd ywys.
(ll. 1219–20)

Perhaps two points are to be drawn from his usage: that he
had a written source, a narrative lay, which he loosely calls a
lay of Bretayn, and that by 1400 this term designated a form
loosely equated with *tale* and *romance* (each a chronicle in
this context).

In the following pages an attempt will be made to show
that a *lay of Bretayn* could have existed. Nothing definitely
rules out this possibility and much confirms it. The lost lay
may be assumed to resemble the lays of Marie de France, but,
according to the present thesis, would be an imitation—a much
closer imitation than, for example, *Lai d'Haveloc.* No evidence
points definitely to an English intermediary in couplets, such
as *Landavall,* which precedes *Sir Launfal.*

Apart from its meter *The Erl of Tolous* has the external
form of a Breton lay as well as the contents. It runs to 1224
lines, which would presumably expand a much shorter original
in couplets. It moves fast and directly, except for the following
elegiac stanza, which follows the battle between the Emperor
of Germany and Sir Barnard:

Many a sted there stekȝd was,
Many a bold baron in that place
Lay burlyng yn his blod.
So moch blod there was spylt,
That the feld was ovyrhylt,

> As hyt were a flod.
> Many a wyfe may sytt and wep,
> That was wont soft to slep,
>   And now con they no god.
> Many a body and many a hedd,
> Many a doghty knyȝt there was dedd,
>   That was wyld and wod.
>   (ll. 97–108)

The prologue and epilogue, of course, contain mainly a prayer and statement of theme and have no exact counterpart in an Old French Breton lay.

With the exception of the bourgeois horse-dealer, the characters of *The Erl of Tolous* belong to the highest level of society and are invested with courtly qualities. As Emperor of Germany, Sir Dioclesian is a "bold man and stout," Sir Barnard, "an hardy man and a strong," and Dame Beulyboon, "god, in alle thyng, / Of almesded and god beryng."[26] The latter's character is revealed when she unsuccessfully urges the Emperor, her husband, to restore Sir Barnard's lands. In the war which follows, Sir Barnard is determined to fight, "As y am trewe knyght."[27] The fighting once started, emphasis is on heroism and physical conflict.

Two minor characters illustrate typical feudal loyalties. When the "faithful" Sir Tralabas promises to introduce Sir Barnard to Dame Beulyboon, he will receive his freedom in return for this favor, which is at the same time treachery to his lord, the Emperor. But his loyalty remains strong, though to preserve it means breaking his word to Sir Barnard:

> Yn that covenaunt in þys place
> My trouth y plyght to thee;

[26] Ll. 16, 31 and 40–41.
[27] L. 54.

Y schell hold thy forward god,
Tbryng the, wyth mylde mod,
  In syght hur for to see;
And therto wyll y kep counsayl
And never more, wythoute fayl,
  Agayn the to bee;
Y schall be treu, by goddes ore,
To lese myne own lyfe therfore;
  Hardely tryst to me!
                    (ll. 218–228)

On reaching the German court he will kill the enemy then in his power and tries to do so at the earliest opportunity. For good or bad, his loyalty compares with the more innocent loyalty of the Queen's young carver, who is used by the conspiring knights as a tool in their plot to embarrass the Queen. Since he wants to please her, he cannot refuse their offer of a chance to participate in the entertainment.

Love, in the *Erl of Tolous*, is so vital throughout as to unify the entire poem. Sir Barnard undertakes the defense of Dame Beulyboon only because he is her lover. It is not Courtly Love, but a compromise suggesting it. Although she is already married when he first sees her, he finds marriage no insurmountable barrier to a devoted lover.

Whan the erl saw hur in syght,
Hym thought, sche was so bryght,
  Os blossom on the tre;
Of all the syghts that ever he sy,
Raysyd nevyr none hys hert so hy:
  Sche was so bryght of blee!
                    (ll. 331–336)

Sche stod stylle in that place
And schewed opynly hur face

> For love of that knyght.
> > (ll. 337–339)

Occasionally Sir Barnard chafes under conventions, which technically, however, should not concern the courtly lover:

> "Lord god full of myght
> Leve, y were so worthy a knyght,
> > That y myght be hur fer,
> And that sche no husband hadd:
> All the gold, that evyr god made,
> > To me were not so der!"
> > > (ll. 367–372)

When he looks at the ring which she gives him as a pledge, he is anxious for other gestures of love:

> > My der derlyng,
> On thy fyngyr thys was,
> Well ys me, y have thy grace,
> > Of the to have thys ryng!
> Yf evyr y gete grace of þe quen,
> That any love be us betwen,
> > Thys may be our tokenyng.
> > > (ll. 402–408)

Sir Barnard's love, very sympathetically treated, contrasts with the "derne love" of the two conspiring knights, Dame Beulyboon's attendants. These fail in their duty to the Emperor and secretly love her:

> Nothyr of othyr wyst ryght noght,
> So derne love on them wroght,
> > To deth they were ner dyght
> > > (ll. 390–392)

Both suffer the torment, loss of complexion and other signs.

But their love becomes base passion when each divulges his secret and agrees to a cooperative plan to enjoy her. All the while, as far as the evidence indicates, Sir Barnard's love is pure:

> For hur he morned nyt and day,
> And to hymselfe can he say,
> He wold aventure hys lyfe
> (ll. 925–927)

Finally, however, it is Christianized to the extent that it leads to marriage, which comes after the Emperor's opportune death.

Although love and the various qualities of character are prominent, something else gives *The Erl of Tolous* its essential courtliness. It is the trial by champion, which by the late fourteenth century changed from a purely legal to a chivalric institution. The details of a trial are clearly presented. When Dame Beulyboon "betrays" her lord, she becomes punishable according to law:

> The lawe wyll, þat sche be brent,
> Be god, that boght us der.
> (ll. 839–840)

At the special inquiry, her defense appears hopeless, since Sir Antore's corpse is perfect evidence against her.

> They myȝt not fynd in þer counsayl
> Be no law, wythoute fayl,
> To save herr fro the ded.
> (ll. 880–882)

An old knight, knowing her reputation and suspecting her two accusers, proposes a trial by champion, which will indicate a divine judgment through the champion's prowess:

> No mo wyll preye hyt but þey two,
> We may not save hur fro woo,
>   For soth, os y you say,
> In hur quarell but we myȝt fynd
> A man, þat were god of kynd
>   Durst fyght agayn þem tway.
>   (ll. 895–900)

Since his own character is flawless, Sir Barnard arises within the prescribed time to defend her, but must first be assured of her innocence, since even ideal love is capable of doubts:

> Yf he wyst, that she had ryght,
> He wold aventure hys lyfe to fyght
>   For that lady free.   (ll. 922–924)

> Yf y may wytt, þat sche be trew,
> They, þat hur accused, schall rew,
>   But they stynte of ther stryfe. (ll. 928–930)

Still in doubt he receives from the horse-dealer a strong assurance, and still stronger one from the abbot, her uncle and confessor. Sir Barnard remains unconvinced, however, until disguised as a monk he finds out for himself on hearing confession. Immediately convinced of her innocence, he challenges her accusers:

> Y prove on hur, þou sayst not ryght.
> Lo here my glove wyth þe to fyght
>   Y undertake thys case;
> Os false men, y schall you ken,
> Yn redd fyre schall ye bren,
>   Therto god gyve me grace
>   (ll. 1099–1104)

213

According to rule the knights participating in the trial swear an oath and commence. They wear armour and are mounted. After a brief encounter, Sir Barnard, still disguised as a monk, overcomes the accusers and thus proves that the defendant is innocent.

The lack of technical detail in this description does not alter the impression that the author is familiar with trial by champion. Of the weapons customarily used, only a spear is mentioned, not the sword. Nothing is said about the lists, the time of day, the spectators and the usual officers, the constable and marshall. But there is sufficient detail, as is indicated above, to explain the author's intent.

He must have written *The Erl of Tolous* to satisfy a current interest in trial by combat. By his time the "progress of chivalry somewhat changed the character of the judicial duel, investing it with a religious ceremonial and tingeing it with a romantic hue which did not belong to its purely legal stages."[28] The judicial duel as such was passing from English law, and in its place the duel of chivalry remained and was common, especially during the reigns of Edward III and Richard II, primarily to try cases of treason. Thomas Plantagenet, Duke of Gloucester and uncle of Richard II, who in 1372 became high constable of England, some time thereafter codified in *The Ordenaunce and Fourme of Fightyng within Lists*, the rules of trial by combat.[29] What is significant is that he mentions in his dedication a renewed interest in this form of trial, which grew during the reigns of Edward III and Richard II;

[28] George Neilson, *Trial by Combat* (Glasgow, 1890), p. 8. For detailed differences between the two kinds of trial see pp. 188–190.

[29] *The Black Book of the Admiralty*, ed. Sir Travers Twiss (London, 1871), I, 300, n. 1.

and the interest is great enough to call for written rules:[30]

> A vous tres excellent et trespuissant prince Richard par
> le grace de Dieu roy dAngleterre et de France, seigneur
> dIrlande et Acquitayne, monstre le vostre humble lige a
> vous, sil vous plaist, Thomas dec de Gloucestre, vostre
> connestable dAngleterre, que comme pleusurs battailles
> dedens lices darmes ont este en vostre royalme dAngleterre
> ore tarde, si bien ou temps et present mon dit seigneur
> et pere vostre aiel, que Dieu face pardon, comme en vostre
> temps et present, plus que ne furent long temps devants.

If this association of *The Erl of Tolous* with a late interest in
trial by combat is warranted, as it seems to be, one further
point follows. The poem may have appeared earlier than the
fifteen hundreds, ordinarily given as the date of composition.

The Erl of Tolous, in conclusion, may have a lost original
in Old French, even a "Breton lay," which at best would be
an imitation. It departs somewhat from the courtliness of the
Breton lay written in octosyllabic couplets. Although it represents love and the courtly qualities, it stresses an external
feature of chivalry—the trial by combat presented for its own
sake. This, in terms of interest, seems to be the climax of the
poem. Sir Barnard is viewed more closely as a participant in
the formalized trial than as the subject of an internal struggle.
His struggle, in fact, is resolved into a simple test of courage—
aided by love—and little more. *The Erl of Tolous*, further,
bears out exactly what was said of *Sir Launfal* and suggested
of the other Breton lays written in tail-rhyme stanzas. These
externalize chivalry by emphasizing spectacle. Sir Barnard's
trial by combat satisfies the same interest as the combat scenes

---

[30] P. 300.

added to *Sir Launfal,* which, in fact, were never intended by the first known *Lanval* poet, Marie de France.

IV. EMARE

Emare, like *The Erl of Tolous,* relates a widely diffused legend found in many forms, the chronicle, *chanson de geste,* the didactic poem, the miracle-play and the chapbook story. A single manuscript survives, *Cotton Caligula Aii,* preserved in the British Museum and copied between 1446 and 1460.[31] *Emare* was written in Yorkshire, probably around 1400, by an itinerant minstrel:[32]

> Menstrelles þat walken fer and wyde,
> Her and þer in euery a syde,
>   In mony a dyverse lond,
> Sholde, at her bygynnyng,
> Speke of þat ryghtwes kyng
>   That made both see and sonde
> Who-so wylle a stounde dwelle,
> Of mykylle myrght y may ȝou telle.
>   (ll. 13–20)

It tells substantially the same legend as Chaucer's *Man of Law's Tale* and Gower's "The Tale of Constance" in the *Confessio Amantis:*[33] Emare is the only daughter of an em-

---

[31] E. Rickert, ed. *Emare,* EETS ES No. 99 (London, 1908), Introduction, pp. ix and x. All quotations are from her edition. Ed. Rumble, pp. 97–133.

[32] Pp. xviii and xxxviii. But Trounce, *MÆ,* III (1934), 45, claims "East Anglia, perhaps even . . . Suffolk, I suggest for a date the turn of the century [i.e., c. 1400]." See *MED,* P & B, p. 40.

[33] Margaret Schlauch, "The Man of Law's Tale," *Sources and Analogues of Chaucer's Canterbury Tales,* p. 155; see also p. 160 for a bibliography of writings on the Constance-saga; and *Chaucer's Constance and the Accused Queens* (New York: 1927), by the same author.

peror, Sir Artyus, and Dame Erayne. While still an infant, she loses her mother and is carefully reared by Abro, who teaches her manners and sewing. At court Sir Artyus lives a widower's life with occasional amusements and while entertaining Sir Tergaunte, king of Sicily, is presented with a cloth set with precious stones and prepared by an emir's daughter. In three corners of the cloth the stories of Ydoyn and Amadas, Tristan and Isolt and Floris and Blancheflor are separately portrayed; and, in the fourth, the love of the emir's daughter and the son of the Sultan of Babylon; years before, when Sir Tergaunte's father conquered Babylon, he seized the cloth and later gave it to his son. After Sir Tergaunte's departure the Emperor calls home Emare, by now a lady of courtesy and beauty. When she wears a robe cut from the rich cloth, she so attracts her father that he desires, with the Pope's permission, to marry her. She refuses and is abandoned in an open boat without food or water and with only the robe for cover.

The Emperor, repenting, vainly sends out searchers after her. Drifting for a week she reaches a distant land called Galys, is found on the shore by the steward, Sir Kadore, and, when questioned, says her name is Egare. Brought to a nearby castle she recovers rapidly and impresses everyone, including the King of Galys, with her courtesy, needlework and, above all, her beauty. The King presently insists that she become his queen, even in spite of protests from the Queen-mother, who is suspicious of Emare's beauty. After the marriage and the King's subsequent departure for France to fight the Saracens, Emare has a son, whose birth Sir Kadore announces in a letter to the King. By trickery, however, the Queen-mother intercepts the letter and substitutes another, which explains that the infant is a devil with three heads. When the grief-stricken

217

King replies that Emare should be well attended until his return, the letter is confiscated by the Queen-mother, at whose castle the messenger again stops. Her forged letter specifies that Emare and infant be put to sea in an open boat.

Emare accepts her lot with Christian resignation and, adrift for over a week, is finally rescued on the coast of Rome by a merchant named Jurdan, who shelters her and her son for over seven years. Meanwhile, when the King of Galys discovers the Queen-mother's treachery, he has her exiled and stripped of name and property. After seven years of mourning he goes to Rome to do penance for his part in Emare's presumed death and there stays at the same house with her and her son. In a happy scene, King, Queen and Prince are finally reunited. Their happiness increases when they recognize in Rome the aged Emperor, doing penance also, who makes the Prince his heir.

Although conflicting references to a source are made throughout the text, to a *song*, a *story* which is told, a *romance*, a *tale*, these may be a conventional device to gain authority, as they seem to be also in *The Erl of Tolous*:[34]

> Her name was called Emare
>> As I here synge in songe.   (ll. 23–24)

> And, as þe story telles in honde,
> The stones þat yn þys cloth stonde,
>> Sowȝte þey were fulle wyde.   (ll. 115–117)

> In romans as we rede   (l. 216)

> As y haue herd menstrelles syng yn saw,

[34] Flora Ross Amos, *Early Theories of Translation* (New York, 1920), pp. 23–39.

> Hows ny lond myȝth she non knowe,
> A-ferd she was to go.   (ll. 319–321)

> She was so fayr and gent,
> The kynges loue on her was lent,
> In tale as hyt ys tolde.   (ll. 403–405)

> A greete feste þer was holde,
> Of erles and barones bolde,
> As testymonyeth þys story.
> Thys ys on of Bretayne layes,
> That was vsed by olde dayes,
> Men callys "playn þe garye." (ll. 1027–1032)

Yet, as in *The Erl of Tolous*, the genre of the source is given; the present work is one of the *Breytayne layes* (l. 1030), meaning a narrative *lay* or *conte*, and the source is a *tale* (l. 405) or *romans* (l. 216). Unhappily, the poet complicates his explanation by claiming that he has heard the heroine's name in *song* (l. 24), which must be distinct from the narrative forms mentioned.

The personal names clearly point to a French original, not necessarily a Breton lay: *Cesyle, Golys, Artys, Dame Erayne, Segramour, Kadore, Iurdan, Tergaunte, Abro, Ydoyne, Amadas, Florys, Blawncheflour, Trystram* and *Isowde, Emare* and *Esgare*. Certain common nouns are equally significant: *acyse, crepawtes, perydotes*.[35] If the original is French, it cannot be dated later than the first half of the thirteenth century, when certain other versions of the story, all containing references to the robe, were prepared.[36]

---

[35] Rickert, Introduction, pp. xxviii and xxix.

[36] See ll. 82–180 and Rickert, Introduction, pp. xxx–xxxi. The analogues to which she refers are *La Mankine, Enikel, La Comtesse d'Anjou* and *Historia del Rey de Hungria*. See also for a discussion of analogues Alfred Gough, *On the Middle English Metrical Romance of Emare* (Dissertation, U. of Kiel, 1900), pp. 19–22.

If, besides "hagiography, pseudo-history, and moral instructions, our story also contains motives drawn from the general body of migratory plots, superstitions, and popular beliefs commonly known as folklore,"[37] the form of *Emare* as a Breton lay may be difficult to make out. It is a short poem, first of all, 1035 lines, containing the specialized prologue and epilogue typical of the tail-rhyme romance. Although it is not set in Brittany, it calls itself a Breton lay and bears the characteristic double-title which is parodied in *Lai du Lecheor*:

> Thys ys on of Brytayne layes,
> That was vsed by olde dayes,
> Men callys "playne þe garye."
> (ll. 1030–32)

How little it differs from any of the folk versions of the same story will be interesting to see. *Emare* has been described as "singularly bare of figures, containing only seven similes,"[38] and, as romance, called "poor stuff," written by an imitator of the tail-rhyme style and not a continuation.[39]

The characters, with the exception of Iurdan, the merchant, are represented in very general terms as courtly. First, the Emperor and Empress receive summary treatment:

> She was fulle of loue and goodnesse,
> So curtays lady was none.   (ll. 35–36)

> He was curtays in alle þyne,
> Both to alde and to ȝynge,
> And welle kowth dele and dyght   (ll. 40–42)

---

[37] Schlauch, "The Man of Law's Tale," p. 161.

[38] Rickert, Introduction, p. xxiii.

[39] Trounce, *MÆ* iii (1934), 44. Rickert, Introduction, pp. xviii and xix, finds *Emare* metrically "unique among romances of this class in its mixtures of stanza forms"; 29 of the 86 stanzas rhyme a a b a a b c c b d d b, with slight variations.

> The emperour of gentylle blode,
> Was a curteys lord and a gode,
> In alle maner of thynge.   (ll. 75–77)

The King of Galys, who reputedly marries outside his class, thereby loses prestige:

> For he weddede so poerly
> On me, a sympulle lady
> He is a-shamed sore.
>   (ll. 631–633)

He remains courageous, fights the Saracens as enemies of God and is honest to the point of punishing his own mother for her abuse of Emare. The latter is characterized as

> curteys yn alle þyng,
> Both to olde and to ʒynge;
> Her loued bothe gode and ylle
>   (ll. 724–726)

In *Emare* the treatment of love is uneven. Sir Artyus is married with little ceremony to Dame Erayne, who bears Emare. Nothing significant is said thereafter until the long description of the cloth which Sir Tergaunte gives his host, Sir Artyus. In its four corners the true love of certain well-known characters from romance is represented in great detail. Although the effect of the passage is to prepare the reader for another example of "true love," ironically the very opposite follows: when Emare wears a garment cut from the cloth, she receives from her father a proposal of marriage, which she rejects. The description of the cloth, which is out of proportion with the rest of the story, is present in certain analogues and seems to have been carried over into *Emare* for its own richness and without regard for its effect.[40] The next significant instance of love, where the King of Galys is enamored of Emare and finally marries her, is treated briefly and should be mentioned because it ends, as ideal love should, happily and with a reunion of the lovers.

Although these passages give a superficial impression of courtliness, certain others so emphasize "nurture"—breeding, upbringing, training—as to confuse courtliness with manners.[41] While still very young Emare, for example, is sent to Abro to learn courtesy and

> Golde and sylke for to sewe,
>   Among maydenes moo.
> Abro towȝte þys mayden smalle,
> Nortur þat men vseden in sale,
>   Whyle she was in the bowre.
> She was curtays in alle thynge,
> Both to old and to ȝynge.
>
> (ll. 59–65)

Reaching Galys after her voyage, Emare instructs in needle-work and is so skillful that Sir Kadore calls her the "konnyngest wommon" in the world.[42] She instructs her son as well, so that

[40] Rickert, Introduction, pp. xxx–xxxi. The rich cloth in *Fraisne*, on the other hand, functions variously and is given suitable, and no more, prominence.

[41] See in *OED nurture* as a substantive, dating in this sense from around 1330. Manners and courtesy are distinguished in Fred B. Millett, "English Courtesy Literature before 1557," *Bureau of the Departments of History and Political and Economic Science in Queen's University, Kingston, Ontario*, No. 30 (Kingston, 1919), p. 1: "If it be not hair-splitting to distinguish between manners and courtesy, we may say that courtesy is manners raised to the dignity of a system, organized and directed towards the exemplification of a social ideal." The emphasis on manual skills such as needlework, of course, is not original with *Emare*. See Rickert, Introduction, p. xxxvi; also n. 7.

[42] Ll. 373–378, 427–429 and 731–732.

later, in the recognition scene, he impresses the King of Galys, actually his father, with his good manners:

> When þe kyng ys serued of spycerye,
> Knele downe hastylye,
>   And take hys hond yn þyn;
> And when þou hast so done,
> Take þe kuppe of golde sone,
>   And serue hym of þe wyn
>   (ll. 853–858)

The banquet which follows is described with a precision that leaves no doubt about the minstrel's purpose (ll. 866 ff.)

His purpose, to stress manners as a mark of breeding, is paralleled in contemporary books of courtesy. These, in fact, "are concerned with practical nurture for anyone with aspirations to breeding rather than to knightly courtesy, which was intended only for the chosen few whose birth made them worthy of such instruction."[43] In *Lytylle Childrenes Lytil Boke* or *Edyllys be*, a striking contrast illustrates the identification of courtesy with manners through 1480, when the work was written:[44]

> For clerkis that the vij artez cunne,
> Seyn þat curtesy from hevyn come
> Whan Gabryelle oure lady grette,
> And Elizabeth with Mary mette.
> Alle vertues arne closide yn curtesye
> And alle vices yn vylonye.
>   (ll. 3–8)

---

[43] H. Rosamond Parsons, "Anglo-Norman Books of Courtesy and Nurture," *PMLA*, XLIV (1929), 451.
[44] Ed. F. J. Furnivall, EETS OS. No. 32 (London, 1894).

Without any transition, *curtesye* is exemplified, for the benefit of a child, to be sure:

> Loke þhye hondis be wasshe clene,
> That no fylthe on thy nayles be sene
> Take þou no mete tylle grace be seyde
> And tylle þou see alle thyng arayde.
>
> (ll. 9–12)

Curtesy, in this text, means manners, and, to the composer of *Emare*, may mean little more. The emphasis is on external details and hardly on the familiar virtues—fidelity, *largesse* and the like—around which courtly romance is built. Perhaps the explanation is that we expect too much of Abro and the education of a medieval woman.

Considered as a whole, however, *Emare* should not be thought of as a dramatized book of courtesy. Its heroine, like Freine, as the model of Christian patience and trust could easily become the subject of a saint's life:[45]

> She was dryven toward Rome,
> Thorow þe grace of God yn trone,
> That all þyng may fulfylle.
>
> (ll. 679–681)

She submits to the most trying abuse only because she knows that the future will bring relief. She is primarily a sufferer and afterward "the konnyngest wommon," skilled in courtesy and, as an anticlimax, needlework. The poem in which she appears, more than anything else suggests hagiography, yet retains courtly elements. These support the judgement that at some point in history the Constance-legend was given the appear-

---

[45] See Dieter Mehl, "Die kürzeren mittelenglischen 'Romanzen' und die Gattungsfrage," *DVLG*, xxxviii (1964), 522.

ance of a Breton lay by an imitator more interested in the faithful transmission of his legend than in the content of the Breton lay.

V. SIR GOWTHER

Sir Gowther, which tells a story equally widespread, presents the historian of the Breton lay with the same difficulties as Emare. It not only has no known source in Celtic literature, but is found in many countries, Spain, Portugal, France and England, and in a variety of forms, exemplum, chronicle, ballad, play, pantomime and opera. It is roughly the same story as the better known Robert the Devil and, like it, is probably unrelated to any historical incident, involving here a duke of Normandy.[46] It is preserved in only two manuscripts, 19.3.1 (f.11ª–27ᵇ) of the Advocates' Library, Edinburgh, dating from the second half of the fifteenth century, and Royal MS. 17 B. XLIII, dating from the same period and now held by the British Museum.[47] The date of composition is the late fourteenth century and the place, the Northeast Midlands.[48] There is no reason for considering Sir Gowther anything but the work of an itinerant minstrel, vying perhaps with the com-

[46] The identification of Robert the Devil with any of the dukes of Normandy is rejected by Karl Breul, whose edition of Sir Gowther (Oppeln, 1886) is used in this study; see pp. 107–134. E. Löseth, ed. Robert le Diable, Roman d'Adventure (Paris, 1903), pp. xxx–xxxvii summarizes opinion. For a study of analogues see Breul, pp. 45–134, to which "La Fille Vendue au Diable," Folk Songs of French Canada, ed. Marius Barbeau and Edward Sapir (New Haven, 1925) should be added. Breul, pp. 100–101, lists the differences between Sir Gowther and Robert the Devil.

[47] Breul, pp. 1–4. MED, P & B, p. 43. Two recent editions are: Rumble, pp. 179–204; C. Novelli, U. of Notre Dame diss. DA, xxvi, 1634.

[48] Trounce, MÆ, iii (1934), 40.

poser of *Sir Launfal, The Erl of Tolous* and *Emare*.[49]

When the Duchess of Austria, childless for more than ten years, prays for a child *by any means*, she is visited by a man resembling the Duke, who after lying with her, reveals himself a devil. Frightened, she blesses herself, but tells the Duke that an angel appeared and instructed her to expect a child. The child is born and christened Gowther and soon grows so strong as to kill his wet nurses and bite even his own mother. At fifteen he forges a heavy sword which only he can bear, and so terrorizes everyone, including the religious, that the Duke, his supposed father, dies of grief and the Duchess is heartbroken. When an earl calls Gowther a devil's son, Gowther forces his mother at sword's point to identify his real father. Horrified, he reaches Rome on foot and there confesses to the Pope, who as penance directs him to eat only what he can snatch from dogs and to remain silent until he receives a sign from heaven. Beginning his penance Gowther visits the court of Germany where he is called "Hob the Fool." When the Saracens seek by force the Emperor's daughter, who is dumb, he prays for help, is heavily armed and, unrecognized except by the Emperor's daughter, thrice routs the enemy before being wounded. Perceiving his wound, the maiden falls off the castle and is thought dead. When she revives, she gains her speech and relates that Gowther is the unknown knight of great heroism. The Pope, present originally for her funeral, recognizes the sign from God and absolves Gowther. After his marriage to the Emperor's daughter, Gowther rules Germany; the earl, left in charge of Austria, formally takes over that country and marries Gowther's widowed mother. A model

---

[49] Breul, pp. 2 and 40–41.

Christian, Gowther is considered after his death a saint, works miracles and intercedes for those desiring help.

The immediate source of *Sir Gowther*, unfortunately, has never been determined. Certain conflicting references to a source found in *The Erl of Tolous* and *Emare* appear again, but somewhat changed:

> A lai of Breyten long y soȝght
> And owt þerof a tale have broȝht,
>   þat lufly is to tell.   (ll. 28–30)

> þes lordys to bed con hom bown
> And knyȝttys and ladys of renown:
>   þus þis romans told   (ll. 541–543)

> þis is wreton in parchemyn,
> A story bote gud and fyn,
>   Owt off a lai of Breyteyn.   (ll. 751–753)

The present work is called a *tale* (l. 29), which has as its source a *romans* (l. 543) and a *lai of Breyten* (l. 28); again, the *lai of Breyten* must be a *narrative lay* or *conte*, which would yield a *story* (l. 752).

The "lai of Breyten" from which the minstrel drew has been tentatively identified as *Tydorel*,[50] already considered in Chapter 2, but the similarities are only general. A happy marriage goes unblessed by children. When a child is born, his father is a supernatural being, of whom the husband has no knowl-

---

[50] Florence Leftwich Ravenel, "Tydorel and Sir Gowther," *PMLA*, xx (1905), 153–177. Ogle, "The Orchard Scene in *Tydorel* and *Sir Gowther*," pp. 37–43, traces the "sadness of the man and the wife over their childless state, the wife's prayers to 'Mary mild,' the description of the scene in the orchard, the appearance of the supernatural lover" to the Apocryphal Story of Anna, the wife of Joachim. For a study of story-patterns see Smithers, pp. 66 ff.

edge. The child, who has great mental and physical powers, discovers his supernatural origin by accident and forces his mother to relate the details. No Breton lay corresponding exactly to *Sir Gowther* survives in Old French, and the only reason for supposing that there ever was one is the author's claim, as well, of course, as the negative evidence which the external appearance of the poem offers: although the setting is Austria, Rome and Germany, *Sir Gowther* does have the appropriate length 756 lines and the typical epilogue.

It has long been felt, on the other hand, that *Sir Gowther* lacks the courtliness of a Breton lay.[51] Although it opens promisingly as the Duke of Austria marries and amid great splendor holds a tournament, it soon loses the reader in the business of Gowther's nursery. When the infant kills his wet nurses, he causes their knightly husbands to complain with amusing understatement:

> Kynȝtus geydyre hom in samun
> And seyd to þe duke, hit was no gamun
> To lose hor wyffus soo
>
> (ll. 121–123)

The youthful Gowther forges his own sword and, still willful and unchastised, is ironically knighted in the hope of amendment. His unknightly adventures include every kind of sin. He refuses to attend Mass, burns convents, breaks up marriages, abuses widows and goes to whatever extremes. After his pilgrimage to Rome, however, he attends the court of Germany, but as a penitent, where he meets the Emperor's daughter:

[51] Thomas Warton, *History of English Poetry*, ed. W. Carew Hazlitt (London, 1871), pp. 163–164.

> Þat meydon was worþely wroȝt,
> Bote feyr, curteys and free.
> (ll. 377–378)

Love is minimized, and Gowther receives her as a simple reward for his bravery against the Saracens. These have felt the iron of his sword, especially the Sultan, who is described at disproportionate length:

> Þo sawdyn bare in sabull blacke
> ·iij·lyons rampand, withowt lacke,
> All of silver schene.
> Won was corvon with golys redde,
> A nodur with gold in þat steyd,
> To thyrde with aser, y wene,
> and his helmyt full rychely fret,
> With charbuckolus stonus sett
> And dyamondus betwene,
> And his batel evele areyd
> And his baner brodly dyspleyd;
> Cone aftur tyde hom tene.[52]
> (ll. 577–588)

This careful description, recalling a similar passage in *Sir Degare*, indicates with the evidence already considered that *Sir Gowther* is more concerned with courtly setting than with courtliness itself.

In content, it resembles a saint's life, since it plainly stresses the "life, death, and miracles of some person accounted worthy to be considered a leader in the cause of righteousness."[53] It demonstrates, in fact, in a theoretic case, how depraved one

[52] Medieval English, French, Spanish and Saracenic records reveal no coat of arms answering exactly this description. Leo A. Mayer, *Saracenic Heraldry* (Oxford, 1933), p. 9, claims that the lion is rare in Saracenic armory.

[53] Gerould, *Saints' Legends*, p. 5.

can be and still do penance. Gowther's life, accordingly, falls
into two parts. The "warlocke greytt," begotten by a devil,
could begin life no worse, and his chances of salvation seem
small. He lives in sin until the knowledge of his origin forces
him to reform. The second part of his life deals with grace—
his confession to the Pope and the penance which he performs. The sign from God, ending his uncertainty, comes
before battle with the Saracens. Even after the second of the
three engagements, his thoughts are so fixed on sin and penance that he hardly rejoices in the victory:

> He had no þoȝt, bot of his syn,
> And how he myȝt is soule wyn
>   To þo blys, þat god con by.
>
> > (ll. 538–540)

Beginning a life of grace as "goddees chyld" he founds an
abbey and is beloved for his charities. After his death he

> Was beryd at to same abbey,
>   Þat hymselfe gart make;
> And he is a varre corsent parfytt
> And with cryston pepull wele belovyd.
>   God hase done for his sake
> Myrrakull, for he was hum hold,
> Þer he lyse in schryne of gold,
>   Þat suffurd for goddus sake.
>
> > (ll. 725–732)

As "a varre corsent parfytt" he has powers of intercession.

> Who so sechys hym with hart fre,
> Or hor bale bot mey bee,
>   For so god has hum hyȝt.
>
> > (ll. 745–747)

His miracles are numerous:

> For he garus þo blynd to see
> And þo dompe to speyke, parde,
>   And makus þo crakyd ryght
> And gyffus to þo mad hor sytte
> And mony odur meracullus yytte
>   Þoro þo grace of god allmyȝt.
>
> (ll. 739–744)

The poet can hardly be charged with having concealed his intention:

> Grace he had to make þat eynd,
>   Þat god was of hym feyn.
>
> (ll. 749–750)

One of the two manuscripts, therefore, *Royal 17. B. XLIII*, of the British Museum, ends interestingly, if not appropriately, "Explicit Vita Sancti."

Since *Sir Gowther* has the courtly setting, but lacks the treatment of love found in a Breton lay, its claim to a Breton origin may be explained as an appeal to authority. It resembles more closely a saint's life, based on a fictitious character whose reformation, worked by grace, becomes an object lesson in morality. That grace is always effective, is so emphasized that the poem becomes unmistakably didactic. As has been proposed,[54] *Sir Gowther* may be said to be, like *Emare*, religious in nature, while *Sir Launfal* and *The Erl of Tolous*, the remaining lays in tail-rhyme stanzas, are secular. Whatever the ultimate validity of this pair of terms, of the four only *Sir Launfal* is counted with the first Breton lays through a translation. After it comes *The Erl of Tolous*, which has the

---

[54] Trounce, *MÆ*, iii (1934), 49–50.

appropriate contents. *Emare* and the present poem are at best imitations.

It may prove significant to observe together the four lays as they identify their genre. Three of the four call themselves a *tale*, a general enough term, yet one which translates exactly Marie's designation *conte*. While *Emare*, the fourth, is one of the Breton lays or, we would say, a narrative lay, it is the equivalent of *conte* or *tale* when read in context, as one would agree at once.

VI. SOME GENERALIZATIONS

Perhaps the composer of each of the Middle English lays would accept as true of his own intention Marie's opening of *Guigemar* (ll. 19–21): "Les contes que jo sai verais, / dunt li Bretun unt fait les lais, / vos conterai assez briefment." She will tell more or less simply the tales from which the Bretons composed their lyrical lays. At the same time, even as she simplifies, she will form ancient tales according to her present view of the past:

> Mult unt esté noble barun
> cil de Bretaigne, li Bretun.
> Jadis suleient par pruësce,
> par curteisie e par noblesce
> des aventures que oeient,
> ki a plusurs genz aveneient,
> faire les lais pur remembrance
> qu'um nes meist en ubliance.
> (*Equitan:* ll. 1–8)

These lines stress the courtliness which Marie de France gave Breton and other tales as she composed before 1189 the first

narrative lays. This form, for practical purposes, may be identified as a short narrative either calling itself a Breton lay,
derived from the same adventure as a lyric lay, or set in Brittany or Britain and having as its subject matter *courtoisie*
preserved as an ideal of the past for a feudal society. The
aspects of love which Marie develops have been variously
interpreted. After her death, as imitators continued to write
lays, some close to hers in general appearance, the term *Breton
lay*, which insured a ready audience, was applied to short
didactic poems in the Courtly Love tradition, to examples of
the fabliau and even to any short serious poem, whatever its
content or story-pattern. During the fourteenth century and
slightly later, when English was already the language of the
court, translators made available in Middle English certain Old
French lays, and some English writers produced original imitations of the form.

The practice, admittedly loose, of regarding the English
Breton lays not as tales but as short romances has led to the
following grouping according to poetic style: Breton lays in
(1) octosyllabic couplets, (2) decasyllabic couplets and (3)
tail-rhyme stanzas. *Lai le Freine, Landavall, Sir Orfeo* and *Sir
Degare*, all in octosyllabic couplets and dating from the first
half of the fourteenth century, are the earliest Middle English
Breton lays. Of these, the first two as rather close translations
of Marie de France can be called true lays. Since *Sir Orfeo*,
probably based on a missing *Lai d'Orphéy*, offers the proper
courtly contents, its source is presumed to be a thirteenth-
century imitation. *Sir Degare*, judging from its contents, is a
native English imitation made up of available materials and
lacking, of course, an original in Old French. A final imitation,
but in decasyllabic couplets, Chaucer's *Franklin's Tale*, dating

from the end of the century, so emphasizes a courtly theme as to resemble vaguely the didactic poetry described in Chapter II. During the middle of the fourteenth century there must have been other examples, now lost, which kept alive the tradition after the preparation of the *Auchinleck* MS., dated c. 1330–40.

The Breton lay of the period 1350–1400 or slightly later is written also in the style of the tail-rhyme romance. It is popular poetry and, generally speaking, stresses merely chivalric setting. Of the four examples, only *Sir Launfal* is a translation of Marie de France; its two interpolated passages add physical action not found in the original. The other three examples are called Breton lays merely to attract readers. *The Erl of Tolous* comes close to Marie de France in content, yet presents the trial by combat for its own sake and as a kind of spectacle. *Emare* and *Sir Gowther*, really didactic works of a religious nature, can be compared to saints' lives and certainly lack the love and adventure vital to courtly literature.

APPENDIX

Guigemar: "Die Liebesverbundenheit besteht in Leid und doch ist dies Leid dem Menschen notwendig."

Lanval: "Wahre Liebe darf unter keinen Umständen die Diskretionspflict verletzen, auch wenn diese noch so schwerer Belastung unterworfen wird."

Eliduc: "Der zwischen zwei Frauen stehende Mann bringt die drei Beteiligten in einen Konflikt zwischen *crestienté* und *amor*."

Chievrefueil: "Die Liebenden gehören zusammen; wenn Schicksalfugungen sie auseinanderreissen, müssen sie sterben."

Yonec: "Liebe ist von roher Eifersucht bedroht: sie sollte sich ihr nicht verraten."

Les deus amanz: "Tod die Folge von zu viel Liebe."

Bisclavret: "Wenn Ehebruch in manche Fallen gerichtfertigt werden kann, so nimmer ein feiger Verrat."

235

Milun: "Die Liebenden werden durch das Kind, das ihrer Verbindung entstammt, geeint."

Le Fraisne: "Die Ehe wird vom Schicksal zu guter Letzt doch zwischen den Menschen gestiftet, die füreinander bestimmt sind."

Equitan: "Die Allgewalt der Liebe treibt zu Sünde und Tod."

Laostic: "Wenn such *vilenie* die Liebe stören will, so bleibt trotz seines Erfolges der verrat gemein und wahre Liebe ist ewig und unzerstörbar."

Chaitivel: "Das Problem der Ausschliesslichkeit und Wechselseitigkeit einer Liebe."

> Spitzer, "Marie de France—Dichterin von Problemmärchen," pp. 289 ff.

BIBLIOGRAPHY

I. Primary Sources

Alanus de Insulis. *Anticlaudian*, PL, ccx, 485–576.

Andreas Capellanus. *De Amore Libri Tres*, ed. Amadeu Pagès. Castello de la Plana, 1930.

Bicket, Robert. *Le Lai du Cor*, ed. Fredrik Wulff. Paris, 1888.

————. *Le Lai du Cor*, ed. Heinrich Dörner. Strasbourg, 1907.

Boccaccio. *De genealogia deorum gentilium* in *Opere*, ed. V. Romano. Scrittori d'Italia, No. 201. 2 vols. Bari, 1951, I.

Boethius. *The Theological Tractates and the Consolation of Philosophy*, LCL. London and New York, 1918.

————. *The Paris Psalter and Meters of Boethius*, ed. George Philip Krapp. The Anglo-Saxon Poetic Records, v, New York, 1932.

Caesar. *Commentarii de Bello Gallico* in *Commentarii*, ed. Bernard Kubler. 4 vols. Leipzig, 1893–97, I.

Chaucer, Geoffrey. *The Text of the Canterbury Tales*, edd. John M. Manly and Edith Rickert. 8 vols. Chicago, 1940.

————. *The Works of Geoffrey Chaucer*, ed. F. N. Robinson. 2nd ed. Boston and New York, 1957.

Chrétien de Troyes. *Philomena*, ed. C. de Boer. Paris, 1909.

————. *Sämtliche Werke*, ed. Wendelin Foerster. 5 vols. Halle, 1884–1932.

237

Denis Pyramus. *La Vie Seint Edmond le Rei*, ed. Florence Ravenel. Bryn Mawr College Monographs, v, 1906.

Early English Meals and Manners, ed. F. J. Furnivall. EETS, OS 32. London, 1894.

Emare, ed. Edith Rickert. Chicago, 1907.

Evans, Thomas. *Old Ballads, historical and narrative*. London, 1784.

The Erl of Tolous and the Emperes of Almayn, ed. Gustav Lüdtke. Sammlung englischer Denkmäler in Kritischen Ausgaben, No. iii. Berlin, 1881.

Faral, Edmond. *Les Artes Poétiques du XIIe et du XIIIe Siècle*. Paris, 1924.

Floire et Blanceflor, ed. E. du Méril. Paris, 1856.

French, Walter Hoyt, and Charles Brockway Hale, edd. *Middle English Metrical Romances*. New York, 1930.

Galeran de Bretagne, ed. A. Boucherie. Montpellier, 1888.

"Guiron," published in *Le Roman de Tristan*, ed. Joseph Bédier. 2 vols. Paris, 1902, i.

Henri d'Andeli. *Le Lai d'Aristote*, ed. Alexandre Héron. Rouen, 1901.

Henryson, Robert. *The Poems of Robert Henryson*, ed. G. Gregory Smith. 3 vols., STS, XLV–XLVII. Edinburgh and London, 1914.

Das anglonormanische Lied vom Ritter Horns, edd. R. Brede and E. Stengel. Marburg, 1883.

Ille et Galeron, ed. E. Löseth. Paris, 1890.

Laȝamon, *Brut*, ed. Sir Frederic Madden. 3 vols. London, 1847.

Libeaus Desconus, ed. Max Kaluza. Leipzig, 1890.

Le Lai de Guingamor, Le Lai de Tydorel, edd. E. Lommatzsch and M. Wagner. Romanische Texte No. 6. Berlin, 1922.

"Le Lai de l'Épervier," ed. Gaston Paris. *Romania*, vii (1878), 1–21.

"Le Lai de l'Épine," ed. Rudolf Zenker, *ZfRPh*, xvii (1893), 232–255.

"Le Lai de l'Oiselet," ed. Raymond Weeks. *Medieval Studies in Memory of Gertrude Schoepperle Loomis*. Paris and New York, 1927, pp. 341–353.

"Le Lai de Nabaret," in *Charlemagne, An Anglo-Norman Poem of the Twelfth Century*, ed. Francisque Michel. London, 1836, pp. 90–91.

Le Lai d'Haveloc and Gaimar's Haveloc Episode, ed. Alexander Bell. Publications of the University of Manchester, No. clxxi. Manchester, 1925.

Le Lai d'Ignaure ou Lai du Prisonnier, ed. Rita Le Jeune. Académie

Royale de Langue et de Littérature françaises de Belgique, Textes Anciens, III. Brussels, 1938.

"Le Lai du Conseil," ed. Albert Barth, *Romanische Forschungen*, XXXI (1911–12), 799–872.

"Le Lai du Cort Mantel," ed. Frederick A. Wulff, *Romania*, XIV (1885), 343–380.

The Middle English Lai le Freine, ed. Margaret Wattie. Smith College Studies in Modern Languages, X (1929), No. 3.

"Lais Inédits de Tyolet, de Guingamor, de Doon, du Lecheor et de Tydorel," ed. Gaston Paris, *Romania*, VIII (1879), 29–72.

"Le Lai du Trot," ed. Evie M. Grimes, *RR*, XXVI (1935), 313–321.

The Lays of Desiré, Graelent and Melion, ed. Evie M. Grimes. New York, 1928.

The Lay of Haveloc the Dane, ed. Walter W. Skeat. Oxford, 1902.

Marie de France, *Das Buch vom Espurgatoire S. Patrice der Marie de France und Seine Quelle*. ed. Karl Warnke. Bibliotheca Normannica, IX. Halle, 1938.

————. *Die Fabeln der Marie de France*. Bibliotheca Normannica, VI. Halle, 1898.

————. *Die Lais*, ed. Karl Warnke. Bibliotheca Normannica, III, 3rd ed. Halle, 1925.

————. *Lais*, ed. Alfred Ewert. Blackwell, Oxford, 1947.

————. *Lai di Maria di Francia*, ed. F. Neri. Turin, 1946.

"Der altfranzösische Narcisuslai," ed. Alfons Hilka, *ZfRPh*, XLIX (1929), 633–675.

Narcisus, edd. M. M. Pelan and N. C. W. Spence. Publications de la Faculté des Lettres de l'Université de Strasbourg, No. 147. Paris, 1964.

Otto of Freising, *Chronicon*, ed. G. H. Pertz, M. G. H., XX. Hanover, 1868.

Ovid. *Heroides and Amores*, tr. Grant Showerman. LCL. London and New York, 1925.

————. *Metamorphoses*, tr. Frank J. Miller. LCL. 2 vols. London and New York, 1928.

Ovide Moralisé, ed. C. de Boer. Amsterdam, 1915–38.

The Owl and the Nightingale, edd. J. H. G. Grattan and G. F. H. Sykes. EETS, ES, CXIX. London, 1935.

Petrus Helias. Selections in C. Thurot, *Notices et extraits des manuscrits de la bibliothèque impériale*, No. 22. Paris, 1868.

Piramus et Tisbé, ed. C. de Boer. Paris, 1921.

Priscian. *Institutiones*, ed. M. Hertz in *Grammatici Latini*, ed. H. Keil. Leipzig, 1855, ii.

Renart, Jehan. *Le Lai de l'Ombre*, ed. John Orr. Edinburgh, 1948.

Robert le Diable, Roman d'Aventure, ed. E. Löseth, SATF. Paris, 1902.

Le Roman de Renart, ed. Ernest Martin. 3 vols. Strasbourg, 1882–87.

Le Roman de Tristan, ed. Joseph Bédier. 2 vols. Paris, 1902.

Rumble, Thomas C., ed. *The Breton Lays in Middle English*. Detroit, 1965.

Sargent, Helen C., and George Lyman Kittredge, edd. *English and Scottish Popular Ballads*. Boston, 1932.

Scalachronica, The Reigns of Edward I, Edward II and Edward III as Recorded by Sir Thomas Gray, tr. Sir Herbert Maxwell. Glasgow, 1907.

Sir Degarre nach der gesamten Überlieferung und mit Untersuchungen über die Sprache und den Romanzenstoff, ed. Gustav Schleich. Englische Textbibliothek, No. 19. Heidelberg, 1929.

Sir Degarree, ed. Muriel B. Carr. University of Chicago Diss., 1923.

Sir Gowther, ed. Karl Breul. Oppeln, 1886.

————, ed. C. Novelli. University of Notre Dame Diss. (DA, xxvi, 1634).

Sir Landeval, ed. Rudolf Zimmermann. Königsberg, 1900.

"Sir Launfal," ed. George Lyman Kittredge, *AJPh*, x (1889), 1–33.

————, ed. A. J. Bliss. Nelson's Medieval & Renaissance Library. London, 1960.

Sir Orfeo, ed. Oscar Zielke. Breslau, 1880.

————, ed. A. J. Bliss. Oxford English Monographs. Oxford, 1954.

Strengleikar eða Liodabok, edd. R. Keyser and C. R. Unger. Christiania, 1850.

Thomas of Woodstock, *The Ordinaunce and Fourme of Fightyng within the Lists*, in *Black Book of the Admiralty*, ed. Sir Travers Twiss. London, 1871, i, 301–329.

Towneley Plays, ed. Alfred W. Pollard, EETS, ES 71. London, 1897.

Trivet, Nicholas, *Annales Sex Regum Angliae*, ed. Thomas Hog. London, 1845.

II. Secondary Sources

Ackerman, Robert W. "Middle English Literature" in *The Medieval Literature of Western Europe*, ed. John H. Fisher. New York, 1966.

Acta Sanctorum quotquot orbe coluntur, etc. Bollandist Society of Brussels, 1643–1925.

Ahlström, Axel. "Marie de France et les Lais Narratifs," *Kungl. Vetenskaps-och Vitterhets-Samhälles, Handlingar*, 3rd Series, XXIX, No. 3. Göteborg, 1925, 1–37.

————. *Studier i den Fornfranska Lais-Litteraturen.* Upsala, 1892.

Alden, Raymond MacD. *English Verse.* New York, 1903.

Amos, Flora Ross. *Early Theories of Translation.* New York, 1920.

Archer, Jerome. "On Chaucer's Source for 'Arveragus' in the *Franklin's Tale*," *PMLA*, LXV (1950), 318–322.

Atkins, J. W. H. *English Literary Criticism: The Medieval Phase.* Cambridge, 1943.

Baldwin, Charles Sears. *An Introduction to English Medieval Literature.* New York, 1922.

————. "Cicero on Parnassus," *PMLA*, XLII (1927), 106–112.

————. *Three Medieval Centuries of Literature in England.* Boston, 1932.

Baring-Gould, Sabine. *A Book of Brittany.* rev. ed. London, 1932.

Barrow, Sarah F. *The Medieval Society Romance.* New York, 1924.

Baugh, A. C. "The Authorship of the Middle English Romances," *Annual Bulletin of the Modern Humanities Research Association*, XXII (1950), 13–28.

————. "Improvisation in the Middle English Romance," *Proceedings of the American Philosophical Society*, CIII (1959), 418–454.

Baum, Paull Franklin. *The Principles of English Versification.* Cambridge, Mass., 1926.

Bédier, Joseph. *Les Fabliaux.* 5th ed. Paris, 1925.

————. "Les Lais de Marie de France," *Revue des Deux Mondes*, CVII (1891), 835–863.

Bell, Alexander. "Gaimar's Early 'Danish' Kings," *PMLA*, LXV (1950), 601–640.

Bellows, H. A. *The Relations between Prose and Metrical Composition in Old Norse Literature.* Harvard University diss., 1910.

Bennett, H. S. *Chaucer and the Fifteenth Century.* The Oxford History of English Literature, Vol. II, Part 1. Oxford, 1947.

Biller, Gunnar. *Étude sur le style des premiers romans français en vers (1150–1175).* Göteborg, 1916.

Bordman, Gerald. *Motif-Index of the English Metrical Romances,* FFC, LXXIX, No. 190. Helsinki, 1963.

Borrmann, Otto. *Das kurze Reimpaar bei Chrestien von Troyes mit besonderer Berücksichtigung des Wilhelm von England.* Erlangen, 1907.

Bossuat, Robert. *Manuel bibliographique de la littérature française du moyen âge.* Paris, 1951; Supplement I, 1955; II, 1961.

Brandl, Alois. "Spielmannsverhaltnisse in frühmittelenglischer Zeit," *Sitzungsberichte der königlich preussischen Akademie der Wissenschaft,* XL (1910), 873–892.

Brereton, Georgine E. "A Thirteenth Century List of French Lays and Other Narrative Poems," *MLR,* XLV (1950), 40–45.

Brinkmann, Hennig. *Zu Wesen und Form mittelalterlichen Dichtung.* Halle, 1928.

Bromwich, R. "A Note on the Breton Lays," *MÆ,* XXVI (1957), 36–38.

Bruce, James D. *The Evolution of Arthurian Romance from the Beginnings down to the Year 1300.* 2 vols. Göttingen and Baltimore, 1923.

Brugger, E. "Die Lais der Marie de France," *ZfSL,* XLIX (1926–27), 116–155.

————. "Eigennamen in den Lais der Marie de France," *ZfSL,* XLIX (1926–27), 201–252 and 381–484.

————. "Ueber die Bedeutung von Bretagne, Breton in mittelalterlichen Texten," *ZfSL,* XX (1898), 79–162.

Bryan, W. F., and Germaine Dempster, edd. *Sources and Analogues of Chaucer's Canterbury Tales.* Chicago, 1941.

Bush, Douglas. *Mythology and the Renaissance Tradition in English Poetry.* Minneapolis, 1932.

Buttenweiser, H. "Popular Authors of the Middle Ages: The Testimony of the Manuscripts," *Speculum,* XVII (1942), 53.

Caplan, Harry. "The Four Senses of Scriptural Interpretation," *Speculum,* IV (1929), 282–290.

Carpinelli, Francis. *Explicator,* XIX (1960), Item 13.

Carr, Muriel Bothwell. Review of George Patterson Faust, *Sir Degare*, *MLN*, LIII (1938), 115.

Chambers, E. K. *Arthur of Britain*. London, 1927.

————. *Mediaeval Stage*. 2 vols. Oxford, 1903.

Comfort, William W. "The Essential Difference between a *Chanson de Geste* and a *Roman d'Aventure*," *PMLA*, XIX (1904), 64–74.

Cooke, John Daniel. "Euhemerism: a Mediaeval Interpretation of Classical Paganism," *Speculum*, II (1927), 396–410.

Christensen, Parley A. "The Beginnings and Endings of the Middle English Metrical Romances," *Stanford University Abstracts of Dissertations* (1928), II, 105–110.

Crosby, Ruth. "Chaucer and the Custom of Oral Delivery," *Speculum*, XIII (1938), 413–432.

————. "Oral Delivery in the Middle Ages," *Speculum*, XI (1936), 88–110.

Cross, Tom P. "Celtic Elements in the Lays of Lanval and Graelent," *MP*, XII (1915), 585–644.

————. "The Celtic Fée in Launfal," *Kittredge Anniversary Papers*. New York, 1913, pp. 377–410.

————. "The Celtic Origin of the Lay of Yonec," *Revue Celtique*, XXI (1910), 413–471.

Cummings, Hubertis Maurice. *The Indebtedness of Chaucer's Works to the Italian Works of Boccaccio*. University of Cincinnati Studies, Series II, Volume X (Part 2), pp. 181–197.

Damon, S. Foster. "Marie de France: Psychologist of Courtly Love," *PMLA*, XLIV (1929), 968–996.

Davies, Constance. "Classical Threads in 'Orfeo,' " *MLR*, LVI (1961), 161–166.

————. " 'Ympe Tre' and 'Nemeton,' " *N & Q*, IX n.s. (1962), 6–9.

————. "L'uevre Salemun," *MÆ*, XXIX (1960), 173–183.

DeGhellinck, J. "Nani et Gigantes," *Bulletin du Cange*, XVIII (1945), 25–29.

Dempster, Germaine. "A Further Note on Dorigen's Exempla," *MLN*, LIV (1939), 137–138.

————. "Chaucer at Work on the Complaint in the Franklin's Tale," *MLN*, LII (1937), 16–23.

————. *Dramatic Irony in Chaucer*, Stanford University, Publications in Languages and Literatures, IV (1932).

De Riquer, Martín. "La 'aventure,' el 'lai' y el 'conte' en Maria de Francia," *Filologia Romanza*, Anno II, Fasc. 1, No. 5 (1955), pp. 1–19.

Dictionary of National Biography, edd. Leslie Stephen and Sidney Lee. 22 vols. London, 1908–09.

Donovan, M. J. "The *Anticlaudian* and Three Passages in the *Franklin's Tale*," *JEGP*, LVI (1957), 52–59.

———. "Breton Lays," in J. Burke Severs, ed. *A Manual of the Writings in Middle English 1050–1500*, fascicule 1 (New Haven, 1967), pp. 133–143; 292–297.

———. "Herodis in the Auchinleck *Sir Orfeo*," *MÆ*, XXVII (1958), 162–165.

———. "*Lai du Lecheor*: A Reinterpretation," *RR*, XLIII (1952), 81–86.

———. "Priscian and the Obscurity of the Ancients," *Speculum*, XXXVI (1961), 75–80.

———. "*Sir Degare*: ll. 992–7," *MS*, XV (1953), 206–208.

Duff, J. Wight. *A Literary History of Rome in the Silver Age*. New York, 1935.

Dunlap, A. R. "The Vocabulary of the Middle English Romances in Tail-Rhyme Stanzas," *Delaware Notes*, 14th Series (1941), pp. 1–42.

Dunn, Charles W. *William of Palerne, History, Legend, and Romance*. Harvard University Diss., 1947.

———. *The Foundling and the Werwolf*. University of Toronto Department of English Studies and Texts, No. 8. Toronto, 1960.

Dupin, Henri. *La Courtoisie au Moyen Âge*. Paris, 1931.

Eberwein, Elena. *Zur Deutung mittelalterlicher Existenz*. Kölner Romanistische Arbeiten, VII. Bonn and Cologne, 1933.

Edel, Marie. *The Relations between Prose and Metrical Composition in Early Irish Literature*. Radcliffe College Diss., 1935.

Ellis, George. *Specimens of Early English Metrical Romances*. 3 vols. London, 1805.

Engels, Joseph. *Études sur l'Ovide Moralisé*. Groningen, 1945.

Everett, Dorothy. "A Characterization of the English Medieval Romances," *Essays and Studies by Members of the English Association*, XV (1929), pp. 98–121. Rptd. in *Essays on Middle English Literature*, ed. P. Kean. Oxford, 1955.

———. "The Relation of Chestre's 'Launfal' and 'Lybeaus Desconus,'" *MÆ*, VII (1934), 29–49.

Fahnestock, E. A Study of the Sources and Composition of the Old French Lai d'Haveloc. New York, 1915.

Faral, Edmond. Recherches sur les sources latines des contes et romans courtois du moyen âge. Paris, 1913.

Faust, George Patterson. Sir Degare: A Study of the Texts and Narrative Structure. Princeton Studies in English, No. 11 (1935).

Ferguson, Mary. "Folklore in the Lais of Marie de France," RR, LVII (1966), 3–24.

Fischer, Erna. Die Lautbestand des südmittelenglischen Octovian, verglichen mit seinen Entsprechungen im Lybeaus Desconus und im Launfal. Anglistische Forschungen, LXIII. Heidelberg, 1927.

Flum, F. N. "Additional Thoughts on Marie de France," RomN, III (1962), 53–56.

Foulet, Lucien. "English Words in the Lais of Marie de France," MLN, xx (1905), 108–110.

————. "Marie de France et la Légende de Tristan," ZfRPh, xxxII (1908), 161–183.

————. "Le Prologue du Franklin's Tale et les Lais bretons," ZfRPh, xxx (1906), 698–711.

————. "Les Strengleikar et le lai du Lecheor," Revues des Langues Romanes, LI (1908), 97.

————. "Marie de France et les Lais bretons," ZfRPh, xxIx (1905), 19–56 and 293–322.

————. "The Prologue to Sir Orfeo," MLN, xxI (1906), 46–50.

————. "Thomas and Marie in their Relations to the Conteurs," MLN, xxIII (1908), 205–208.

Fox, John C. "Marie de France," The English Historical Review, xxv (1910), 303–306; xxvI (1911), 317–326.

Francis, E. A. "The Trial in Lanval," Studies Presented to Mildred K. Pope, Manchester, 1939, pp. 115–124.

————. "Marie de France et son Temps," Romania, LXXII (1951), 74–91.

Frantzen, J. J. A. A. "Ueber den Einfluss der mittellateinischen Literatur auf die französische und die deutsche Poesie des Mittelalters," Neophilologus, IV (1918), 358–371.

Frappier, J. "Remarques sur la structure du lai, Essai de définition et de classement," La Littérature narrative d'imagination. Colloques de Strasbourg, avril 1959, pp. 23–39.

French, Walter Hoyt. Essays on King Horn. Cornell Studies in English, xxx. Ithaca, 1940.

Frey, John A. "Linguistic and Psychological Couplings in the Lays of Marie de France," *SP*, LXI (1964), 3–18.

Friedensburg, Ferdinand. *Die Symbolik der Mittelaltermünzen.* 3 vols. Berlin, 1913–22.

Friedman, J. B. "Eurydice, Heurodis, and the Noonday Demon," *Speculum*, XLI (1966), 22–29.

Gennrich, Friedrich. *Grundriss einer Formenlehre des mittelalterlichen Liedes.* Halle, 1932.

Gerould, Gordon Hall. "King Arthur and Politics," *Speculum*, II (1927), 33–51.

————. "King Arthur and Politics Again," *Speculum*, II (1927), 448.

————. *Saints' Legends.* Boston and New York, 1916.

————. "The Social Status of Chaucer's Franklin," *PMLA*, XLI (1926), 262–279.

Getty, Agnes. "Chaucer's Changing Conceptions of the Humble Lover," *PMLA*, XLIV (1929), 213–214.

Gough, Alfred Bradly. *On the Middle English Romance of Emare.* Kiel diss. 1900.

Griffin, Nathaniel E. "The Definition of Romance," *PMLA*, XXXVIII (1923), 50–70.

Gröber, Gustav. *Grundriss der romanischen Philologie.* Strasbourg, 1888–1902.

Gros Louis, K. R. R. "Robert Henryson's *Orpheus and Eurydice* and the Orpheus Traditions in the Middle Ages," *Speculum*, XLI (1966), 643–655.

Grosse, R. *Der Stil Chrestiens von Troies.* Französischen Studien, I (1881).

Guillaume, Gabrielle. "The Prologues of the *Lay le Freine* and *Sir Orfeo*," *MLN*, XXXVI (1921), 458–464.

Gunther, Werner W. "Probleme der Rededarstellung," *Die neueren Sprachen*, Beiheft No. 13 (1928), pp. 1–160.

Guyer, F. E. "The Dwarf on the Giant's Shoulders," *MLN*, XLV (1930), 398–402.

Hallauer, Marguerite. *Das wunderbare Element in den Chansons de Geste.* Basel, 1918.

Hamer, Enid. *The Metres of English Poetry.* London, 1930.

Hamilton, Jean I. *Landschaftsverwertung im Bau höfischer Epen.* Bonn diss., 1932.

Hamilton, Marie. "Notes on Chaucer and the Rhetoricians," *PMLA*, XLVII (1932), 403–409.

Harrison, Benjamin S. "The Rhetorical Inconsistency of Chaucer's Franklin," *SP*, xxxii (1935), 55–61.

Hart, Walter M. "The *Franklin's Tale*," *Haverford Essays*, Haverford, 1909.

Haskins, Charles Homer. "Henry II as a Patron of Literature," *Essays in Medieval History Presented to Thomas Frederick Tout*. Manchester, 1925, pp. 71–77.

———. *The Renaissance of the Twelfth Century*. Cambridge, Mass., 1927.

Hatcher, A. G. "Lai du Chievrefueil, 61–78 and 107–113," *Romania*, lxxi (1950), 330–344.

Hatzfeld, H. "Esthetic Criticism Applied to Medieval Romance Literature," *Romance Philology*, i (1947–48), 319.

Heather, P. J. "Color Symbolism: Part I," *Folk-Lore*, lix (1948), 165–183; Parts II and III, lx (1949), 208–216 and 266–276.

Hertz, W. *Spielmannsbuch*. Stuttgart-Berlin, 1886.

Hibbard, Laura A. *Medieval Romance in England, A Study of the Sources and Analogues of the Non-Cyclic Metrical Romances*. New York, 1924. Rptd. 1959. (See Loomis, Laura Hibbard)

Highet, Gilbert. *The Classical Tradition*. New York and London, 1949.

Hiller, Friedrich. *Tydorel, ein Lai der Marie de France*. Rostock diss., 1927.

Hoepffner, Ernest. *Aux Origines de la Nouvelle Française*. The Taylorian Lecture, 1938; Oxford, 1939.

———. "La Chanson de Geste et les Débuts du Roman Courtois," *Mélanges de Linguistique et de Littérature Offerts à M. Jeanroy*. Paris, 1928, pp. 427–437.

———. "La Géographie et l'Histoire dans les Lais de Marie de France," *Romania*, lvi (1930), 1–32.

———. *Les Lais de Marie de France*. Paris, 1935.

———. "Marie de France et les Lais Anonymes," *Studi Medievali*, iv (1931), 1–31.

———. "Pour la Chronologie des Lais de Marie de France," *Romania*,, lix (1933), 351–370; lx (1934), 36–66.

Hofer, S. "Bemerkungen zur Beurteilung des Horn- und Mantellai," *RF*, lxv, (1953), 38.

Holmes, Urban T. *A History of Old French Literature*. New York, 1937.

———. "Further on Marie de France," *Symposium*, iii (1949), 335–339.

————. "New Thoughts on Marie de France?" *SP*, xxix (1932), 1–10.

————. "Old French *Yonec*," *MP*, xxix (1931), 225–229.

Holthausen, F. "Zu Emare," *Anglia Beiblatt*, xiii (1902), 46–47.

————. "Zu mittelenglischen Romanzen," *Anglia*, xlii (1918), 425–429.

Hoops, Reinald. *Der Begriff 'Romance' in der mittelenglischen und frühneuenglischen Literatur.* Anglistische Forschungen, No. 68. Heidelberg, 1929.

Hulbert, James R. "Hypothesis concerning the Alliterative Revival," *MP*, xxviii (1931), 405–422.

Hunt, R. W. "Studies on Priscian in the Eleventh and Twelfth Centuries," *Mediaeval and Renaissance Studies*, i (1941–43), 211–212.

Jones, Paul John. *Prologue and Epilogue in Old French Lives of Saints before 1400.* Philadelphia, 1933.

Jusserand, J. J. *English Wayfaring Life in the Middle Ages*, tr. L. T. Smith. New York and London, 1889.

Kaluza, M. "Thomas Chestre, Verfasser des Launfal, Libeaus Desconus und Octovian," *Englische Studien*, xviii (1893), 165–190.

Kastner, L. E. *A History of French Versification.* Oxford, 1903.

Kellett, E. E. *Fashion in Literature, A Study of Changing Taste.* London, 1931.

Ker, W. P. *Epic and Romance.* London, 1922.

————. *Form and Style in Poetry.* London, 1928.

————. "Metrical Romances, 1200–1500," *The Cambridge History of English Literature.* 14 vols., Cambridge, 1908, i, 308–334.

Kern, Otto. *Orpheus.* Berlin, 1920.

Kinsky, Georg. *A History of Music in Pictures.* London and Toronto, 1930.

Kitchin, George. *A Survey of Burlesque and Parody in English.* Edinburgh, 1931.

Kittredge, George Lyman. "Chaucer's Discussion of Marriage," *MP*, ix (1912), 436–467.

————. "Sir Orfeo," *AJPh*, vii (1886), 176–202.

Klibansky, R. "Standing on the Shoulders of Giants," *Isis*, xxvi (1936–37), 149.

Kölbing, E. "Vier Romanzen-handschriften," *Englische Studien*, vii (1884), 178–191.

————. "Zu Chaucers Sir Thopas," *Englische Studien*, xi (1887), 506–507.

Kolls, Anton F. H. *Zur Lanvalsage, Eine Quellenuntersuchung.* Berlin, 1886.

Krappe, Alexander H. "The Celtic Provenance of 'The Lay of Tydorel,'" *MLR*, xxiv (1929), 200–204.

Kusel, Peter. *Guingamor, Ein Lai der Marie de France.* Rostock diss., 1922.

Lambley, Kathleen. *The Teaching and Cultivation of the French Language in England during the Tudor and Stuart Times.* Publications of the University of Manchester, French Series, No. III. Manchester, 1920.

Lawrence, W. W. "Satire in Sir Thopas," *PMLA*, l (1935), 81–91.

Leach, H. G. *Angevin Britain and Scandinavia.* Harvard Studies in Comparative Literature vi. Cambridge, Mass., 1921.

Legge, M. Dominica. *Anglo-Norman Poetry in the Cloisters.* Edinburgh, 1950.

————. *Anglo-Norman Literature and its Background.* Oxford, 1963.

Lerner, Luise. *Studien zur Komposition des höfischen Romans im 13. Jahrhundert.* Münster in Westf., 1936.

Levi, Ezio. *Studi sulle Opere di Maria di Francia.* Florence, 1922.

————. "Sulla Cronologia delle Opere di Maria di Francia," *Nuovi Studi Medievali,* i (1923), 41–72.

Lewis, C. S. *The Allegory of Love: A Study in Medieval Tradition.* Oxford, 1936.

————. "What Chaucer really did to *Il Filostrato*," *Essays and Studies by Members of the English Association,* xvii (1932), pp. 56–75.

Loomis, Gertrude Schoepperle. "The Old French *Lai de Nabaret*," *RR,* xiii (1922), 285–291.

————. *Tristan and Isolt.* London and Frankfort, 1913.

Loomis, Laura Hibbard. "Chaucer and the Auchinleck MS: 'Thopas' and 'Guy of Warwick,'" *Essays and Studies in Honor of Carleton Brown.* New York, 1940, pp. 111–128.

————. "Chaucer and the Breton Lays of the Auchinleck MS.," *SP,* xxxviii (1941), 14–33.

————. "The Auchinleck MS and a Possible London Bookshop of 1330–1340," *PMLA,* lvii (1942), 595–627.

Loomis, Roger Sherman. *Arthurian Tradition and Chrétien de Troyes.* New York, 1949.

————. "Sir Orfeo and Walter Map's De Nugis," *MLN,* li (1936), 28–30.

————. ed., *Arthurian Literature in the Middle Ages*. Oxford, 1959.

Lowes, John Livingston. *Convention and Revolt in Poetry*. Boston and New York, 1919.

————. "The Franklin's Tale, the Teseide, and the Filocolo," *MP*, xv (1918), 689–728.

Magoun, F. P., Jr. "Norman History in the 'Lay of the Beach,'" *MLN*, lvii (1942), 11–16.

————. "Scottish History in the 'Lay of Gurun,'" *Studia Neophilologica*, xiv (1942), 1–24.

————. Review of Margaret Wattie, *The Middle English 'Lai le Freine,'* *Speculum*, v (1930), 239–241.

Mâle, Émile. *L'Art Religieux du XIIIe Siècle en France*. Paris, 1902.

Manly, John M. "Chaucer and the Rhetoricians," *Proceedings of the British Academy*, xii (1926).

————. "Sir Thopas, a Satire," *Essays and Studies by Members of the English Association*, xiii (1928), pp. 52–73.

Mathew, Gervase. "Ideals of Knighthood in Late Fourteenth-Century England," *Studies in Mediaeval History Presented to Frederick Maurice Powicke*. Oxford, 1948, pp. 354–362.

Mayer, Leo A. *Saracenic Heraldry*. Oxford, 1933.

McNeill, John T., and Helena Gamer. *Medieval Handbooks of Penance*. Columbia University Records of Civilization Sources and Studies, No. XXIX. New York, 1938.

Mead, W. E. *The Medieval Feast*. London, 1921.

Mehl, Dieter. "Die kürzeren mittelenglischen 'Romanzen' und die Gattungsfrage," *DVLG*, xxxviii (1964), 513–533.

Meissner, R. *Die Strenglolkar, Ein Beitrag zur Geschichte der altnordischen Prosaliteratur*. Halle a. S., 1902.

Middle English Dictionary, ed. Hans Kurath. "Plan and Bibliography." Ann Arbor, 1954.

Millett, Fred B. "English Courtesy Literature before 1557," *Bulletin of the Departments of History and Political and Economic Science in Queen's University, Kingston, Ontario*, No. 30 (1919).

Mitchell, Phillip M. "Scandinavian Literature," in *ALMA*, pp. 462–471.

Moore, Olin. *The Young King Henry Plantagenet, 1155–1183 in History, Literature and Tradition*. The Ohio State University Studies, Vol. II, No. 12 (1925).

Muscatine, Charles. "The Emergence of Psychological Allegory in Old French Romance," *PMLA*, lxviii (1953), 1160–82.

Nagel, Erich. *Marie de France als dichterische Persönlichkeit*. Erlangen, 1929.

Neilson, George. *Trial by Combat*. London, 1890.

Nitze, William A. "Perceval and the Holy Grail: An Essay on the Romance of Chrétien de Troyes." *University of California Publications in Modern Philology*, 28. Berkeley and Los Angeles, 1944.

Nykrog, Per. *Les Fabliaux*. Copenhagen, 1959.

Oakden, J. P. *Alliterative Poetry in Middle English: The Dialectal and Metrical Survey*. Publications of the University of Manchester, No. ccv, English Series No. xix. Manchester, 1930.

————. *Alliterative Poetry in Middle English: A Survey of Traditions*. Publications of the University of Manchester, No. ccxxxvi, English Series No. xxii. Manchester, 1935.

Ogle, Marbury B. "The Orchard Scene in *Tydorel* and *Sir Gowther*," *RR*, xiii (1922), 37–43.

Pansa, Giovanni. *Ovidio nel medioevo e nella tradizione popolare*. Sulmona, 1924.

Papworth, J. W., and A. W. Morant. *An Alphabetical Dictionary of Coats of Arms Belonging to Families of Great Britain and Ireland and Forming an Ordinary of British Armorials*. London, 1874.

Paré, G., A. Brunet, P. Tremblay. *La Renaissance du XIIe Siècle: Les Écoles et l'enseignement*. Publications de l'Institut d'Études médiévales d'Ottawa. Paris and Ottawa, 1933.

Paris, Gaston. "Le Lai de l'Ombre, publié par Joseph Bédier," *Romania*, xix (1890), 609–610.

————. "Oeuvres de Henri d'Andeli," *Romania*, xi (1882), 137–144.

Parsons, H. Rosamond. "Anglo-Norman Books of Courtesy and Nurture," *PMLA*, xliv (1929), 383–451.

Patch, Howard R. "Chaucer and Medieval Romance," *Essays in Memory of Barrett Wendell* (Cambridge, Mass., 1926), pp. 93–108.

————. *The Other World according to Descriptions in Medieval Literature*. Smith College Studies in Modern Languages, New Series. Cambridge, Mass., 1950.

Pearsall, Derek. "The Development of Middle English Romance," *MS*, xxvii (1965), 91–117.

Potter, M. A. *Sohrab and Rustum*. Grimm Library, No. 14. London, 1902.

Rajna, Pio. "Le Origini della novella narrata dal *Frankelyn* nei *Canterbury Tales* del Chaucer," *Romania*, xxxii (1903), 204–267.

Rand, Edward Kennard. *Ovid and His Influence*. Boston, 1926.

251

Ravenel, Florence. "*Tydorel* and *Sir Gowther*," *PMLA*, xx (1905), 1952–77.

Reinhard, John R. "The Literary Background of the *Chantefable*," *Speculum*, i (1926), 157–196.

Ritson, Joseph. *Ancient English Metrical Romances*. 3 vols. London, 1802.

Robertson, D. W., Jr. "Marie de France 'Lais'-Prologue 13–16," *MLN*, LXIV (1949), 336–338.

⸺. "Love Conventions in Marie's *Equitan*," *RR*, XLIV (1954), 241–245.

Saintsbury, George. *A History of English Prosody from the 12th Century to the Present Day*. 3 vols. New York, 1906.

Sandison, Helen E. *The Chanson d'Aventure in Middle English*. Bryn Mawr, Pa., 1913.

Sarton, G. "Aristotle and Phyllis," *Isis*, xiv (1930), 8–19.

⸺. "Standing on the Shoulders of Giants," *Isis*, xxiv (1935–36), 107–109.

Schiött, E. *L'amour et les amoureux dans les lais de Marie de France*. Lund, 1889.

Schipper, Jakob. *A History of English Versification*. Oxford, 1910.

Schlauch, Margaret. *Chaucer's Constance and the Accused Queens*. New York, 1927.

⸺. "English Short Fiction in the 15th and 16th Centuries," *Studies in Short Fiction*, III (1966), 393–434.

Schofield, William Henry. "Chaucer's Franklin's Tale," *PMLA*, xvi (1901), 405–449.

⸺. *Chivalry in English Literature*. Harvard Studies in Comparative Literature, II. Cambridge, Mass., 1912.

Schürr, F. "Komposition und Symbolik in den Lais der Marie de France," *ZfRPh*, L (1930), 556–582.

Serjeantson, Mary S. "The Dialects of the West Midlands in Middle English," *RES*, III (1927), 330–331.

Severs, J. Burke. "The Antecedents of *Sir Orfeo*" in *Studies in Medieval Literature in Honor of Professor Albert Croll Baugh*, ed. MacEdward Leach. Philadelphia, 1961, pp. 187–207.

⸺. "Appropriateness of Character to Plot in the 'Franklin's Tale,'" *Studies in Language and Literature in Honour of Margaret Schlauch*. Warsaw, 1966, pp. 385–396.

⸺, ed. *A Manual of the Writings in Middle English 1050–1500*, 1st fascicule. New Haven, 1967.

Slover, Clark H. " 'Sire Degarre': A Study of a Mediaeval Hack Writer's Methods," *The University of Texas Bulletin*, Studies in English No. 11 (1930), pp. 5–23.

Smalley, Beryl. *The Study of the Bible in the Middle Ages*. New York, 1952.

Smithers, G. V. "Story-patterns in Some Breton Lays," *MÆ*, XXII (1953), 61–92.

Spencer, Theodore. "Chaucer's Hell: A Study in Mediaeval Convention," *Speculum*, II (1927), 184–185.

Spitzer, Leo. "Marie de France—Dichterin von Problem-märchen," *ZfRPh*, L (1930), 29–67.

————. "The Prologue to the *Lais* of Marie de France and Medieval Poetics," *MP*, XLI (1943), 96–102.

Stemmler, Theo. "Die mittelenglischen Bearbeitungen zweier Lais der Marie de France," *Anglia*, LXXX (1962), 243–263.

Stokoe, William C., Jr. "The Sources of *Sir Launfal*: Lanval and Graelent," *PMLA*, LXIII (1948), 392–404.

Strong, Caroline. "History and Relations of the Tail-Rhyme Strophe in Latin, French, and English," *PMLA*, XXII (1907), 371–421.

Stubbs, William. *Seventeen Lectures on Medieval and Modern History*. 3rd ed. Oxford, 1900.

Tatlock, J. S. P. "Astrology and Magic in Chaucer's Franklin's Tale," *Kittredge Anniversary Papers*. Boston, 1913, pp. 339–350.

————. *The Scene of the Franklin's Tale Visited*. Chaucer Society Publications, Second Series, No. 51. London, 1914.

Taylor, Henry O. *The Medieval Mind, A History of the Development of Thought and Emotion in the Middle Ages*. 2 vols. New York, 1925.

Thompson, Stith. *The Folktale*. New York, 1946.

Trounce, A. McI. "The English Tail-Rhyme Romances," *MÆ*, I (1932), 81–108, 168–182; II (1933), 34–57, 189–198; III (1934), 30–50.

Utley, F. L. "Arthurian Romance and International Folktale Method," *RP*, XVII (1964), 596–607.

Voretzsch, Karl. *Introduction to the Study of Old French Literature*, tr. Francis du Mont. New York, 1931.

Warnke, Karl. "Die Quelle des Esope der Marie de France," *Festgabe für Hermann Suchier*. Halle, 1900, pp. 161–284.

Warren, Frederick M. "Notes on the Romans d'aventure," *MLN*, XIII (1898), 339–351.

Wathelet-Willem, J. "Le mystère chez Marie de France," *Revue belge de Philologie et d'Histoire*, xxxix (1961), 661–686.

Warton, Thomas. *History of English Poetry*, ed. W. Carew Hazlitt. 4 vols. London, 1871.

Wells, John E. *A Manual of the Writings in Middle English, 1050–1400.* 9 Supplements, Connecticut Academy of Arts and Sciences. New Haven, 1916–41.

Wells, Whitney H. "Chaucer as a Literary Critic," *MLN*, xxxix (1924), 255–268.

West, C. B. *Courtoisie in Anglo-Norman Literature*. Oxford, 1938.

Whiting, B. J. "Old Maids Lead Apes in Hell," *Englische Studien*, lxx (1935–36), 337–351.

Whitney, Marian P. "Queen of Mediaeval Virtues: Largesse" in *Vassar Mediaeval Studies*. New Haven, 1923, pp. 183–215.

Wienert, Walter. *Die Typen der griechisch-römischen Fabel*. FFC No. 56. Helsinki, 1925.

Wilamowitz-Moellendorff, Ulrich von. *Die Glaube der Hellenen*. Berlin, 1932.

Williams, H. F. "The Anonymous Breton Lays," *RS*, xxxii (1964), 76–84.

Wilmotte, W. "Marie de France et Chrétien de Troyes," *Romania*, lii (1926), 353–355.

Wilson, R. M. *Early Middle English Literature*. London, 1939.

————. "More Lost Literature in Old and Middle English," *Leeds Studies*, v (1936), 25–26.

Wind, Bartina H. "L'Idéologie courtoise dans les lais de Marie de France" in *Mélanges de linguistique romane et de philologie médiévale offerts à Maurice Delbouille*. 2 vols. Gembloux, 1964, ii, 741–748.

Winkler, Emil. *Französische Dichter des Mittelalters II*. Sitzungsberichte der kaiserlichen Academie, Philologie-historie, 188. Vienna, 1918.

Wolf, Ferdinand J. *Ueber die Lais, Sequenzen und Leiche*. Heidelberg, 1841.

Worcester, David. *The Art of Satire*. Cambridge, Mass., 1940.

Young, Karl. "Chaucer's 'Troilus and Criseyde' as Romance," *PMLA*, liii (1938), 37–63.

————. "Chaucer's Use of Boccaccio's Filocolo," *MP*, IV (1906), 169–177.

Zupitza, Julius. "Zum Lay le Freine," *Englische Studien*, X (1886), 41–48.

————. "Zum Sir Launfal," *Archiv*, LXXXVIII (1892), 69–70.

INDEX OF AUTHORS

257

INDEX OF WORKS AND
MANUSCRIPTS

SUBJECT INDEX OF BRETON LAY
AND OTHER GENRES

266